THE PERFECT
AFTERNOON TEA
RECIPE BOOK

THE PERFECT
AFTERNOON TEA
RECIPE BOOK

More than 160 classic recipes for sandwiches,
pretty cakes and bakes, biscuits, bars, pastries, cupcakes,
celebration cakes and glorious gâteaux

ANTONY WILD and CAROL PASTOR

HERMES
HOUSE

Contents

Introduction

In 1615 the first use of a word relating to tea is recorded in the English language, when an East India Company associate in Japan, Mr Wickham, writes to his friend Mr Eaton asking him to buy a "pot of the best sort of chaw in Meaco", the place where the tea was grown for the Shogun, the chief military commander. It took a Portuguese princess, however, to introduce the British to the pleasures of drinking tea. In the summer of 1662 Catherine of Braganza arrived in England to become the bride of King Charles II. On landing at Portsmouth, the first thing she did was to ask for a cup of tea, taking the welcoming party completely by surprise (they had been preparing to serve her a glass of weak ale). Luckily a potential diplomatic crisis was averted by a retainer in her entourage who was able to produce the tea, and so the English Court was introduced to an old custom of the Portuguese nobility. Portugal's long trading association with China and Japan had made the Portuguese accustomed to what was still, at the time, a novelty in England, and certainly one that the Court had previously looked upon with some suspicion.

Catherine's endorsement of tea meant that the unfamiliar beverage suddenly became all the rage in London society – music to the ears of the directors of the East India Company. Founded by Royal Charter in 1600, the company had been created to compete with the success of the Portuguese in capturing the hugely valuable spice trade from the east. But the company had failed to dislodge its rivals, and its fortunes had fluctuated wildly. Its traders were aware of the existence of tea but at the time, the English were reluctant to take up

tea-drinking as a habit. Tea was to be found on sale at some of London's coffee houses, albeit in a medicinal role, but it was not until the arrival of Catherine in England that the habit of drinking tea became established.

Tea becomes the English drink of choice

As tea-drinking spread, the East India Company directors realized the popularity of the product. A Mrs Harris was hired to serve the drink at all the company meetings in the fine silver teapot presented to his fellow directors by Lord Berkeley in 1670. Two of the hallowed traditions of English business – the tea-lady and the tea-break – therefore owed their genesis, appropriately enough, to the company that first imported tea.

By the end of the 17th century, tea was in its ascendancy, with everyone from peasant farmer to the highest nobility in the land regularly drinking the beverage. Beer, the traditional drink of the working classes, was less popular, and so was coffee in the coffee houses – but tea triumphed behind the drawing room doors of the middle classes, demanding to be served. This Portuguese habit had taken the English by storm, although it was modified to reflect the unique character of the English. Fabulous outdoor tea gardens flourished at Vauxhall, Ranelagh Gardens and elsewhere in London. Here the fashionable set could see and be seen, and be entertained all the while as they took tea. Porcelain pots (their design adapted from Chinese wine jugs) were imported to brew the beverage in, and milk and sugar were added to the mix. The directors of the East India Company, which had the monopoly on the trade with China, rubbed their hands with glee: tea had become the single most valuable item of their trade.

The rise and fall of 'afternoon tea'

Tea was firmly established as the drink of choice, but the invention of 'afternoon tea', now seen as the quintessential English custom, did not occur until the 19th century. Although the innovation is usually attributed to the 7th Countess of Bedford, in fact the new habit was the result

Left The famous tea clipper, the Cutty Sark, *was designed to be the fastest of its kind in the world. Her maiden voyage was made to China in early 1870, and she returned later that year with the first of eight cargoes of almost 1,500 tonnes of tea. This method of transporting tea was later superseded by steamships, which were more suited to navigating the newly built Panama Canal.*

Above Taking tea with friends in the afternoon was a social
ritual valued by polite society.

of the complex series of social and economic changes
wrought over time by industrialization. Luncheon had
been invented to fill the gap between breakfast and
dinner, but this was a light meal. The evening meal of
dinner was now served later than at any other time, and
so a light snack in the afternoon became the way to stave
off hunger. The custom of taking afternoon tea quickly
became one of the defining rituals of English social life,
giving rise to all manner of fashionable china and silver
tea services as well as appetizing new snacks to
accompany it. Many of the scenes in Oscar Wilde's most
enduring play, *The Importance of Being Earnest* (1895),
revolve around the afternoon tea table, its cakes and
cucumber sandwiches, and when accused by a friend of
eating too much, Algernon is able to respond with
complete assurance, "I believe it is customary in good
society to take some slight refreshment at five o'clock."

Initially a purely domestic phenomenon, by the end
of the 19th century the serving of afternoon tea had
been adopted by the large hotels which were springing
up all over Britain – and in far-flung reaches of the
British Empire. Elegant cafés followed suit, and even
when silver cake stands and cucumber sandwiches were
no longer to be found in homes, they could still be found
there. The tradition continued widely until the 1970s.

After that date cafés increasingly became self-service.
Working practices changed for most people and with
them came new social habits. Only a few bastions of the
old tradition remained – mainly the grand hotels and
the occasional little teashop in a quaint rural town, with
gingham tablecloths and homemade cakes.

A renaissance for afternoon tea

In the 1990s an increasing interest in quality teas
conspired against the all-pervasive buzzing coffee bar
boom, to remind people that there was a way of eating
and drinking socially in an unhurried, elegant manner
and in a way that appealed to people's sense of
nostalgia. Afternoon tea returned to the national
consciousness. While tea leaves remain an imported
commodity, afternoon tea lends itself perfectly to the
increasing trend towards the use of locally sourced
ingredients in homemade delicacies. In hotels,
department stores and cafés across Britain, the public
ritual of afternoon tea is once again enacted for the
pleasure of thousands every day.

Although the fashionable private salons for taking
afternoon tea in the style of the Countess of Bedford
may no longer be found, the tradition of afternoon tea
is maintained, but as a treat rather than on a daily basis.
An enormous variety of teas have become available now,
and keen cooks can exert their talents over a range of
traditional and newly created delicacies.

The afternoon tea table

The new 19th-century phenomenon of afternoon tea was not only good for tea importers, it heralded a growth in several attendant industries, such as the production of fine china and porcelain tea services and the manufacture of silverware.

The East India Company made huge profits out of the tea that they brought from China, and so did the government, who applied hefty taxes to the product. To increase sales, the importers quickly realized that their new customers needed something in which to brew the tea. The Chinese were used to brewing tea in powdered form in a teacup, but towards the end of the 14th century larger leaved teas had become popular, requiring a brewing vessel, and the Chinese, who had made growing and brewing tea a skill akin to that of wine production, had adapted their traditional wine pots to this purpose, adding a handle and a spout.

The first appearance of the teapot

This appealing Chinese design found favour with the English when they became interested in drinking tea, and many stoneware pots of this kind were exported back to England. These in turn spawned imitators, principally in Staffordshire, and the familiar 'Brown Betty' teapot evolved, a utilitarian vessel, with a high sheen glaze, reputed to make the best pot of tea. While not the most elegant of teapots, it has the virtue of durability – and given the sheer quantity of tea being brewed in Britain at the time, that was not to be underestimated. The design of the Brown Betty has stood the test of time and can still be seen in many households to this day, although today, every colour imaginable is available to co-ordinate with kitchen decor and home furnishings.

Fine china

Such workaday items as the Brown Betty teapot, however, were not suited to the elegant style of service that tea drinking demanded among the fashionable, well-heeled set. Consequently, it was Chinese porcelain which lent the most lustre to the new custom in Britain. This was the era of the craze for 'Chinoiserie', when Chinese silks, wallpapers, screens and porcelain were the must-have items for any distinguished household.

Below The fine tradition of taking afternoon tea necessitated an equally elegant tea service in which to present it.

Below Industrialization meant that pottery was widely available for everyone to purchase at reasonable cost.

Above Every fashionable house, teashop or hotel tearoom possessed an attractive fine china tea service, as porcelain became the material of choice for making and serving tea.

The East India Company's merchants started to exploit these markets, eventually involving themselves in the design and production process in China. Many a noble house in the 18th century would display dinner services of fine porcelain emblazoned with their coats of arms, hand-painted on the other side of the world. Teapots, teacups and saucers were now added to the shopping list among a growing range of other tea-serving items.

The Chinese dominance of the porcelain industry, could not last, however. German alchemists discovered the formula for making porcelain, and later Josiah Wedgwood of England was credited with industrializing the production of pottery on a scale never seen before. It was not long before other manufacturers followed suit. Elements of Chinese designs such as the ubiquitous 'Willow Pattern', 'Blanc de Chine' and others were shamelessly plundered, and remain popular even now.

It was not just the demand for teapots that fuelled the porcelain boom. During the 18th century British tea drinkers discovered a taste for black teas (as opposed to the green teas they had drunk initially) and found that these bitter teas worked particularly well with the addition of milk and sugar. This was good news for dairy farmers, West Indian sugar planters and porcelain manufacturers, who produced suitable vessels for the new additions. Then, in the last century, along came the idea of afternoon tea with its cakes and sandwiches, and yet more items were required to make up a tea service.

Silverware and linen

Alongside the East India Company – who retained their monopoly on the tea trade with China until 1834 – and porcelain manufacturers, others benefited commercially from the fashion for tea. Silver manufacturers were required to create sugar tongs, strainers, teaspoons, cake stands and small cutlery to enhance the daintiness of the offering, as well as teapots, milk jugs and sugar bowls for the top-notch tearooms. Linen mills, embroiderers and lacemakers did well likewise in producing tablecloths and napkins – even the innovation of the humble doily was a spin-off from the unstoppable growth in demand for tea.

But the teapot always was and remains the undisputed star of the proceedings. Over the years endless sleek styling and technical innovations in design have been dedicated to the teapot over its illustrious career. What makes it all the more curious, in Britain at least, is that the conservative, ever-reliable earthenware teapot remains the default teapot of choice in many households – and for that we have to thank an anonymous 14th-century Chinese craftsman.

The etiquette of afternoon tea

Over two centuries of tradition have led to a wealth of customs and codes of behaviour that must be followed if you wish to display proper tea-time manners in genteel society. Smart clothes and good manners are always welcomed at the tea table.

When serving afternoon tea the hostess should bring all the essential items to the tea table on a large tray. The tray should be set down on the table and the individual items arranged appropriately. Platters of sandwiches and cake stands should be placed in the middle of the table and the teapot should be positioned with the spout facing the hostess, or pourer. In front of each guest a teacup should be placed on a saucer with a teaspoon resting on the right side, a small plate with a fork for eating cake (or knife if you are serving anything that requires spreading) and a napkin. The milk jug (pitcher) and sugar bowl should be arranged near the centre.

Pouring the tea perfectly

A warm teapot should be filled immediately when the water boils, and be brought to the table on a tray where it can stand while the tea brews. When the tea is ready to pour, the pourer should take the teapot to each guest

and pour carefully into each cup. Tea is traditionally served in a cup holding 120ml/4fl oz of liquid and should be three-quarters filled with tea. The size is not imperative, but a teacup should be shallower and wider than a coffee cup to allow the tea to cool slightly before drinking.

Demure tea drinking

Once the tea has been poured, guests may add milk or lemon (offered in delicate slices) and sugar. It is preferable to use gentle to-and-fro movements with the teaspoon rather than wide, noisy circular motions. The spoon should then be placed on the saucer to rest.

If seated at the table, the correct etiquette is to lift the teacup only to drink the tea and replace it on the saucer between sips. If there is no table, the saucer should be held in the left hand on your lap and the teacup in your right hand. It should be returned to the saucer when not in use. The cup should be held daintily by the handle

Below If scones are served at tea, split in half, butter, then top with jam and finish with a dollop of clotted cream.

Below Sandwiches should always be served in delicate fingers, triangles or squares, to enable graceful eating.

Above A properly arranged tea tray is loaded with a teapot, a cake stand, cake knife, teacups and saucers, side plates, napkins, forks, teaspoons, sugar bowl and milk jug.

between the thumb and fingers, with the little finger extended for balance. Never hold the teacup in the palm of your hand or loop your fingers through the handle. And by no means wave the cup around.

Tea should be drunk in small, silent sips from the cup with as much grace and elegance as possible.

Elegant eating

The correct size of plate to use for serving sandwiches, cakes, pastries and other delicacies at afternoon tea is between 15 and 20cm (6 and 8in). The hostess must ensure that guests are provided with the necessary cutlery for the food that is served. It is customary to serve wafer-thin sandwiches cut into dainty triangles and with crusts removed from purposely designed bread and butter plates. Finger food can also be served.

A slice of cake, scones with jam and cream, or a selection of biscuits are appropriate to serve, all in small and dainty sizes.

When enjoying afternoon tea at a table, place the napkin on your lap and, if you leave the table temporarily for any reason, set the napkin on the seat.

All food should be eaten in delicate bites, with the utmost attention to detail. Think about how you will appear to your fellow guests at the tea table. When not in use forks should be rested on the side of the plate with the tines down. Never place them back on the table once they have been used. Similarly, place used knives on the side of the plate.

A social event

Above all, afternoon tea is a sociable occasion to be enjoyed with friends and family. So remember to smile and make polite conversation (between mouthfuls, of course) and savour this most quintessential of English afternoon traditions.

A perfect pot of tea

Whether your preference is for green, black, herbal or flavoured, there is nothing more refreshing in the afternoon than a pot of freshly brewed tea. Aficionados have maxims of their own on what constitutes the perfect cup of tea, and many blends are mentioned here, but they all agree that utmost care should be taken in making it. Step-by-step instructions for brewing are given. If you prefer a cool drink on a hot day, or you wish to offer a choice, there are also some suggestions for alternative drinks to serve at the tea table.

Left: For the best taste, purists believe tea should be drunk without the addition of milk, sugar and lemon.

Teas of the world

There is a bewildering number of teas, with quality ranging from the fabled imperial 'monkey-picked' tea of China, so called because it was collected from inaccessible locations, to the rare Ceylon 'Silver Tips', and from 'speciality' blends like Earl Grey to machine-harvested, blended black teas.

India, China and Sri Lanka dominate the tea-producing world. Together India and China produce more than half of all tea consumed. India produces enormous amounts of tea – its 14,000 plantations employ one million people. Kenya, Turkey, Indonesia and Malawi are also tea producers. Teas sold purely by their particular country or region of origin, for example those from India and Sri Lanka, are known as speciality teas.

Left India has three tea-producing regions – Darjeeling, Assam and Nilgiri – and a blend of teas from these plantations produces Indian tea.

first crop of the year is known as the 'first flush' and has a fanatical following in northern Germany. Darjeelings are all grown for export.

Assam, the other leading Indian tea, comes from the valley of the lower Brahmaputra River where indigenous tea plants were discovered in the 1840s. The Assam Company, which still exists today, pioneered the estate system there. The best Assams have a rich, almost tarry flavour. Lesser ones are often used to give strength to blends such as English Breakfast.

In Sri Lanka too, teas are often packaged according to the plantation or tea garden from which they are hand picked. The government of that country still permits the use of the old colonial name of Ceylon

Speciality teas

These are the aristocrats of the tea world and are considered sufficiently refined and distinctive to be drunk unblended. India and Sri Lanka produce speciality teas as well as

Below Ceylon tea is a black tea, with citrus notes to the flavour, grown on the island of Sri Lanka (formerly Ceylon).

blended teas from plantations in distinct regions. India is best known for its delicate Darjeelings and robust Assams. Assam is also known as British tea because of the British inclination to take strong-flavoured tea with milk and sugar.

The region of Darjeeling produces the 'champagne of teas', prized for its light colour and fine flavour. The

Below Assam tea, manufactured from leaves picked in the Assam region of India, has a full-bodied flavour.

Right In a tea plantation in Assam, India, workers pluck 'two leaves and a bud' by hand in the traditional way. The leaves at the tip are younger and finer than the rest of the bush.

in connection with its fine, golden teas. The two best known are the pungent Uvas of the east and softer Dimbulas of the west. China, like India and Sri Lanka, produces many speciality teas.

Tea blends

A blend is a mixture of leaves from different plantations. Blends occur in India as well as other countries, though, like olive oil and wine, blended tea is not for the purist. Some blends are machine-harvested teas and all play an undistinguished role in the proprietary mixtures of tea that are widely sold.

A few anomalies exist however, defined as speciality tea, but created from a blend, none more so than the blend known as Earl Grey, the best selling speciality tea of all. This blend of black teas is flavoured with essence of bergamot, and tea companies frequently claim to have some unique access to the original

Below Darjeeling tea, named after the Darjeeling region of West Bengal in India, has a unique much sought-after muscatel flavour.

recipe. However, Earl Grey, the popular British prime minister who saw the Reform Act through Parliament in the 1830s, almost certainly had nothing to do with its formulation. Although the blend is supposedly of Chinese origin, in fact the bergamot fruit is a spontaneous mutation of the bitter orange, and has never been grown in China.

Below Earl Grey tea is infused with bergamot, the pungent oil of a citrus fruit. It is one of the most popular 'speciality' teas in Britain and North America.

Earl Grey tea is best enjoyed black, or with a splash of milk, or a slice of lemon.

Another blend which has speciality tea status is 'English Breakfast' (also known as 'Irish' and 'Royal Breakfast') which could consist of teas from anywhere, the only consensus being that they should be of a reasonably high quality and have a strong flavour.

Below English Breakfast tea is a blended tea with a strong flavour intended to be offset by the addition of milk and sugar.

Right Jasmine tea is a green tea or black China tea with added jasmine petals, which are valued for their delicate floral flavour.

Picking tea

Tea is picked from the plant *Camellia sinensis,* which is a hardy bush, not unlike the common privet hedge, and is kept to a height of about 1.2m (4ft) on tea plantations. The quality and taste of tea are affected by many factors including the time of year that the tea is picked, the way it is picked, the climate of the region where the plantation is situated, the altitude and direction that the plantation faces, as well as the quality of the soil. Consecutive years may produce completely different qualities of crop from the same plantation.

The tea plants are dormant through the winter, turning green in spring. The youngest 'two leaves and a bud' are handpicked from the bush in early spring, and then sometimes up to two or three times a week at peak harvest times. The first tips picked in spring have

collected the most essential oil and for this reason are known as 'golden tips' – the most expensive picking.

Tea manufacturing

Broadly speaking, there are three principal methods of treating tea leaves and all are carried out on or near the tea plantation. Leaves can

be immediately 'fired', that is quickly heated in a metal pan to dry them out, the leaves being gently rolled at the same time. This method produces green tea, the backbone of the China tea industry.

The second method involves 'withering' (a gentle initial drying), and then the leaves are cut and torn by machines opening their cell structure up to oxidation, or 'fermentation' as the industry calls it. The blackened fragments of the tea leaves are then dried further in their final stage of production, and finally graded by size. 'Orange Pekoe' and 'Broken Orange Pekoe' are the two largest sizes remaining, the smallest being 'Fannings' and 'Dust'. These sizes of leaf are black teas, which form about 90 per cent of the world's production today.

Halfway between green and black teas is 'Oolong', a semi-fermented tea mainly produced in China and Taiwan, and much prized by connoisseurs for its peachy flavour. Oolong is often referred to as a blue-green tea because of the colour of the leaves of the plant.

Below Green tea is becoming the drink of choice for those concerned with improving their health.

Below White tea, with its delicate, sweet flavour, is made from very young, tender leaves that are quickly fired.

Right Oolong tea is halfway between green and black tea in appearance and flavour. The best have a hint of peaches in the taste.

To the main varieties of green, black and Oolong teas must be added other variations. The most well known of these are Lapsang Souchong, a Chinese black tea which has been smoked over a fire of spruce, and Jasmine tea, a green or black China tea blended with jasmine petals.

Black teas

The black teas that dominate today were initially developed by the British on new plantations in Sri Lanka and India. Not wishing to emulate the extremely labour-intensive production methods of China, the British pioneered the idea of using machinery to speed the process up and bring the price down. Black teas were effectively the first industrialized teas, and enjoyed great worldwide commercial success. As a result the tea-producing colonies that made up the British empire started consuming teas in vast quantities too. Today India, the world's largest producer, has to import tea in order to feed the habit they acquired from the British. The British tea 'estate' system was successfully exported to Britain's East African colonies, with the result that some of the finest blending teas in the world now come from Malawi and Kenya. Their bright orangey flavour makes these teas a brisk, refreshing brew.

Green teas

Almost all green teas originate in China – where tea has been produced for more than 2,000 years – and Japan, where a Buddhist monk introduced it in the 9th century and where it became central to Japan's famous tea ceremonies. In fact, 80 per cent of the tea that China produces is green tea, the daily drink of the Chinese people. Green tea was widely drunk in Europe before black tea became more popular. The health benefits of green tea in protecting against heart disease and certain types of cancer have been widely recognized of late, and it is now better known in the West than it used to be. Specialists can now be found dealing only in green tea. The most common of the Chinese green teas is 'Gunpowder'. In this variety the leaves are tightly rolled into pellets. The astringent 'Sencha' is the best known of the Japanese tea varieties.

White teas

This little known tea variety comes from the same plant as green tea, black tea and Oolong tea, but it is uncured and unoxidized. The fresh leaves have a white downy coat. Once picked, they are fast-dried rather than roasted. White tea comprises buds and young leaves, which have been found to contain less caffeine than older leaves. White teas are thought to be the most beneficial to health, since they contain greater numbers of antioxidants, which are known to help fight cancers. However, this tea needs brewing for a long time in order for the flavour to be released.

Below Lapsang Souchong, a Chinese tea, has a smoky flavour derived from drying the tea leaves over spruce fires.

Herbal and flavoured teas

The average cup of tea contains about half the amount of caffeine as an equivalent cup of coffee. Many people, however, are concerned about consuming excessive quantities of caffeine. For them, herb and fruit teas, or tisanes, are the ideal substitute.

Herbal and fruit teas frequently, but not always, contain no 'real' tea (derived from the bush *Camellia sinensis*). The case against caffeine has led to an enormous surge in demand for herbal and fruit teas. Many of these tisanes offer a range of delights for the palate, and some herb teas may have genuine medicinal properties. The key issue in this respect is the level of essential oils left in the plant material used in the blends.

An anomaly exists here too: 'Moroccan mint' sounds as if it should be pure mint, but in fact is mint blended with black tea. The result of this proliferation is that the grocer's shelf is a minefield for those wanting to drink 'healthy', caffeinate-free tea. Reading the packet carefully is the only solution.

Herbal teas

The essential oils in all herb teas decay with oxidation and time, so the best way to reap the benefits is to buy them fresh, or preserved in sachets. Depending on where you live, some herb teas can be grown in your garden or window box, and there is something particularly pleasing about drinking a preparation of the leaves of a plant that you have grown yourself.

Chamomile tea is traditionally associated with inducing sleep and a calmed state – making a fresh brew with leaves just picked ensures the essential oils go into the brew. Other popular herb teas include

Below Ginger tea is made using slices of the ginger root, which can be bought in supermarkets and health stores.

Above Chamomile tea can be made using fresh or dried flowers.

peppermint and fennel, which act as aids to digestion, lime flower, nettle and verbena. Tea manufacturers have made considerable efforts over the last few years to create blends claiming specific effects. Teas with names like 'Tranquillity', 'Yogi' and 'Detox' are available, but check the essential oil content before you buy.

Below Mint tea is easy to make, using the fresh herb peppermint. Pick a sprig and infuse in boiling water.

Above Ginseng tea is said to have many health benefits. The tea is made from the fleshy root.

Fruit teas

The packets of fruit blends claim no such medicinal effects, and are drunk purely for their flavour, which like any new tea, is an acquired taste. However, it is possible to buy fruit teas that use purely natural ingredients, as opposed to artificial or 'nature identical', meaning created in a laboratory to replicate the flavour it purports to be. Such fruit flavours may well be tasty, but they have never had the benefit of sunshine or a warm breeze.

Beware though, many fruit teas have black tea as a base and are

Below Naturally caffeine free, Rooibos is derived from the plant of that name.

flavoured with the fruit rind or dried fruit as part of the manufacturing process. Lemon tea, made by adding lemon slices to black tea, may well be the precursor of fruit teas. Always read the label carefully.

Below Nettle tea is made from the young leaves of stinging nettles. Its flavour is unlike any other.

Above Fruit teas can be caffeine-free infusions of dehydrated fruits.

A healthy balance

Many tea drinkers regard herb and fruit teas with suspicion, but these infusions are becoming increasingly popular as the health issues surrounding caffeine consumption become more widely recognized.

The art of brewing tea

The key ingredient of a perfect cup of tea is easily taken for granted – it is none other than water. This should be freshly drawn, which means that the cold tap should be allowed to run for half a minute, at least, before the kettle is filled.

Water that has been sitting in the pipes overnight is stale and flat. Likewise twice-boiled water is dull and lifeless, so empty the kettle before filling it with fresh. The hardness of your water supply has a great influence on the quality of your tea. Some manufacturers even go to the lengths of making specific blends for specific areas. Very soft water mutes the nuances of flavour in a tea, and very hard water tends to dull the appearance of the brew and can create an unpleasant scum. Filtering the water before boiling always improves its performance.

1 Always warm the pot before measuring in the tea. Either hold the inverted pot over the spout of the kettle as it boils, or swill the teapot with boiling water before adding the tea leaves.

2 There is no fixed amount of tea that one should use – the old adage of 'one spoon per person and one for the pot' is a vague guide. Large leaf teas occupy more volume than small leafed ones, and the measure should be adjusted accordingly.

3 Tea brews best at boiling point, so pour the water on to the tea leaves as soon as the water boils. Stir briskly. Allow to stand for at least 3 minutes before pouring.

4 Pour the tea through a tea strainer.

Adding lemon: Many people drink black tea with a slice of lemon for added zest – something that makes the tea purists shudder. Never add milk to tea that is flavoured with lemon.

Adding milk: To temper the bitterness of black tea, milk can be added. When everyone drank the same blends of tea, old-fashioned polite protocol used to require that milk be poured into the cup before the tea. There are so many varieties of tea on offer these days that the tradition doesn't seem so appropriate.

Adding sugar: As with the addition of lemon, sweetness is all a matter of individual preference. White sugar can be added to black tea, tea with milk and lemon tea.

Making tea with fresh herbs

The same general rules apply for brewing herbal infusions from fresh leaves as they do for brewing tea from dried leaves. The exception is fresh ginger tea made using thin slices of peeled root ginger: this should be allowed to steep for at least 5 minutes.

1 The difference here with making tea is that you need to pick your own leaves, so correct plant identification is crucial. Use a sprig of your chosen herb per person.

2 Either add the herb to the warmed teapot or, if you are making an individual cup, you could put the sprig straight into the cup. Remember, the leaves will remain visible.

3 Pour on boiling water and allow the herb to steep. When it has reached the desired strength, strain the liquid into the cup if you used a teapot, and enjoy.

Cold drinks for hot summer days

Homemade, thirst-quenching soft drinks, freshly made with quality ingredients, are enjoyable to make and taste nothing like the manufactured sugary drinks that are sold commercially. These are deliciously refreshing on hot summer days.

Still lemonade

Fresh lemonade is often seen on the menu in smart contemporary cafés and teashops.

MAKES 4–6 GLASSES

3 unwaxed lemons
115g/4oz/generous ½ cup caster (superfine) sugar

1 Pare the skin from the lemons with a vegetable peeler. Put the lemon rind and sugar into a bowl, add 900ml/1½ pints/3¾ cups boiling water and stir well until the sugar dissolves.

2 Cover and leave to cool. Squeeze the juice from the lemons. Add it to the flavoured water, mix well and strain into a jug (pitcher). Chill and serve in tall glasses with ice.

Energy 115kcal/489kJ; Protein 0.2g; Carbohydrate 30.4g, of which sugars 30.4g; Fat 0g, of which saturates 0g; Cholesterol 0mg; Calcium 17mg; Fibre 0g; Sodium 2mg.

Barley water

Like lemonade, barley water is an old-fashioned drink. It is usually served cold, but is equally delicious as a hot drink.

MAKES 10 GLASSES, TO DILUTE

50g/2oz/⅓ cup pearl barley, washed
rind and juice of 1 lemon
caster (superfine) sugar, to taste
mineral water, to serve

1 In a large pan cover the pearl barley with cold water. Bring to the boil and simmer for 2 minutes. Strain.

2 Return the barley to the rinsed pan. Add the lemon rind and 600ml/1 pint/ 2½ cups water. Bring to the boil over medium heat and simmer for 1½–2 hours, stirring occasionally.

3 Strain the liquid into a jug (pitcher), add the lemon juice, and sweeten to taste. Leave to cool. Dilute to taste.

Energy 38kcal/161kJ; Protein 0.4g; Carbohydrate 9.4g, of which sugars 5.3g; Fat 0g, of which saturates 0g; Cholesterol 3.8mg; Calcium 21mg; Fibre 0g; Sodium 0.5mg.

Fresh orange squash

Using a juicer rather than squeezing out the juice means you maximize the quantity and reduce the amount of wastage.

MAKES 550ML/18FL OZ/2½ CUPS, TO DILUTE

90g/3½oz/½ cup caster (superfine) sugar
6 large oranges
still or sparkling mineral water, to serve

1 Put the sugar in a small, heavy pan with 100ml/
3½fl oz/scant ½ cup water. Heat gently, stirring until
the sugar has dissolved. Bring to the boil and boil
rapidly for 3 minutes until the mixture is syrupy.
Remove from the heat and leave to cool.

2 Using a parer, or sharp
knife, cut away the skins
from three of the six
oranges. Chop the flesh
into pieces small enough
to fit through the funnel
of a juicer.

3 Chop the remaining oranges, with skins on, into
similar-size pieces.

4 Push all the orange pieces through the juicer, then mix
with the sugar syrup. Pour into a bottle or jug (pitcher)
and store in the refrigerator. To serve, dilute the orange
squash to taste with still or sparkling mineral water.

Energy 725kcal/3093kJ; Protein 11.4g; Carbohydrate 179.1g, of which sugars 179.1g;
Fat 1g, of which saturates 0g; Cholesterol 0mg; Calcium 518mg; Fibre 17g; Sodium 55mg.

Ruby red berry squash

*This intensely coloured, fruity-flavoured drink uses
blackberries or blueberries, or both, to make a sweet squash.*

MAKES 350ML/12FL OZ/1½ CUPS, TO DILUTE

350g/12oz/3 cups blackberries or blueberries
130g/4½oz/scant ¾ cup golden caster
   (superfine) sugar
sparkling mineral water, to serve

1 Remove any tough stalks or leaves from the fruit.
Wash the fruit thoroughly and allow to dry.

2 Push handfuls of the fruit through a juicer.

3 Put the sugar in a small, heavy pan with 100ml/
3½fl oz/scant ½ cup water. Heat gently until the sugar
dissolves, stirring with a wooden spoon, then bring to
the boil and boil for 3 minutes until syrupy. Leave
until completely cool.

4 Mix the fruit juice with
the syrup in a jug
(pitcher). Chill in the
refrigerator. For each
serving pour about
50ml/2fl oz/¼ cup fruit
syrup into a glass.

5 Add ice and top up with sparkling mineral water.

Energy 712kcal/3020kJ; Protein 4.2g; Carbohydrate 184.8g, of which sugars 170.8g;
Fat 0g, of which saturates 0g; Cholesterol 0mg; Calcium 69mg; Fibre 7g; Sodium 8mg.

Real vanilla milkshake

This is a milkshake for connoisseurs: it is the cream of the crop and definitely one to linger over. Nothing beats the flavour of milk infused with a vanilla pod.

MAKES 2 GLASSES

1 vanilla pod (bean)
400ml/14fl oz/1⅔ cups full cream (whole) milk
200ml/7fl oz/scant 1 cup single (light) cream
4 scoops vanilla ice cream

1 Using a sharp knife, score the vanilla pod down the centre. Place in a small pan, pour the milk over and bring slowly to the boil. Remove from the heat. Leave to go cold.

2 Remove the vanilla pod and scrape out the seeds with the tip of a knife. Put the seeds in a blender or food processor with the milk and cream. Blend until combined.

3 Add the vanilla ice cream to the mixture and blend well until it is thick and frothy. Serve immediately.

Energy 648kcal/2687kJ; Protein 15.8g; Carbohydrate 36.4g, of which sugars 36.3g; Fat 49.6g, of which saturates 30.8g; Cholesterol 83mg; Calcium 475mg; Fibre 0g; Sodium 205mg.

Strawberry and apple slush

Sweet, juicy strawberries make wonderfully fragrant juices. This juice has an almost perfect consistency that is not too thick and not too thin. Serve over crushed ice.

MAKES 2 GLASSES

300g/11oz/2½ cups ripe strawberries
2 small, crisp eating apples
10ml/2 tsp vanilla syrup

1 Hull the strawberries. Slice a couple of the most perfect-looking strawberries, and reserve them for the decoration. Roughly chop the apples into large chunks.

2 Push the fruits through a juicer. Stir in the syrup.

3 Half fill two glasses with ice, if you like. Pour over the juice. Decorate with strawberry slices.

COOK'S TIP
Vanilla syrup can be bought from large supermarkets.

Energy 78kcal/331kJ; Protein 1.4g; Carbohydrate 18.8g, of which sugars 18.8g; Fat 0.2g, of which saturates 0g; Cholesterol 0mg; Calcium 28mg; Fibre 2.7g; Sodium 24mg.

Elderflower cordial

There is a freshness and intensity of flavour in homemade cordials that is very rarely present in their commercial counterparts. Use to make sorbets as well as drinks.

MAKES 12 GLASSES

10 fresh elderflower heads
2–3 limes, sliced
675g/1½lb/3¼ cups sugar
5ml/1 tsp each citric acid and cream of tartar
1 litre/1¾ pints/4 cups boiling water

1 Thoroughly wash and pick over the elderflowers. Put them in a large bowl with the sliced limes. Add the sugar, citric acid and cream of tartar. Set aside for 2 hours.

2 Pour in the boiling water and leave to stand for 24 hours.

3 Strain the syrup into sterilized bottles and seal them tightly shut.

4 The cordial will keep, chilled, for 2–3 months. To serve, dilute with about twice as much water.

Energy 222kcal/947kJ; Protein 0g; Carbohydrate 59g, of which sugars 59g;
Fat 0g, of which saturates 0g; Cholesterol 0mg; Calcium 8mg; Fibre 0g; Sodium 2.8mg.

Cinnamon iced coffee

For those who prefer coffee to the traditional afternoon drink, this beverage is perfect for hot summer days. Lightly flavoured with cinnamon it is a smooth and relaxing drink.

MAKES 2 LARGE GLASSES

5ml/1 tsp ground cinnamon
400ml/14fl oz/1⅔ cups full cream (whole) milk
40g/1½oz/3 tbsp caster (superfine) sugar
300ml/½ pint/1¼ cups strong cold espresso coffee
cinnamon sticks, to serve

1 Put the cinnamon and 100ml/3½fl oz/scant ½ cup of the milk in a small pan with the sugar. Bring the milk slowly to the boil, then remove from the heat and leave to cool.

2 Turn the cinnamon milk into a large jug (pitcher) or bowl. Add the remaining milk and the coffee and whisk well, using a hand-held electric wand, until frothy. Pour into glasses with ice, if you like. Serve with cinnamon stick stirrers.

Energy 218kcal/915kJ; Protein 7.1g; Carbohydrate 30.8g, of which sugars 29.9g; Fat 8.2g,
of which saturates 5.1g; Cholesterol 28mg; Calcium 251mg; Fibre 0g; Sodium 88mg.

Baking
techniques

Good quality ingredients are the foundation of well-made cakes, so information is provided on the characteristics of basic ingredients such as sugar, eggs, flour, fats and spices. Using quality baking equipment is vital for cake-making. Few items of bakeware are needed, and the essentials are all included. The many methods of making cakes such as creaming, all-in-one, rubbing-in, melting and whisking, are illustrated with photographs and described step by step to help you achieve perfect results. To finish a beautiful cake you may like to add some fabulous decorations – working with sugarpaste, marzipan, glacé icing and making crystallized flowers are all included here. The final section explains what can go wrong in baking and the reasons why, and offers problem-solving advice.

Left: Eggs, sugar, butter and flour are the basic ingredients for making delicious cakes for afternoon tea. Chocolate adds richness.

Essential ingredients

Basic ingredients have different properties, and these, combined with the particular cake method, are what makes such a wide variety of bakes possible. Most cakes are made by mixing sugar with fats, flour and eggs and then adding a variety of flavourings.

Sugar

Not only added for sweetness, sugars produce the structure and texture that make a cake tender, so it's important to use the correct type:
Caster (superfine) sugar is available in white and golden unrefined varieties. It blends easily with fats when beaten or 'creamed' into light sponge mixtures.
Granulated sugar may be coarse white or golden and unrefined and is used for toppings.
Demerara (raw) sugar is golden in colour and has a grainy texture.

Below, clockwise from bottom left Caster sugar, runny honey, granulated sugar, demerara sugar, soft light and dark brown sugar, black treacle, golden syrup, icing sugar and muscovado sugar are all sweeteners with differing flavours.

It is often used for recipes where sugar is melted over heat, or as a decorative topping.
Soft light and dark brown sugars cream well and usually form the base of a fruit cake or are used in recipes where a rich flavour is required. To prevent them from drying out store them in an airtight container.
Muscovado (molasses) sugar is natural and unrefined with an excellent dark colour and richer flavour. It makes fruit cakes and gingerbreads extra special.
Icing (confectioners') sugar is sold as a fine white powder or as an unrefined golden variety. It is used for icings, frostings and decorations. Store the sugar in a dry place, as it tends to absorb moisture. Sift the sugar at least once, or preferably twice before you use it, as it may

Above Eggs are essential to make cakes rise. Buttermilk adds a tangy flavour.

form hard lumps during storage.
Golden (light corn) syrup, honey, treacle and molasses are thick liquid sugars. They can be used in cakes made by the melting method.

Eggs

Although eggs are often stored in the refrigerator, better baked results will be achieved if they are at room temperature when they are used. The eggs will whisk better than those kept refrigerated and achieve more aeration. Aeration gives more volume but also allows the eggs to blend into mixtures more easily. Cold eggs will tend to curdle a mixture more quickly.

Medium size (US large) eggs are used in the recipes in this book, unless otherwise stated in the recipe.

Dried egg-white powder gives excellent results and can be substituted in royal icing recipes, or in recipes where you are unsure about the suitability of using raw egg whites. **Raw eggs are unsuitable for the elderly, pregnant women, babies and young children.**

Flours

Plain (all-purpose) flour provides the structure of a cake but contains nothing to make it rise. Richer cakes that do not need raising agents are made with plain flour.

Self-raising (self-rising) flour has raising agents mixed into it. These create air in the batter to make a cake rise, so self-raising flour is used for sponges and light mixtures that contain little or no fruit. If you have only plain flour, add 12.5ml/2½ tsp baking powder to every 225g/8oz plain flour to make it into a self-raising flour.

Wholemeal (whole-wheat) and brown flours contain bran from the wheat, which provides a good texture with extra fibre. This tends to keep cakes and breads moist and

Above, clockwise from left Baking powder, bicarbonate of soda, cream of tartar are all raising agents used in cake making.

Above, clockwise from bottom left Plain, strong, wholemeal, brown, and self-raising flours, each add texture and bulk to cakes.

gives a mellow flavour. If you are substituting brown flour for white in a recipe, you will need to add extra liquid, as the bran in brown flour will absorb more fluid.

Gram flour is made from ground chickpeas and retains moisture.

White flours can be kept in a cool dry place for up to six months, but wholemeal flours will not keep for as long because they have a higher fat content. Check the use-by date on packs of all types of flour. Flour is best stored in an airtight container, which should be thoroughly washed and dried before refilling. Don't add new flour to old, as eventually small micro-organisms that look like tiny black specks may form, and will spread into new flour. Make sure all flour is kept dry, as damp flour weighs more and therefore alters the measurements in a recipe, which could lead to failure.

Raising agents

There are a number of raising agents that, when added to flour, make cakes rise. They produce an airy and light texture. As they are added in small quantities, it is important to be accurate when measuring them out.

Baking powder is a ready-made mixture of bicarbonate of soda (baking soda) and cream of tartar. When liquid is added, the powder bubbles and produces carbon dioxide, which expands with heat during baking and creates an airy texture in the cake.

Bicarbonate of soda (baking soda) is a gentler raising agent than baking powder and is often used to give heavy melted or spicy mixtures a lift. It can create a bitter flavour if too much is added.

Cream of tartar is a fast-acting raising agent that works immediately once it touches liquid, so bake the mixture as soon as possible after adding it.

Buttermilk

When added to recipes that use bicarbonate of soda buttermilk acts as a raising agent. The acidity in the buttermilk combined with the bicarbonate of soda produces carbon dioxide, which raises the mixture as it cooks. If buttermilk is not available, make your own souring agent by mixing 290ml/10fl oz low-fat yogurt or milk with 5ml/1 tbsp lemon juice.

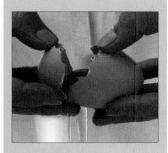

SEPARATING EGG WHITES

AND YOLKS
When separating egg whites from their yolks, tip the whites into a cup one at a time so that if there are any specks of yolk or pieces of shell in the cup, you can remove these easily. If yolk is present in a bowl of whites it will prevent whisking and aeration. Even a tiny speck of yolk will stop the whites from whisking up to a foam and you will have wasted the whole mixture.

Above, clockwise from left Vegetable shortening, soft margarine, hard block margarine, butter and oil.

Above, clockwise from left Raisins, currants, glacé and crystallized fruit and sultanas.

Above, from left to rigtht Whole nutmegs, cinnamon sticks, cloves and ground ginger.

Fats

As well as giving flavour and texture to cakes, fats improve their keeping qualities. For cake-making (apart from mixtures that use the rubbed-in method), always use fats at room temperature to make mixing them into the other ingredients easier. Fat and sugar should be beaten to a smooth, rather than grainy, batter.

Butter and hard block margarine can be interchanged in a recipe, but butter will always give the best flavour to cakes, so it is well worth spending that little extra.

Soft tub margarine is suitable only for all-in-one sponge recipes where all the ingredients are quickly mixed together in one bowl. These cakes usually require an extra raising agent. Don't overbeat recipes using soft tub margarine, as the mixture will become wet and the cake will sink. Do not substitute this fat for butter or block margarine as it is a totally different kind of fat, and it will not produce the same results.

Vegetable shortenings are flavourless but can be used to produce very pale, light cakes.

Cooking oils can be used successfully in moist cakes such as

carrot cake. As they do not hold air, the mixture cannot be creamed and these cakes have a dense texture.

Fruits

Sultanas (golden raisins), raisins and currants are usually sold pre-washed and cleaned, but it is still worth picking them over for pieces of stalk and grit. Dried fruit benefits from soaking in dark sherry, brandy or rum, which will make the fruits extra plump and succulent.

Glacé (candied) and crystallized fruits, such as cherries, ginger or angelica, need to be rinsed and dried before use to wash away their sugary

coating. If you do not do this, the sticky coating may cause the fruits to sink during baking.

Use fresh fruit when it is in season, because out-of-season fruits often have less taste. Sharp-tasting berries may be partly cooked in the oven first with sugar and butter before they are added to the batter. Mandarins or clementines can be boiled and puréed (skin and all) to make distinctive, zesty cakes. Dates (fresh or dried), raisins, prunes, sultanas and ready-to-eat dried apricots are frequently used in batters. Freshly squeezed juice, grated rind and quince paste also add flavour.

Herbs and spices

Frequently used spices for baking include nutmeg, ground ginger, cinnamon, cloves and mixed (apple pie) spice, which all add warm and fragrant tones to cakes. Dried spices have a long shelf-life but will not keep indefinitely and will gradually lose aroma and flavour. Buy them in

Left, clockwise from left Whole hazelnuts, whole walnuts, blanched almonds and ground almonds.

Right, clockwise from top left
Unsweetened cocoa powder, milk, white
and plain chocolate.

small quantities when you need them. Light and heat will affect the flavour of spices, so keep them out of the light. For a longer life, store them in a cool dry place.

If you add spices to hot mixtures, don't measure them into the mixture straight from the jar, as steam may get into the jar causing the spice to become damp and deteriorate.

Nuts

Because nuts are expensive and will deteriorate quickly, buy them in small quantities. If you buy a large pack of nuts that you are not going to use immediately, you can freeze them for up to six months.
Almonds are bought blanched, slivered, flaked (sliced), ground or whole. To remove the skins from shelled almonds, place the nuts in boiling water for 2–3 minutes. Drain and rub off the skins. Ground nuts have a fine, powdery texture.
Hazelnuts are bought whole, skinned, unskinned or ground.

Below Vegetables and herbs may not
appear to be likely baking ingredients,
but many work well together.

Walnuts contain more oil than most other nuts and will quickly become rancid, so don't buy them in bulk. Walnut halves are more expensive, so if you need chopped walnuts, buy walnut pieces.

Chocolate

For a professional finish and fine flavour buy the best quality chocolate. Good chocolate is sleek and shiny and will snap easily. It also contains a higher percentage of real cocoa fat, which gives a superior flavour and texture. The amount of cocoa fat or solids will be noted on the wrapper of any chocolate. Those marked as 70 per cent or more cocoa solids will give the best results.
Cocoa powder needs to be cooked so that its full flavour will be released. Blend it with boiling water to make it into a paste, then cool it before adding to a recipe.
Drinking chocolate contains milk powder and sugar. Don't substitute it for cocoa powder, as it will spoil the flavour of a cake.
White chocolate may be difficult to work with. Grate it finely, or, if melting it, keep the temperature low.

Alcohol

The alcohol content of any drink you add will evaporate during baking leaving a luxurious flavour.

MELTING CHOCOLATE

Melting chocolate needs care and attention. To melt chocolate, break the bar into small pieces and put it in a heatproof bowl standing over a pan of warm water. Make sure the bowl containing the chocolate is dry and that steam cannot get into the bowl. Heat the water to a gentle simmer and leave the bowl to stand for five minutes.

Calvados (apple brandy) enhances cakes made with pears, apples, or quince. Amaretto (almond-flavoured liqueur) adds to the flavour of peach, almond and apricot bakes. Marsala (fortified wine) has a special affinity with pears, chocolate and coffee. Blackcurrant liqueur is perfect for blackcurrant treats.

Cheese

French Brie and soft herb and garlic cheese add a light tart flavour to savoury recipes. Cheddar, Parmesan and Stilton each add robust flavour.

Vegetables

Versatile ingredients in bakes, vegetables, should be finely grated before they are added to the batter. Use courgettes (zucchini), marrow (large zucchini), pumpkin, squash, onions, carrots, beetroot (beet) and sweet potato for sweet and savoury flavours.

Basic equipment

For successful cake-making you need an oven that will retain an accurate and even temperature and some basic equipment. If you're new to baking, start off with some mixing equipment and a few pans. A 900g/2lb loaf tin, a muffin tin and a 20cm/8in cake pan are useful sizes to have.

Baking papers, paper cases and foil

For lining tins and baking sheets use baking parchment, which is non-stick, or greaseproof (waxed) paper. Paper cases can be purchased in many different and convenient sizes to fit round or square cake tins (pans) or cupcake and muffin tins. Waxed paper is a useful surface to pipe royal iced decorations on to, as they will peel away easily once dry. Kitchen foil is handy for wrapping rich fruit cakes or for protecting wrapped cakes in the freezer.

Baking sheets

Choose large, heavy-duty baking sheets that will not buckle at high temperatures. Non-stick sheets are useful, but avoid thin, cheaper bakeware, which may bend during baking and cause sloping cakes or burnt edges.

Below Paper cases can be purchased to fit an exact tin size, but you can make your own lining from sheets of baking parchment, if you like.

Above Mixing bowls, wooden spoons, palette knives or metal spatulas, flexible scrapers and a skewer or cake tester are basic items of baking equipment.

Bowls

You'll need a set of different sizes of bowls for mixing and beating small and large amounts of cake batters, eggs, cream and other liquids.

Electric whisk

A hand-held electric whisk makes quick work of whisking cake batters and egg whites, and is an invaluable aid for cake-making.

Flexible scraper

A flexible scraper is perfect for getting the maximum amount of cake batter out of a bowl. These become softer with use.

Grater

A grater with a fine and a coarse side is useful for grating citrus rinds, chocolate and marzipan. You can also use a zester for citrus rinds.

Kitchen scales

Good kitchen scales are a vital piece of equipment for a baker. Old-fashioned scales with a pan and a set of weights are equally as good as a modern set with a digital display screen as long as they are accurate.

Measuring spoons and cups

Use a set of standard measuring spoons for accurate measuring of small quantities of ingredients. Sets of plastic or metal measures are sold specifically for this purpose. Remember that all spoon measures

Above Essential equipment includes sieves, graters, scissors, a pastry brush and a palette knife or metal spatula.

should be level. Standard kitchen tablespoons or teaspoons may be inaccurate measures.

Metric and imperial measures are given in the recipes. Follow one set of measurements only, as they are not exact equivalents.

Graded measuring cups are used in many countries in place of kitchen scales and are handy for quick measuring. A measuring jug (cup) is vital for liquids and it needs to be graduated in small measures.

Below An electric mixer and whisk are helpful and time-saving kitchen tools, making light work of beating cake batters.

Oven

Each recipe usually begins with the oven setting (unless some form of preparation needs to be done in advance). It is important to preheat the oven to the correct temperature before putting a cake in to bake. Before you switch on the oven, it is also important to arrange the shelves to the correct position.

Fan-assisted ovens circulate hot air around the oven and will heat up very quickly. If you are using a fan oven, you will need to reduce the temperature stated in the recipe by 10 per cent; for example, if the baking temperature is 180°C/350°F/Gas 4, reduce it to 160°C/325°F/Gas 3. If the oven is too hot, the outside of a cake will burn before the inside has had time to cook. If it is too cool, cakes may sink or not rise evenly. Try not to open the oven door until at least halfway through the baking time when the cake has

had time to rise and set, as a sudden drop in temperature will stop the cake rising and it will therefore sink.

Palette knives or spatulas

These are ideal for many jobs including loosening cakes from their tins (pans), lifting cakes and smoothing on icing and frostings.

Pastry brush

A pastry brush is necessary to brush glazes over cakes and to brush melted butter into tins. Brushes wear out and start to shed bristles if used regularly, so keep a spare one handy.

Scissors

These are essential for cutting lining papers to size and snipping dried fruits or nuts into chunks.

Below Measuring jugs, kitchen scales, measuring spoons and cups are essential for baking.

Left A selection of tins in different sizes and shapes increases the range of baked goods you can make.

deep-set muffin holes for larger individual cakes.

Fairy cake, bun or patty tins are similar to muffin tins but have shallower indentations in the individual tins for making smaller cakes. Line each indentation with a paper case.

Ring moulds and Kugelhopf tins are round metal moulds with a hole or funnel in the centre and are specially designed for baking angel cakes and ring-shaped cakes. Grease these moulds well with melted butter and put small strips of baking parchment in the base of plain ring moulds to aid the release of the cake.

Wire racks

These cooling racks allow air to circulate around the hot baked cakes so that they will cool without becoming moist underneath.

Sieves

A large wire sieve (strainer) is useful for sifting flour and dry ingredients. A smaller nylon sieve can be kept just for icing (confectioners') sugar.

Skewer or cake tester

A thin metal skewer is used to test if the inside of a cake is cooked.

Spoons

Keep a large wooden spoon aside just for baking, for beating mixtures, butters and creaming. Don't use one that has been used for frying savoury things such as onions, as the flavours may taint the cake batter. Use a metal spoon for folding flour into cake batter.

Tins

Always use the size of tin (pan) stated in the recipe. If you use too large a tin, your cake may be too shallow when it is baked. Too small a tin may cause a peak in the mixture to form, which will then crack or sink in the middle.

Choose good-quality rigid bakeware. When buying new tins, remember that top-quality tins will last longer and give better results. Non-stick coatings on some of the new ranges of bakeware need almost no greasing and cakes turn out beautifully, as do cakes cooked in the new heatproof flexible-type muffin and loaf moulds.

Sandwich tins and shallow round tins are designed to bake light sponges quickly.

Loaf tins in small and large sizes are ideal for teabreads and loaf cakes.

Deep round and square heavy-duty cake tins are ideal for baking rich fruit cakes.

Springform tins are round baking tins that have a clipped side that can be loosened and removed easily from delicate bakes such as light sponges or cheesecakes. A loose-based tin makes a good substitute.

Muffin tins are available in sets of six or 12 indentations and have

---

ROUND OR SQUARE TINS AND COMPARABLE SIZING
If you use a tin (pan) that is a different size from the one stated in the recipe, the baking time, height, texture and appearance of the cake may be affected, as the quantity of mixture you have prepared will not be correct for that size of tin. Although you can use a square tin instead of a round tin, the equivalent sizes are not exactly equal, as they involve a 2.5cm/1in size difference. A square tin will have a larger area than its round equivalent; for example, a 20cm/8in round cake tin will take the same quantity of mixture as an 18cm/7in square tin.

Successful cake-making

Paying attention to the detail of a recipe will help to ensure a perfect cake. So, get all your equipment ready and prepare your cake tin. Take care with accurate measuring, and know how to test that the cake is cooked so that your hard work is rewarded with a delicious treat.

Assembling the ingredients
Ensure that you have all the necessary ingredients before baking.

Sifting flour makes a superfine product that is light and airy.

Accurate weighing and measuring
Recipes usually specify imperial, metric or cup weights and you must stick to one set only and never combine these weights, as they are not exact equivalents. If the measurements are muddled, it will affect the quality of the baked goods.

1 All spoon measurements must be level using a recognized set of metric or imperial spoon measures. Never estimate weights, as you will rarely achieve an accurate result. Do not measure ingredients over the mixing bowl in case you spill too much.

2 As ingredients must be measured exactly, use good kitchen scales for weighing or graded measuring cups and scoops. These cups should be levelled for accurate measuring unless the recipe calls for a 'generous' cup.

Preparing tins
When recipes give instructions on how to prepare and line tins (pans), don't be tempted to skimp on them, or you may ruin the baked cake. If using tins without a non-stick coating, give them a light greasing before use. Line the base of a tin to help the cake turn out easily.

1 Apply a thin film of melted butter with a pastry brush, or rub around the tin with kitchen paper and a little softened margarine. Ensure the corners are adequately coated or the baked cake may stick.

Lining the sides of the tin

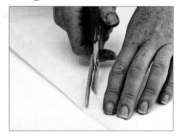

1 Cut a piece of baking parchment 2.5cm/1in wider than the depth of the tin and long enough to fit around the circumference. Make a fold along one long edge of the strip, about 2.5cm/1in deep. Snip this folded edge at regular intervals with sharp scissors. The snipped edge is the bottom edge.

2 Line the sides of the tin using the strip, with the snipped edge at the base, lying flat. Smooth the baking parchment flat against the greased sides of the tin. It should adhere easily. Lightly grease any overlap of the edges so that it doesn't protrude into the cake batter. Lightly grease the snipped edges. If your tin has a loose base this step will stop the baking batter from escaping and burning on the oven base.

Lining for a fruit cake

1 Tins for rich fruit cake batters are double-lined on the inside and lined on the outside. Cut a piece of baking parchment large enough to fold double and to stand 5cm/2in higher than the tin sides before continuing as for Lining the Sides of the Tin. A layer of brown paper wrapped around the outside protects the cake from forming a dark crust.

Lining the base of a tin

1 Place the tin on a sheet of baking parchment and draw around it with a pencil. Cut out the shape.

2 Fit the rounds of paper in the base of the tin to cover the snipped edge of the side lining.

Lining a baking tray

1 Cut a sheet of paper larger than the tray. Cut into each corner, then press in place.

Coating with flour

1 To coat with flour, tip a spoonful into the greased tin, then tip away the excess. This gives a golden edge.

Filling a cake tin with batter

1 Pour cake batter into the centre of the cake tin and spread it out to the edges with a knife. The batter should be spread evenly to ensure even baking. Do this lightly without removing too much air from the batter. Rub off any drips.

Checking to see if a cake is cooked

There are several clues to help determine whether a cake is ready. Has it baked for the suggested time? The baking times may need reviewing if you know that your oven temperature is inaccurate, if other items are being cooked at the same time, or if the oven door is opened in the baking process.

1 Cakes should be golden, risen and firm to the touch when pressed lightly in the centre. Lighter sponges and cakes should be a pale golden colour and the sides should shrink away slightly from the sides of the tin.

2 To test to see if a cake is baked through, insert a thin warmed skewer into the deepest part of the centre, which should take longest to bake. If the cake is cooked, the skewer should come out perfectly cleanly with no mixture sticking to it. If there is mixture on the skewer, bake the cake for a little longer and test again.

Releasing from the tin and cooling cakes

As freshly baked cakes are very fragile, they need time to stand in the tin to cool for a short time to firm them. Sponges and delicate cakes need 3–4 minutes standing time, but rich fruit cakes are very soft when freshly baked, so leave these in the tin for longer. To give a good shape to the edges, very rich fruit cakes such as wedding cakes should be left in the tins to go cold.

1 Loosen the cake sides by running a small metal spatula around the inside of the tin between the lining paper and the tin.

2 Turn the cake out to go cold on a wire rack. Put a wire rack on top of the cake tin, then turn the whole thing over so that the cake is upside down. Use oven gloves to protect your hands. Peel away the lining papers from the base of the cake while it is warm. Turn the cake back the right way up. Leave the cake to go completely cold before icing and storing.

Storing cakes

Make sure cakes are completely cold before storing, otherwise condensation will form in the tin and this can cause the cakes to go mouldy. Plastic food containers will encourage cakes to keep moist, so are ideal for storing richer sponges, but an airtight cake tin is necessary to keep fatless sponge-type cakes dry.

Cakes with fresh cream fillings and decorations need to be kept in the refrigerator and ideally eaten on the day of filling with cream.

Fatless sponges such as Swiss rolls (jelly rolls), will keep for only 1–2 days. Sponges with added fat will store for 3–5 days and richer cakes, such as creamed sponges, will keep for up to 1 week. Light fruit cakes will store for 2 weeks in a tin but rich fruit cakes will keep for up to 3 months after cutting.

If you don't have a large cake container, invert a large mixing bowl over the cake on a plate or flat surface and the cake will stay fresh.

FEEDING A FRUIT CAKE
Fruit cakes fed with alcohol have a mellow flavour.

Prick the surface of the baked cake with a cocktail stick (toothpick) and brush with a little alcohol such as rum, brandy or sweet sherry. The alcohol should infuse the cake.

Storing a rich fruit cake

Rich fruit cakes, such as wedding cakes, will mature in flavour and improve in texture if kept for 3 months before being eaten, especially if you feed them with alcohol two or three times during that 3 months. Store undecorated fruit cakes in their baking papers.

1 Wrap the original wrappings of the rich fruit cake with clean baking parchment and seal with tape.

2 Wrap in a double layer of foil and seal tightly, then store in a cool dry place.

Freezing cakes

Most cakes will freeze well, undecorated. Cool each cake completely, then wrap in strong clear film (plastic wrap) or kitchen foil to exclude as much air as possible. Label and freeze away from strong-smelling foodstuffs such as fish. To use, completely unwrap the cake and thaw it at room temperature on racks, allowing plenty of time for larger cakes.

Different methods of making baked goods

There are just six basic ways to make cakes. Each method gives the cake a different texture and consistency. To get perfect results, it's important to know how the different types of mixtures should be prepared and what to look out for.

Classic creaming method

Light cakes are made by the creaming method, which means that the butter and sugar are first beaten or 'creamed' together. A little care is needed to achieve the perfectly creamed mixture.

1 Use a large bowl, and either an electric whisk or a wooden spoon to beat the fat and sugar together until pale and fluffy. As the sugar dissolves it blends with the fat, lightening it and making it very soft. Have the fat at room temperature to make beating it easier.

2 Now add the eggs one by one, beating after each addition, to form a slackened batter. Eggs for baking are always best used at room temperature to prevent the mixture from 'splitting' or curdling, which will happen with cold eggs.

3 Adding a teaspoon of flour with each beaten egg will help to keep the mixture light and smooth and prevent the mixture from separating. A badly mixed and curdled batter will hold less air and be heavy, or it can cause a sunken cake.

All-in-one method

This one-stage method is quick and easy, and it's perfect for those new to baking, as it does not involve any complicated techniques. It's an ideal method for making light sponges, but softened butter or tub margarine at room temperature must be used.

1 All the ingredients are placed in a large bowl and quickly beaten together using a wooden spoon or an electric mixer for just a few minutes until smooth. Do not over-beat, as this will make the mixture too wet.

Rubbing-in method

This method is used for easy fruit cakes and small buns such as rock buns. In this method, the fat is lightly worked into the flour between cold fingers, in the same way as for making pastry. The fat should ideally be cold.

1 Rub the fat into the flour with your fingertips until the mixture resembles fine crumbs. This can be done by hand or using a food processor. Shake the bowl to allow the larger lumps of fat to rise to the surface, then rub in the larger lumps. Repeat until an even crumb is achieved.

2 Stir in the sugar and other dry ingredients until combined. Stir in enough liquid to give a soft mixture that will drop easily from a spoon.

Melting method

Cakes with a deliciously moist and sticky texture, such as gingerbread, are made by the melting method. These cakes use a high proportion of sugar and syrup and may contain heavier grains such as ground nuts or oats. These cakes benefit from storing for at least a day before cutting, to improve their moisture and stickiness.

1 Over gentle heat and using a large pan, warm together the fat, sugar and syrup, until the sugar granules have dissolved and the mixture is liquid. If the heat is set too high, the sugar will burn before the fat has melted. Stir occasionally, but keep watching so that the sugar does not burn on the base of the pan.

2 Allow the mixture to cool a little before beating in the flour, eggs, spices and remaining ingredients to make a batter. Bicarbonate of soda (baking soda) is often used as a raising agent in this method, to help raise a heavy batter. These cakes rise but the texture is heavier.

Whisking method

Light and feathery sponges are made by the whisking method. These are not easy cakes for beginners, and require a little skill and care. The only raising agent for this method is the air that has been trapped into the mixture during mixing. As the air expands in the heat of the oven, the cake rises. Fatless sponges such as a Swiss roll (jelly roll) are made by whisking.

1 A classic sponge is made by whisking eggs and caster (superfine) sugar together over a pan of hot water until the batter is thick enough to leave a trail when the whisk is lifted away from the bowl. When the mixture is pale, thick and airy, remove from the heat and continue to whisk until the batter is cool and doubled in volume.

2 Add the flour by sifting some over the surface and gently folding it in, using a large metal spoon, until all the flour is evenly blended. A metal spoon will cut through the batter retaining as much air as possible.

3 Be gentle with the mixture; it is essential not to knock out the air bubbles when folding in the flour.

Making fruit cakes

Rich fruit cakes are usually made by the creaming method, then soaked dried fruits and nuts are folded in with the flour.

1 Cream the butter and sugar in a large bowl, add the eggs, a few spoonfuls of flour to stop the eggs curdling and treacle (molasses).

2 Add the flour and any spices, then add the dried fruits last, stirring well to incorporate all the ingredients. The batter for a rich fruit cake is usually quite stiff.

Working with sugarpaste

A versatile medium for all kinds of edible ornaments, sugarpaste can be rolled out like pastry and used to cover cakes of all sizes with a perfectly smooth sweet coating. It can also be stamped, embossed and moulded to make a wonderful range of three-dimensional decorations.

Sugarpaste, also known as fondant, is a combination of liquid glucose, gelatine, glycerine and icing (confectioners') sugar, and can be bought ready-made. You can make it at home, but the availability of some excellent products on the market means it is more convenient to buy it. Sugarpaste is sold vacuum packed in plastic bags. When you use it make sure that during and after use you keep it well wrapped with clear film (plastic wrap), or it will become dry and chalky in texture and unusable. If the paste is too sticky, add a little finely sifted icing sugar to it.

To tint sugarpaste

Subtle tones of sugarpaste often look much more appealing than bright ones, especially if the cakes are for an elegant celebration. If you require a vibrant colour it is better to buy it ready coloured from a sugarcraft store, because the quantities of colour needed make the paste too wet.

1 To colour sugarpaste add a few drops of food colour or a few specks of paste to a ball of sugarpaste. Knead until the colour is evenly distributed.

To mould sugarpaste shapes

Plastic chocolate moulds are a good investment for this skill. The fine texture of sugarpaste makes it ideal for shaping, intricate decorative moulds.

1 Place the paste on a working surface lightly dusted with sifted icing sugar, and knead until it is smooth and free from cracks. Colour it as required.

2 Divide the paste into portions and press each into a decorative mould. Press repeatedly to ensure the paste adheres. Trim the top so that it is smooth and level.

3 Chill for several hours. Press the tip of a knife between the paste and the mould to create an air pocket. Prise out the shape and leave to defrost. Smooth out any knife marks once the sugarpaste has softened sufficiently.

To make stamped sugarpaste flowers

Shaped small-scale cutters are available to suit every theme.

1 Roll out a small ball of coloured sugarpaste on a light dusting of icing sugar to 3mm/¹⁄₈in thick and cut out each shape.

2 Use a ball modelling tool to gently manipulate the sugarpaste flowers into a cup shape, bending the petals up a little. Pipe the centre and add false stamens if you like.

To emboss sugarpaste

Imprint patterns in soft sugarpaste with decorative tools.

1 Use a decorative rolling pin or craft stamp, available from sugarcraft stores, and press firmly on to thinly rolled out paste to leave an imprint. Remove with care.

2 Use a cookie cutter to cut a scalloped circle. Stick to the top of a cupcake with a little royal icing.

To make sugarpaste plunger-cut flowers

With a flower cutter, such as a plunger cutter, you can make perfect small flowers quickly. The plunge mechanism in each cutter pushes the flower out of the cutter and makes the shape of each cupped. You just need to add a contrasting centre to finish them off.

1 Lightly dust the work surface with sifted icing sugar. Roll out a small ball of coloured sugarpaste to 3mm/¹⁄₈in thick using a small rolling pin.

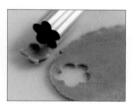

2 Use a plunger cutter (available in different flower shapes) to cut out flowers and lift them gently from the surface using a flat palette knife or metal spatula to avoid squashing the edges of the petals with your fingers.

3 Using a fine plain nozzle and a small quantity of royal icing in a piping bag, pipe a small blob at the centre of each flower.

Working with marzipan

Redolent of medieval feasts, marzipan is a luxurious confection made from ground almonds and fine sugar and is used for covering cakes and making sweets, often coloured and shaped into little fruits, flowers and animals. It can be flavoured with rose or orange flower water.

Marzipan leaves

Marzipan is an ideal material for cutting and moulding decorative shapes such as small pumpkins and other vegetables, fruit, flowers or leaves, all of which make exquisite small decorations for cakes. Small leaves made from rolled-out marzipan can make stunning cake decorations, used by themselves or combined with crystallized or sugarpaste flowers. Try green holly leaves on Christmas cakes, or these autumnal oak leaves.

MAKES 8–10 LEAVES

50g/2oz marzipan, tinted as desired
icing (confectioners') sugar, for dusting

1 Roll out the marzipan thinly. Cut out leaves with a cutter, or cut round a card template using a craft knife. Leave to dry on baking parchment.

2 For curled leaves, drape the shapes over a rolling pin and leave to dry at room temperature for 2 days. Paint the veins and edges with food colouring using a fine artist's brush.

Mouse in the house

Uncoloured natural marzipan, made with egg whites, works best for marzipan shapes that you want to colour because it accepts colour readily.

MAKES 2

50g/2oz marzipan, tinted as desired
small quantity royal icing

1 Take a 2.5cm/1in ball of coloured marzipan and roll it so that it is smooth. Hold the ball between the palms of both hands and gently put pressure on one end to form a cone shape.

2 For the ears, roll two tiny balls of marzipan completely smooth. Use a modelling tool to create the indent. Stick the ears to the sides of the head using water.

3 Make a round black nose. Create indents for the eyes and fill with icing blobs. Add black eyeballs. Paint on the eyebrows with food colouring. Model a black tail.

Spider in the web

It is difficult to tint marzipan black without changing the consistency of it, so for an intense shade buy ready coloured.

MAKES 2

50g/2oz black marzipan
small quantity black and white icing
sprinkles

1 To make the web, cover the top of a cupcake with white glacé icing.

2 Pipe black circles with a fine plain nozzle on top. Starting at the centre and working to the edge, drag a cocktail stick (toothpick) through the lines of icing. Allow to set.

3 Form a smooth round head and a larger round body from marzipan using two balls of black marzipan. Dampen one side of one ball with water and stick the two balls together. Make indentations for the eyes.

4 Roll eight legs and stick under the body using water. Pipe white eyes in the sockets and a smiley mouth. Add black marzipan eyeballs, and sprinkles on the back.

Glacé icing

Also known as water icing, this is the simplest of all icing recipes, and is ideal for decorating small cakes. It's quick to mix, with only two basic ingredients, and provided you take care to get the consistency right it flows easily over the surface and sets to a glossy smoothness.

Glacé icing, made with finely sifted icing (confectioners') sugar and hot water, makes a basic topping that is suitable for many cakes. The icing can be flavoured with vanilla, fruit juice and rind, chocolate, coffee or alcohol, and looks wonderful in delicate, pastel colours. It is important to get the consistency exactly right: too thick and it will not form a super-smooth glossy coating; too thin and it will run over the top and down the sides of the cake. Glacé icing sets to form a crisp surface, but never becomes rock hard. The consistency determines how many cakes the icing covers.

MAKES ENOUGH FOR 16 CUPCAKES

225g/8oz/2 cups icing
  (confectioners') sugar
15–30ml/1–2 tbsp hot water
a few drops of food colouring

Below Icing can be tinted with liquid or paste colours.

1 Sift the icing sugar into a bowl, then gradually mix in the water, a few drops at a time, beating until the mixture is the consistency of cream.

2 Add one or two drops of food colouring (with caution). For a more vibrant colour use paste food colouring, available from specialist suppliers. Stir until evenly coloured.

3 Use the icing immediately, while it is smooth and fluid. Add any further decoration before the icing dries.

Crystallized flower decorations

This traditional method of preserving summer flowers is simple to do and makes charming and very effective decorations for delicately iced cakes. The results can be spectacular, with prettily faded colours and the lingering perfumes of summer.

Popular edible flowers include primroses, violets, cowslips, alpine pinks and roses. Try bright blue anchusa, starry-petalled borage or vivid-red pineapple sage.

Use them individually or try different combinations. Some flowers, such as primroses, cowslips, borage, sage and anchusa, are easy to pull away from their green calyx and can be crystallized whole. Daisies, roses and pinks are often best divided into individual petals, although you might consider treating entire small flowerheads for a real showpiece. Fresh crystallized flowers that retain their moisture need using quickly, but flowers that are dried thoroughly in a warm place for 24–36 hours prior to crystallizing will last for a few months.

selection of petals and/or flowers
1 egg white
50g/2oz/¼ cup caster (superfine) sugar

1 Gather flowers when they are dry, and select clean, perfect specimens. Trim and prepare individual petals or whole flowers. Beat the egg white lightly and put it and the sugar in separate saucers.

2 Pick up each petal or flower and paint the entire surface, front and back, carefully with the egg white, using an artist's brush.

3 Dredge on both sides with caster sugar so that it sticks to the egg white and coats the flower or petal.

4 Lay the flowers and petals on baking parchment and leave them in a warm, dry place until completely dry and crisp. Store in a sealed container.

> **WARNING**
> Raw eggs should not be eaten by pregnant women, babies, young children or the elderly. If in doubt, use powdered egg white for coating the flowers. It will work just as well.

Problem solving

If you accurately measure ingredients and follow the recipe steps carefully, your cakes should work out well each time, but if your cake does not turn out as expected, look at the following problems and solutions to find out what might have happened.

Why do cakes stick to the tin?

• You will not be able to turn a cake out of a tin (pan) if it was not greased sufficiently into all the corners or properly lined with paper.
• Poor-quality tins tend to produce bad results and can buckle in the heat, causing a misshapen cake.
• If the cake has been left in the tin for too long it may have dried to it.

Why does a cake sink?

• Too much raising agent such as baking powder or bicarbonate of soda (baking soda) may have been used in proportion to the amount of flour and other ingredients. It is important to weigh out and measure all the ingredients correctly.

• If the oven is too cool, the cake will be under-baked and sink.
• A mixture that is too wet. This can be caused by over-beating when using soft tub margarine or by adding too much liquid.
• If the mixture was cooked in a tin that is too small, it will not cook through properly. The use of the correct size of tin is important.
• Opening or slamming the oven door during the baking time.
• If the cake is under-baked, particularly in the centre, and the batter there is still damp and heavy, the cake will sink.

What causes a close and heavy texture?

• Too little raising agent, or adding too much fat, egg or flour.
• A mixture that is too dry or too wet.
• If the cake is not whisked or beaten sufficiently to incorporate air, the texture will be coarse.
• Too much sugar in the batter.
• Baking in an oven that is too cool will also affect the texture.
• Fat and sugar not beaten enough before the other ingredients added.

What causes a cake with a dry texture?

• Cakes with a dry texture tend to be crumbly when cut and stale rapidly. This can be caused if the cake is baked too slowly or contains too much raising agent.
• The mixture was not rubbed in or beaten sufficiently.
• The cake was over-baked, making it dry.

Why do small fairy cakes spread?

• Small cakes spread out if the mixture is too wet or if there is too much mixture in each paper case; for best results half-fill the cases.
• Adding too much or too little raising agent.

What causes a dark, hard outer crust?

• Too hot an oven or over-baking in a fan-assisted oven at a high temperature. If you are using a fan-assisted oven you will usually need to turn the temperature down by 10 degrees, or follow your instruction booklet.
• Rich fruit cakes taking several hours to bake should be protected by a double lining inside the tin and by wrapping around the outside of the tin with a layer of brown paper or newspaper.

Why do cakes fail to rise?

• Insufficient raising agent or over-beating a mixture, which knocks out the air.
• If a mixture is too stiff and does not contain enough liquid or is baked in too cool an oven.
• If too large a cake tin was used.
• If the batter was left for a while before baking it will not rise.

Why do large air bubbles and tunnels form in the centre of the cake?

• An uneven texture is caused by under-mixing when adding the flour or liquid.
• If the mixture is too dry it will tend to contain pockets of air instead of the air being distributed throughout the mixture.
• If the flour and raising agent are not sifted in or properly mixed together.

What causes a crack or peak to appear in the top of the cake?

• If the tin is too small and it therefore contains too much mixture, the batter will rise up and the top will form a peak.
• Baking in an oven that is too hot, or baking the cake too near the heat at the top of the oven.
• The mixture is too wet or too dry.
• Too little liquid in the batter.

Why does the fruit sink in a sponge cake?

• All vine fruits must be dry when added to the mixture. Glacé (candied) cherries must be washed of their syrup, dried and tossed in flour to prevent them sinking.
• If the mixture is too wet or if it contains too much raising agent.
• Using too cool an oven or opening the oven door too soon before the end of the baking time.

OTHER PROBLEMS
• **The cake sloped or was uneven** Check that the oven shelves are level. Centre the cake in the oven. Mix the batter thoroughly. Check the oven temperature with a thermometer to ensure it is correct.
• **The cake was lumpy** The ingredients were unevenly mixed.
• **The batter ran out of the pan into the oven base** If a loose-base tin or springform tin was used, ensure it was adequately lined. The tin was too small for the volume of batter. Check the oven shelves are level.
• **The cake went soggy after being stored** The cake was under-baked. It wasn't cold before it was stored or wrapped. It was stored in a warm place.

Fruit jams and jellies

There's nothing to compare with homemade jam, bursting with fruit, spread thickly over
a slice of buttered bread or a delicious warm scone at tea time. Here are six of the most popular
recipes, make them when you have a glut of fruit in the summer months.

Strawberry jam

*Perfectly ripe strawberries are the main
ingredient of this most popular jam.*

MAKES ABOUT 1.3KG/3LB

1kg/2¼lb/8 cups strawberries, hulled
900g/2lb/4½ cups sugar
juice of 2 lemons

1 Layer the hulled strawberries with
the sugar in a large bowl. Cover
with clear film (plastic wrap) and
leave overnight.

2 Put the strawberries into a large
heavy pan. Add the lemon juice.
Gradually bring to the boil, over
low heat, stirring until the sugar
has dissolved.

3 Boil steadily for 10–15 minutes, or
until the jam reaches setting point
(*see box below*). When it is ready,
cool for 10 minutes in the pan.

4 Pour into warm sterilized jars,
filling them right to the top. Cover
and seal while the jam is still
hot and label when the jars are cold.

5 Store in a cool dark place for up
to one year.

SETTING POINT
The point at which jam sets is
105°C/220°F. If you don't have a
sugar thermometer, put 10ml/
2 tsp of the jam on to a chilled
saucer. Chill for 3 minutes, then
push the jam gently with your
finger; if wrinkles form it is
ready. If not, continue boiling,
but keep checking regularly.

Energy 3816kcal/16,259kJ; Protein 12.5g; Carbohydrate 1000.5g, of which sugars 1000.5g; Fat 1g, of which saturates 0g; Cholesterol 0mg; Calcium 637mg; Fibre 11g; Sodium 114mg.

Raspberry jam

For many, this is the best of all jams; it is delicious with scones and cream. Raspberries are low in pectin and acid, so they will not set firmly, but a soft set is perfect for this jam.

MAKES ABOUT 3.1KG/7LB

1.8kg/4lb/10²/₃ cups firm raspberries
juice of 1 large lemon
1.8kg/4lb/9 cups preserving sugar, warmed

1 Put 175g/6oz/1 cup of the raspberries into a large, heavy pan and crush them. Add the rest of the fruit and the lemon juice. Bring to the boil, simmer until soft and pulpy.

2 Add the sugar and stir until dissolved, then bring back to the boil and boil rapidly until setting point is reached.

3 Pour the jam into warmed sterilized jars, filling to the top. Cover and seal the jars. Label when cold, and store in a cold, dark place for up to 6 months.

Bramble jelly

This jelly has an excellent intense, fruity flavour. Make sure you include a few red unripe berries in the pan for a good fruit set.

MAKES ABOUT 900G/2LB

900g/2lb/8 cups blackberries
juice of 1 lemon
about 900g/2lb/4½ cups caster (superfine) sugar

1 Put the fruit, 300ml/½ pint/1¼ cups water and the lemon juice in a large, heavy pan. Cover and cook for 15–30 minutes or until the blackberries are very soft.

2 Ladle into a jelly bag, set over a large bowl. Leave to strain overnight. Discard the fruit pulp. Measure the juice and add 450g/1lb/ 2¼ cups sugar to every 600ml/1 pint/2½ cups juice.

3 Place the sugar and liquid in a large, heavy pan and bring slowly to the boil, stirring all the time. When setting point is reached (see box opposite), skim off any scum and pour into warm sterilized jars. Cover and seal while the jelly is still hot. Label when the jars are cold. Store for up to 6 months in a cool, dry place.

Energy 7542kcal/32,220kJ; Protein 34.2g; Carbohydrate 1963.8g, of which sugars 1963.8g; Fat 5.4g, of which saturates 1.8g; Cholesterol 0mg; Calcium 1.4mg; Fibre 45g; Sodium 162mg.

Energy 3771kcal/16,665kJ; Protein 12.6g; Carbohydrate 986.4g, of which sugars 986.4g; Fat 1.8g, of which saturates 0g; Cholesterol 0mg; Calcium 846mg; Fibre 27.9g; Sodium 72mg.

Apricot conserve

If you miss the short apricot season, you can enjoy the taste of sweet, tangy apricot jam all year round.

MAKES ABOUT 2KG/4½LB

675g/1½lb ready-to-eat dried apricots, soaked
    overnight in 900ml/1½ pints/3¾ cups apple juice
juice and grated rind of 2 unwaxed lemons
675g/1½lb/scant 3½ cups preserving sugar
50g/2oz/½ cup blanched almonds, coarsely chopped

1 Pour the soaked apricots and juice into a preserving pan and add the lemon juice and rind. Bring to the boil, then lower the heat and simmer for 15–20 minutes until soft.

2 Add the sugar to the pan and bring to the boil, stirring until the sugar has completely dissolved. Boil for 15–20 minutes, or until setting point is reached.

3 Stir the chopped almonds into the jam and leave to stand for about 15 minutes, then pour the jam into warmed, sterilized jars. Seal, then leave to cool. Label and store in a cool, dark place for up to one year.

Damson jam

Dark, plump damsons are now commercially available. They produce a deeply coloured and richly flavoured jam.

MAKES ABOUT 2KG/4½LB

1kg/2¼lb damsons or wild plums
400ml/14fl oz/1⅔ cups water
1kg/2¼lb/5 cups preserving sugar

1 Put the damsons in a preserving pan and pour in the water. Bring to the boil, then reduce the heat and simmer gently until the damsons are soft. Add the sugar and stir.

2 Bring the mixture to the boil. Skim off the stones (pits) as they rise to the surface. Boil to setting point. Remove from the heat and leave to cool for 10 minutes.

3 Pour into warmed sterilized jars, cover and seal. Allow to cool, then label. Store in a cool, dark place for 1 year.

Energy 4032kcal/17,163kJ; Protein 40.9g; Carbohydrate 955.2g, of which sugars 953.8g; Fat 31.9g, of which saturates 2.2g; Cholesterol 0mg; Calcium 970mg; Fibre 46.2g; Sodium 142mg.

Energy 4320kcal/18,430kJ; Protein 10g; Carbohydrate 1141g, of which sugars 1141g; Fat 0g, of which saturates 0g; Cholesterol 0mg; Calcium 770mg; Fibre 18g; Sodium 80mg.

Lemon curd

This classic tangy, creamy curd is enduringly popular. It is delicious spread thickly over freshly baked white bread, or used to fill homemade tarts, or as a filling for Victoria sandwich cakes.

MAKES ABOUT 450G/1LB

3 unwaxed lemons
200g/7oz/1 cup caster (superfine)
  sugar
115g/4oz/½ cup unsalted
  butter, diced
2 large (US extra large) eggs and
  2 large egg yolks

4 Stir the mixture constantly over the heat until the lemon curd thickens and lightly coats the back of a wooden spoon.

1 Wash the lemons, then grate the rind into a large heatproof bowl. Squeeze the juice into the bowl.

2 Set the bowl over a pan of gently simmering water and add the sugar and butter. Stir until the sugar has dissolved and the butter melted.

3 Put the eggs and yolks in a bowl and beat together. Pour the eggs through a sieve (strainer) into the lemon mixture, and whisk well.

5 Remove the pan from the heat and pour the curd into small, warmed sterilized jars. Cover and seal immediately. Allow to cool and label. Store in a cool, dark place, ideally in the refrigerator. Use within 3 months. Once opened, it is essential to store the lemon curd in the refrigerator and use quickly.

VARIATION
Use oranges to make orange curd.

Energy 1927kcal/8056kJ; Protein 20.7g; Carbohydrate 212.1g, of which sugars 212.1g; Fat 116.8g, of which saturates 66.2g; Cholesterol 1029mg; Calcium 294mg; Fibre 0g; Sodium 871mg.

Savoury treats

Traditionally, afternoon tea begins with a savoury course. A delectable selection of dainty sandwiches, thinly sliced with crusts removed, tempts the tastebuds and whets the appetite. Served alongside these for a more substantial between-meals filler are rich flaky pastry quiches, homemade sausage rolls, crisp crackers and light and flavourful spreads. This chapter also includes recipes for savoury muffins, which can be made in elegant proportions that work perfectly with the rest of the afternoon tea table. This tempting selection includes subtle Shallot, Thyme and Garlic Cheese Bakes, and filling Brioche with Savoury Pâté Stuffing.

Left: Quiche Lorraine and Leek and Bacon Tarts make fabulous additions to the tea table, offering guests more substantial and filling fare.

Sandwiches

The classic afternoon tea commences with a round of dainty sandwiches, which can be elegantly nibbled while you sip your first cup of freshly brewed tea. The sandwiches can be made of brown or white bread, but should always be cut into small fingers, triangles or squares.

Cucumber sandwiches

Delicate cucumber sandwiches with crusts removed are synonymous with traditional afternoon tea.

SERVES 6

1 cucumber
12 slices white bread
butter, at room temperature, for spreading
salt and ground black pepper

1 Peel the cucumber and cut into thin slices. Sprinkle with salt and put in a colander to drain for 20 minutes.

2 Butter the bread on one side. Trim off the crusts. Arrange the cucumber over six slices of bread and sprinkle with pepper. Top with the remaining bread. Press down lightly.

3 Cut the sandwiches into fingers, squares or triangles. Arrange on a serving plate.

Energy 174kcal/735kJ; Protein 6.8g; Carbohydrate 29.2g, of which sugars 3.3g; Fat 4.2g, of which saturates 1.1g; Cholesterol 5mg; Calcium 92mg; Fibre 1g; Sodium 307mg.

Turkey and cranberry sandwiches

Perfect for the festive tea table, turkey and cranberry sandwiches taste delicious and distinctly moreish.

SERVES 6

12 slices wholemeal (whole-wheat) bread
butter, at room temperature, for spreading
300g/11oz roast turkey, sliced
90ml/6 tbsp cranberry sauce

1 Spread each slice of bread with butter. Cover half of the slices of bread with roast turkey.

2 Spoon 15ml/1 tbsp of cranberry sauce on to the turkey and spread out to the edges. Season with salt and pepper. Top with another slice of bread and press down lightly.

3 Cut each sandwich into quarters diagonally to make small triangles.

Energy 312kcal/1314kJ; Protein 20g; Carbohydrate 35.4g, of which sugars 11.5g; Fat 11.3g, of which saturates 6.2g; Cholesterol 63mg; Calcium 40mg; Fibre 3.5g; Sodium 435mg.

Egg and cress sandwiches

A well-made egg and mayonnaise sandwich is a tasty tea-time snack.

SERVES 6

12 thin slices white or brown bread
butter, at room temperature,
    for spreading
4 small (US medium) hard-boiled
    eggs, peeled and finely chopped
60ml/4 tbsp mayonnaise
1 carton mustard and cress (fine
    curled cress)
salt and ground black pepper
slices of lemon, to garnish

1 Trim the crusts off the bread,
using a sharp knife. Then spread the
slices with soft butter.

2 To make the filling, put the
chopped eggs, mayonnaise,
mustard and cress and seasoning in
a bowl and mix.

3 Spoon on to six slices of bread
and spread out to the edges. Top
each one with another slice of bread
and press down gently. Cut into neat
triangles. Garnish with lemon slices.

COOK'S TIP
These sandwiches will keep well
for 2–3 hours. Cover with damp
kitchen paper, then cover tightly
in clear film (plastic wrap). Chill.

Egg and tuna sandwiches

*A flavourful and popular combination,
tuna fish and egg sandwiches are
perfect at any time of year, and are
made using everyday ingredients.*

SERVES 6

12 thin slices white or brown bread
butter, at room temperature,
    for spreading
4 small (US medium) hard-boiled
    eggs, peeled and finely chopped
50g/2oz canned tuna fish in oil,
    drained and mashed
10ml/2 tsp paprika
squeeze of lemon juice
50g/2oz piece cucumber, peeled
    and thinly sliced
salt and ground black pepper

1 Trim the crusts off the bread, then
spread with butter.

2 To make the filling, mix the eggs
with the tuna, paprika, lemon juice
and seasoning.

3 Cover six slices of bread with the
cucumber, top with the tuna and
finish with another slice of bread.
Cut each sandwich into three
even fingers.

Egg and cress Energy 320kcal/1337kJ; Protein 9g; Carbohydrate 26.8g, of which sugars 1.6g; Fat 20.5g, of which saturates 7.8g; Cholesterol 157mg; Calcium 89mg; Fibre 0.9g; Sodium 450mg.
Egg and tuna Energy 273kcal/1145kJ; Protein 12.3g; Carbohydrate 25.7g, of which sugars 1.2g; Fat 14.6g, of which saturates 6.9g; Cholesterol 154mg; Calcium 58mg; Fibre 3.5g; Sodium 477mg.

Crab sandwiches

Bread and butter served with crab is a classic tea-time treat.

SERVES 6

3 cooked crabs, about 900g/2lb each
12 slices crusty wholegrain bread
butter, at room temperature, for spreading
2 lemons, cut into quarters
rocket (arugula)
salt and ground black pepper

1 Break off the crab claws and legs, then use your thumbs to ease the body out of the shell. Remove and discard the grey gills from the body and put the white meat in a bowl.

2 Scrape the brown meat from the shell and add to the white meat. Season with salt and pepper.

3 Butter the bread and spread the crab meat on half of the slices. Add a squeeze of lemon juice and a little rocket. Top with bread and cut into triangles.

Energy 526kcal/2209kJ; Protein 30.1g; Carbohydrate 56g, of which sugars 2.6g; Fat 21.7g, of which saturates 9.1g; Cholesterol 85mg; Calcium 117mg; Fibre 7.7g; Sodium 1150mg.

Cheese and pickle sandwiches

Sharp, mature cheese is complemented with tangy pickle.

SERVES 6

12 slices white bread, crusts removed
butter, at room temperature, for spreading
300g/11oz hard cheese, such as Cheddar
90ml/6 tbsp pickle
watercress or rocket (arugula), to garnish
salt and ground black pepper

1 Spread each slice of bread with butter. Thinly slice the cheese and arrange the slices over half of the slices, filling to the edges.

2 Spoon 15ml/1 tbsp of pickle on to the cheese and season with salt and pepper, to taste. Spread the pickle out to the edges. Top each one with another slice of bread.

3 Cut each sandwich into three equal portions. Arrange on a plate and garnish with watercress or rocket.

Energy 429kcal/1793kJ; Protein 17.4g; Carbohydrate 31.8g, of which sugars 6.4g; Fat 25.6g, of which saturates 16.5g; Cholesterol 72mg; Calcium 433mg; Fibre 1g; Sodium 972mg.

Roast beef and horseradish sandwiches

Piquant horseradish is a perfect accompaniment for beef.

SERVES 6

1 large crusty white loaf
butter, at room temperature, for spreading
300g/11oz roast beef, thinly sliced
30–60ml/2–4 tbsp horseradish sauce
rocket (arugula)
salt and ground black pepper

1 Using a sharp bread knife, generously cut 12 even slices from the loaf of white bread. Spread each with butter.

2 Allowing about 50g/2oz of beef per sandwich, top half of the slices with meat and horseradish sauce, to taste.

3 Add some rocket to each sandwich. Sprinkle with salt and black pepper. Top each one with another slice of bread, and cut each sandwich diagonally into quarters.

Energy 505kcal/2125kJ; Protein 27.3g; Carbohydrate 58.5g, of which sugars 3g; Fat 19.6g, of which saturates 11g; Cholesterol 79mg; Calcium 148mg; Fibre 1.6g; Sodium 838mg.

Ham and English mustard sandwiches

Cold ham sandwiches are an old-fashioned favourite.

SERVES 6

12 slices seeded bread
butter, at room temperature, for spreading
300g/11oz roast ham, thinly sliced
30–60ml/1–2 tbsp English (hot) mustard
salt and ground black pepper
4 tomatoes and ½ carton cress, to garnish

1 Trim the crusts from each slice of bread, then spread with butter. Top half with thin slices of roast ham, and add English mustard to taste, spreading to the edges.

2 Top each one with a slice of bread and press down gently. Then cut each sandwich into three equal portions. Cut the tomatoes into wedges and chop the cress.

3 Arrange the sandwiches on a plate and garnish with the tomato and cress.

Energy 275kcal/1157kJ; Protein 15.2g; Carbohydrate 28.8g, of which sugars 2.2g; Fat 11.9g, of which saturates 6.3g; Cholesterol 52mg; Calcium 55mg; Fibre 2.6g; Sodium 1171mg.

Potted cheese

This is a great way to use up odd pieces of cheese left on the cheeseboard, blending them with your chosen seasonings before adding alcohol. Garnish with parsley and serve with plain crackers, oatcakes or crisp toast for a delicious start to afternoon tea.

SERVES 4–6

250g/9oz hard cheese, such as
   mature (sharp) cheese
75g/3oz/6 tbsp soft, unsalted
   butter, plus 25g/1oz/1 tbsp extra
   for melting
pinch of dried English (hot)
   mustard
pinch of ground mace
30ml/2 tbsp sherry or port
sprigs of fresh parsley,
   to garnish
ground black pepper

1 Cut the cheese into rough pieces and put them into the bowl of a food processor. Use the pulse button to chop the cheese into crumbs.

2 Add the butter, mustard, mace and pepper and blend until smooth. Taste and adjust the seasoning.

COOK'S TIP
Use finely chopped chives instead of mustard for a change.

3 Blend in the sherry or port.

4 Spoon the mixture into a dish leaving about 1cm/½in to spare on top. Level the surface.

5 Melt the butter in a small pan, skimming off any foam that rises to the surface. Leaving the sediment in the pan, pour a layer of melted butter on top of the cheese mixture to cover the surface. Refrigerate.

Energy 262kcal/1082kJ; Protein 10.7g; Carbohydrate 0.2g, of which sugars 0.2g; Fat 23.6g, of which saturates 15.2g; Cholesterol 70mg; Calcium 290mg; Fibre 0g; Sodium 363mg.

Salmon mousse

This light and delicate mousse is ideal for tea on the lawn on a balmy summer's afternoon.
Garnish it with thinly sliced cucumber, delicious when in season, and lemon wedges. Serve with
thin plain crackers or Melba toast for a satisfying crunch.

SERVES 6–8

300ml/½ pint/1¼ cups milk
1 small onion, thinly sliced
1 small carrot, thinly sliced
2 bay leaves
2 sprigs of parsley or dill
6 whole peppercorns
15ml/1 tbsp powdered gelatine
350g/12oz salmon fillet
75ml/5 tbsp dry white vermouth
25g/1oz/2 tbsp butter
25g/1oz/¼ cup plain
  (all-purpose) flour
75ml/5 tbsp mayonnaise
150ml/¼ pint/⅔ cup whipping
  cream
salt and ground black pepper

1 Put the milk in a pan with half the onion, carrot, herbs and peppercorns. Bring slowly to the boil, remove from the heat, cover and leave to infuse for 30 minutes. Meanwhile, sprinkle the gelatine over 45ml/ 3 tbsp cold water and leave to soak.

2 Put the salmon in another pan with the remaining onion, carrot, herbs and peppercorns. Add the vermouth and 60ml/4 tbsp water. Simmer, covered, for 10 minutes.

3 Flake the fish into a bowl, discarding the skin and bones. Boil the juices in the pan to reduce by half, strain and reserve.

4 Strain the infused milk into a clean pan and add the butter and flour. Whisking continuously, cook until thickened, then simmer gently for 1 minute. Pour into a food processor, add the soaked gelatine and blend. Add the salmon and the reserved cooking juices and pulse briefly.

5 Put into a bowl and stir in the mayonnaise and seasonings. Whip the cream and fold in gently. Pour into an oiled mould, cover and refrigerate for about 2 hours.

Energy 285kcal/1183kJ; Protein 12.6g; Carbohydrate 5.8g, of which sugars 3.2g; Fat 22.7g, of which saturates 8.7g; Cholesterol 57mg; Calcium 73mg; Fibre 0.2g; Sodium 103mg.

Quiche Lorraine

This classic quiche has some delightful characteristics, namely very thin flaky pastry, a really creamy and light, egg-rich filling, and smoked bacon. It makes an indulgent and satisfying first course to an afternoon tea.

SERVES 4–6

175g/6oz/1½ cups plain
    (all-purpose) flour, sifted, plus
    extra for dusting
pinch of salt
1 egg yolk
115g/4oz/½ cup unsalted butter, at
    room temperature, diced

For the filling
6 smoked streaky (fatty) bacon
    rashers (strips), rinds removed
300ml/½ pint/1¼ cups double
    (heavy) cream
3 eggs, plus 3 yolks
25g/1oz/2 tbsp unsalted butter
salt and ground black pepper

1 To make the pastry, place the flour, salt, egg yolk and butter in a food processor and process until blended. Turn on to a lightly floured surface and bring the mixture together into a ball. Leave to rest for 20 minutes.

2 Lightly flour a deep 20cm/8in round flan tin (pan), and place it on a baking tray. Roll out the pastry and use to line the tin. Trim off the excess.

3 Gently press the pastry into the corners of the tin. If the pastry breaks up, just push it into shape. Chill for 20 minutes. Preheat the oven to 200°C/400°F/Gas 6.

COOK'S TIP
To prepare in advance, bake for 5–10 minutes less than advised, until just set. Reheat at 190°C/ 375°F/Gas 5 for 10 minutes.

4 Meanwhile, cut the bacon rashers into thin pieces and grill (broil) until the fat runs. Arrange the bacon in the pastry case (pie shell). Beat together the cream, the whole eggs and yolks and seasoning. Carefully pour into the pastry case.

5 Bake for 15 minutes, then reduce the heat to 180°C/350°F/Gas 4 and bake for a further 15–20 minutes. When the filling is puffed up and golden brown, and the pastry edge crisp, remove from the oven and top with knobs (pats) of butter. Stand for 5 minutes before serving.

Energy 976kcal/4043kJ; Protein 18.1g; Carbohydrate 35.5g, of which sugars 2.2g; Fat 85.8g, of which saturates 48.4g; Cholesterol 519mg; Calcium 149mg; Fibre 1.4g; Sodium 678mg.

Leek and bacon tarts

These versatile tartlets are a favourite of the afternoon tea table. They make a deliciously savoury treat to eat instead of sandwiches. Serve with a mixed leaf salad, which has been tossed in a light lemony dressing. Serve with strong tea.

MAKES 6–8

275g/10oz/2½ cups plain
  (all-purpose) flour
pinch of salt
175g/6oz/¾ cup butter, diced
2 egg yolks
about 45ml/3 tbsp very cold water
salad leaves, to serve

For the filling
225g/8oz streaky (fatty) bacon,
  diced
4 leeks, sliced
6 eggs
115g/4oz/½ cup soft white
  (farmer's) cheese
15ml/1 tbsp mild mustard
pinch of cayenne pepper
salt and ground black pepper

1 Sift the flour and salt into a bowl, and rub in the butter with your fingertips until it resembles fine breadcrumbs. Alternatively, use a food processor.

2 Add the egg yolks and just enough water to combine the dough. Wrap the dough in clear film (plastic wrap) and place in the refrigerator for 30 minutes.

3 Meanwhile preheat the oven to 200°C/400°F/Gas 6.

4 Roll out the pastry thinly and use to line the tartlet tins (pans). Prick the pastry. Bake for 15–20 minutes.

5 Fry the bacon until crisp. Add the leeks and cook for 3–4 minutes Remove from the heat.

6 In a bowl, beat the eggs, soft cheese, mustard, cayenne pepper and seasoning together, then add the leeks and bacon.

7 Pour the filling into the tartlet tins and bake for 35–40 minutes, until golden. Remove the tartlets from the tins, and serve warm or cold with salad leaves.

Energy 487kcal/2026kJ; Protein 15.4g; Carbohydrate 28.2g, of which sugars 1.6g; Fat 35.7g, of which saturates 19.1g; Cholesterol 265mg; Calcium 107mg; Fibre 2.1g; Sodium 681mg.

Finger food

Tasty morsels of food tempt the appetite. Serve these sausage rolls, crackers and cheese straws alongside sandwiches, pâtés and cheeses at tea time as a filling accompaniment. The salty flavours are a winner with children and adults alike.

Sausage rolls

Small sausage rolls rank high in the league of popular tea-time foods.

MAKES ABOUT 16

175g/6oz/1½ cups plain
  (all-purpose) flour
pinch of salt
40g/1½oz/3 tbsp lard, diced
40g/1½oz/3 tbsp butter, diced
250g/9oz pork sausagemeat
  (bulk sausage)
beaten egg, to glaze

COOK'S TIP
Buy pastry readymade if you don't have time to make it.

1 To make the pastry, sift the flour and salt into a bowl. Rub the fats into the flour until the mixture resembles fine crumbs.

2 Stir in 45ml/3 tbsp cold water and gather into a smooth ball of dough. Wrap with clear film (plastic wrap) and chill for 30 minutes.

3 Preheat the oven to 190°C/375°F/ Gas 5. Roll out the pastry on a lightly floured surface to make a rectangle about 30cm/12in long. Cut lengthways into two long strips.

4 Divide the sausagemeat into two pieces and, on a lightly floured surface, shape each into a long roll the same length as the pastry. Place a roll on each strip of pastry. Brush the pastry edges with water and fold them over the meat, pressing the edges together to seal them well.

5 Cut each roll into eight. Turn the rolls over and, with the seam side down and brush with beaten egg. Place on a baking sheet and bake for 30 minutes until crisp and golden. Place on a serving plate and serve hot or transfer to a wire rack to cool.

Energy 125kcal/521kJ; Protein 2.5g; Carbohydrate 10.3g, of which sugars 0.5g; Fat 8.4g, of which saturates 3.9g; Cholesterol 14mg; Calcium 23mg; Fibre 0.4g; Sodium 142mg.

Parmesan thins

These crisp, light, savoury crackers are very moreish – the perfect crunchy bite at tea time.

MAKES 16–20

50g/2oz/½ cup plain (all-purpose) flour
40g/1½oz/3 tbsp butter, softened
1 egg yolk
40g/1½oz/½ cup Parmesan cheese, freshly grated
pinch of salt
pinch of mustard powder

1 Rub together the flour and the butter in a bowl, then work in the egg yolk, the cheese, salt and mustard. Mix with a wooden spoon to bring the dough together into a ball. Shape into a log, then wrap in foil or clear film (plastic wrap) and chill for at least 10 minutes.

2 Preheat the oven to 200°C/400°F/Gas 6. Cut the dough log into thin slices, about 3–6mm/ ⅛–¼in, and arrange on a well-greased baking sheet.

3 Flatten with a fork to give a pretty ridged pattern. Bake for 10 minutes or until crisp. Cool on a wire rack.

Energy 36kcal/148kJ; Protein 1.2g; Carbohydrate 2g, of which sugars 0.1g; Fat 2.6g, of which saturates 1.5g; Cholesterol 16mg; Calcium 29mg; Fibre 0.1g; Sodium 34mg.

Cheese straws

These rich cheesy sticks make a fantastic nibble to begin your afternoon tea. Delicious served still warm.

MAKES ABOUT 10

75g/3oz/⅔ cup plain (all-purpose) flour
40g/1½oz/3 tbsp butter, diced
40g/1½oz mature (sharp) hard cheese, finely grated
1 egg
5ml/1 tsp ready-made mustard
salt and ground black pepper

1 Preheat the oven to 180°C/350°F/Gas 4. Line a baking sheet with baking parchment. Sift the flour, salt and pepper into a bowl. Rub the butter into the flour until the mixture resembles breadcrumbs. Stir in the cheese.

2 Lightly beat the egg with the mustard. Add half the egg to the flour, stirring in until the mixture can be gathered into a smooth ball of dough.

3 Roll out the dough into a 15cm/6in square. Cut into narrow lengths. Place on the baking sheet and brush with the remaining egg. Bake for 12 minutes until golden brown.

Energy 49kcal/206kJ; Protein 1.5g; Carbohydrate 3.9g, of which sugars 0.1g; Fat 3.1g, of which saturates 1.9g; Cholesterol 13mg; Calcium 32mg; Fibre 0.2g; Sodium 39mg.

Sweet marrow bakes

Marrow, flaked almonds, golden syrup and vanilla make an unusual muffin with a delicate flavour. These bakes will remain moist for up to one week, if they are kept in an airtight container, and will also freeze well for a future occasion.

3 In a bowl, beat the oil with the sugar, then add the eggs, one at a time, beating until the mixture forms a pale batter. Add the vanilla and golden syrup and stir well to combine.

4 Add the grated marrow flesh and the sultanas, then stir in the flaked almonds.

MAKES 10 STANDARD MUFFINS

300g/11oz marrow (large zucchini)
100ml/3½fl oz/½ cup olive oil
225g/8oz/1 cup soft light brown sugar
2 small (US medium) eggs
7.5ml/1½ tsp vanilla extract
30ml/2 tbsp golden (light corn) syrup
175g/6oz/generous 1 cup sultanas (golden raisins)
50g/2oz/½ cup flaked (sliced) almonds
250g/9oz/2¼ cups self-raising (self-rising) flour
pinch of salt
7.5ml/1½ tsp mixed (pumpkin pie) spice

1 Preheat the oven to 180°C/350°F/ Gas 4. Lightly grease the cups of a muffin tin (pan) or line them with paper cases.

2 To prepare the marrow, peel and remove the central core of seeds. Grate the flesh. Set aside on kitchen paper to drain.

5 Sift the flour, salt and spice together and fold the mixture lightly into the cake batter. Do not overmix. Divide the batter between the prepared paper cases.

6 Bake for 25–30 minutes, until risen and golden. Leave to stand for a few minutes before turning out on to a wire rack to cool completely. Serve with tea.

Energy 338kcal/1427kJ; Protein 5.7g; Carbohydrate 57.8g, of which sugars 39.1g; Fat 11g, of which saturates 1.6g; Cholesterol 38mg; Calcium 137mg; Fibre 1.8g; Sodium 118mg.

Chilli cheese savouries

Prepare for a whole new taste sensation with these fabulous spicy savoury cakes – they're hot stuff. Sharp cheese, aromatic garlic and the heat of the chilli purée combine in a muffin that is light but filling, with a grainy texture. Serve fresh as a savoury delicacy with tea.

MAKES 12 STANDARD MUFFINS

115g/4oz/1 cup self-raising
  (self-rising) flour
15ml/1 tbsp baking powder
225g/8oz/2 cups fine cornmeal
150g/5oz/1¼ cups grated mature
  (sharp) Cheddar cheese
50g/2oz/¼ cup butter, melted
2 eggs, beaten
5ml/1 tsp chilli purée (paste)
1 garlic clove, crushed
300ml/½ pint/1¼ cups milk

1 Preheat the oven to 200°C/400°F/ Gas 6. Line the cups of a muffin tin (pan) with paper cases.

3 In a small bowl, stir together the melted butter, eggs, chilli purée, crushed garlic and milk until thoroughly combined.

4 Pour the liquid on to the dry ingredients and mix quickly until just combined.

5 Spoon the batter into the prepared paper cases and sprinkle the remaining grated cheese on top.

6 Bake for about 20 minutes, until risen and golden. Leave to cool for a few minutes before transferring to a wire rack to go cold, or serve warm.

2 Sift the flour and baking powder together into a bowl, then stir in the cornmeal and 115g/4oz/1 cup of the grated cheese until well mixed.

Energy 166kcal/698kJ; Protein 5.1g; Carbohydrate 19.3g, of which sugars 4.4g; Fat 8.1g, of which saturates 4.6g; Cholesterol 60mg; Calcium 93mg; Fibre 0.6g; Sodium 96mg.

Savoury cheese muffins

Puffed up and golden with their yummy cheese filling and the merest hint of hot spice, these must top the list of everyone's favourite savoury muffins. Serve them warm and freshly baked, to accompany light sandwiches over a pot or two of tea. Store for up to three days.

MAKES 9 STANDARD MUFFINS

175g/6oz/1½ cups plain
  (all-purpose) flour
10ml/2 tsp baking powder
30ml/2 tbsp caster
  (superfine) sugar
5ml/1 tsp paprika
2 eggs
120ml/4fl oz/½ cup milk
50g/2oz/¼ cup butter, melted
5ml/1 tsp dried thyme
50g/2oz mature (sharp) Cheddar
  cheese, diced

1 Preheat the oven to 190°C/375°F/ Gas 5. Lightly grease the cups of a muffin tin (pan) or line them with paper cases.

2 Sift together the flour, baking powder, caster sugar and paprika into a large bowl. Make a well in the centre. Set aside.

3 Combine the eggs, milk, melted butter and dried thyme in another bowl and beat lightly with a whisk until thoroughly blended.

4 Add the milk mixture to the dry ingredients and stir lightly with a wooden spoon until just combined. Do not overmix.

5 Place a heaped tablespoonful of the mixture in each of the prepared paper cases.

6 Divide the pieces of cheese equally among the paper cases.

7 Top with another spoonful of the batter, ensuring that the cheese is covered.

8 Bake for about 25 minutes, until puffed and golden. Leave to stand for 5 minutes before transferring to a wire rack to cool slightly. These muffins are best served while they are still warm.

Energy 166kcal/698kJ; Protein 5.1g; Carbohydrate 19.3g, of which sugars 4.4g; Fat 8.1g, of which saturates 4.6g; Cholesterol 60mg; Calcium 93mg; Fibre 0.6g; Sodium 96mg.

Corn cakes with ham

These delicious little cakes are perfect to serve as a finger food at an afternoon tea buffet.
If you like, serve them unfilled with a pot of herb butter. The batter will make half the number
of standard muffins, if you prefer. Serve them cold and freshly baked.

MAKES 24 MINI MUFFINS

50g/2oz/scant $^{1}/_{2}$ cup yellow
  cornmeal
65g/2$^{1}/_{2}$oz/generous $^{1}/_{2}$ cup plain
  (all-purpose) flour, sifted
30ml/2 tbsp caster (superfine) sugar
7.5ml/1$^{1}/_{2}$ tsp baking powder
50g/2oz/$^{1}/_{4}$ cup butter, melted
120ml/4fl oz/$^{1}/_{2}$ cup
  whipping cream
1 egg
1–2 jalapeño or other medium-hot
  chillies, seeded and finely
  chopped (optional)
pinch of cayenne pepper
butter, for spreading
grainy mustard or mustard with
  honey, for spreading
50g/2oz oak-smoked ham, sliced,
  for filling

1 Preheat the oven to 200°C/400°F/
Gas 6.

2 Lightly grease the cups of a mini
muffin tin (pan) or line them with
mini paper cases.

3 In a large bowl, combine the
cornmeal, sifted flour, sugar and
baking powder.

4 In another bowl, whisk together
the melted butter, cream, egg,
chopped chillies, if using, and the
cayenne pepper.

5 Make a well in the cornmeal
mixture, pour in the egg mixture
and gently stir in just enough to
blend (do not over-beat – the batter
does not have to be smooth).

6 Drop a spoonful of batter into
each paper case. Bake for
12–15 minutes, until golden.
Leave to stand for a few minutes in
the tin, then transfer to a wire rack
to go completely cold.

7 Split the muffins, spread with a
little butter and mustard and
sandwich together with ham.

Energy 54kcal/227kJ; Protein 1.5g; Carbohydrate 6.8g, of which sugars 1.6g; Fat 2.5g, of which saturates 1.4g; Cholesterol 14mg; Calcium 13mg; Fibre 0.2g; Sodium 43mg.

Bacon, Brie and fresh date savouries

The strong flavours of bacon and fresh dates make a wonderful marriage. With the addition of Brie, these little savouries are delicious and unusual enough to serve in miniature form at the tea table. The batter will make 12–14 standard muffins, if you prefer.

5 When it is cool enough to handle, cut the warm bacon into small pieces and stir it back into the warm juices in the pan. Cover with foil and set aside.

MAKES 24–28 MINI MUFFINS

225g/8oz/2 cups plain
   (all-purpose) flour
pinch of salt
10ml/2 tsp baking powder
10ml/2 tsp caster (superfine) sugar
12 fresh dates, pitted
30ml/2 tbsp olive oil, for frying
15g/½oz/1 tbsp butter, for frying
12 rashers (strips) smoked, streaky
   (fatty) bacon
75g/3oz Brie, diced
150ml/¼ pint/⅔ cup milk
50g/2oz/¼ cup butter, melted
2 eggs, beaten

1 Preheat the oven to 180°C/350°F/ Gas 5. Lightly grease the cups of a mini muffin tin (pan) or line them with mini paper cases.

2 In a large bowl, sift together the flour, salt, baking powder and sugar and set aside.

3 Using a knife dusted with flour, chop the dates into small pieces. Separate out any small clumps and add to the flour mixture.

4 In a frying pan, heat the oil and butter over medium heat, and fry the bacon until crisp, 4 minutes.

6 Mash the Brie as finely as you can into the milk, then mix it into the dry ingredients along with the melted butter, eggs, the fried bacon and any juices from the pan. Mix lightly together until just combined.

7 Fill the prepared paper cases three-quarters full. Bake for 18–20 minutes, until risen and golden.

8 Leave to stand and set for 5 minutes before turning out on to a wire rack. Serve warm, or store for up to 3 days in an airtight container. Warm in a microwave.

Energy 183kcal/724kJ; Protein 4.9g; Carbohydrate 12.2g, of which sugars 0.6g; Fat 11.9.6g, of which saturates 8.3g; Cholesterol 53mg; Calcium 99mg; Fibre 0.8g; Sodium 202mg.

Vegetable muffins

Onions, courgettes, cream cheese and herbs have a healthy appeal. When combined in these vegetarian muffins, they have a sharp and tangy flavour and a moist texture. Serve them warm to accompany finger food. Keep for up to two days in an airtight container.

MAKES 8 TALL MUFFINS

150g/5oz courgettes (zucchini)
250g/9oz/2¼ cups self-raising
  (self-rising) flour
pinch of celery salt or salt
12.5ml/2½ tsp baking powder
5ml/1 tsp caster (superfine) sugar
3.5ml/¾ tsp cayenne pepper
8 spring onions (scallions)
30ml/2 tbsp red onion, grated
10ml/2 tsp malt vinegar
115g/4oz/1 cup soft herb and
  cream cheese
60ml/4 tbsp sour cream
75g/3oz/6 tbsp butter, melted
2 eggs
15ml/1 tbsp mixed fresh parsley
  and thyme, finely chopped
15g/½oz Parmesan cheese
ground black pepper
1 small courgette (zucchini),
  to garnish
olive oil, to drizzle

1 Preheat the oven to 180°C/ 350°F/Gas 4. Lightly grease and line eight dariole moulds with baking parchment.

2 Coarsely grate the courgettes into a bowl.

3 In a large bowl, sift together the flour, salt, baking powder, sugar and cayenne pepper and set aside.

4 Slice the white parts of the spring onions into thin discs and add to the courgettes with the grated red onion. Sprinkle with the vinegar. Season and set aside to marinate.

5 In a small bowl, whisk the cheese into the sour cream, then whisk in the melted butter, eggs and herbs.

6 Pour into the dry ingredients with the Parmesan and grated vegetables and any juices from the bowl. Stir to mix until just combined.

7 Fill the prepared paper cases three-quarters full, and garnish each with four thin slices of courgette cut at a 45 degree angle, if you like. Drizzle lightly with olive oil. Add a few twists of black pepper and bake for 25–30 minutes.

8 Leave to cool slightly, then transfer to a wire rack to go cold.

Energy 291kcal/1215kJ; Protein 6.8g; Carbohydrate 25.8g, of which sugars 1.9g; Fat 18.6g, of which saturates 11.1g; Cholesterol 126mg; Calcium 109mg; Fibre 1.4g; Sodium 154mg.

Walnut, cheese and barleycorn muffins

This recipe uses a mixture of self-raising and barleycorn flour, which contains mixed grains that provide texture as well as flavour. Chopped walnuts add extra crunch. Serve them warm, mid-afternoon with a pot of tea. For a more substantial treat, add a slice of cheese.

MAKES 8 STANDARD MUFFINS

115g/4oz/1 cup self-raising
  (self-rising) flour
10ml/2 tsp baking powder
3.5ml/¾ tsp cayenne pepper
150g/5oz/1¼ cups barleycorn
  bread flour
150g/5oz/1¼ cups mature (sharp)
  Cheddar cheese, grated
2 eggs
50ml/2fl oz/¼ cup milk
100ml/3½fl oz/scant ½ cup
  buttermilk
3.5ml/¾ tsp English (hot) mustard
75g/3oz/6 tbsp butter, melted
30ml/2 tbsp finely chopped
  fresh parsley
25g/1oz/1½ tbsp walnuts, chopped

1 Preheat the oven to 190°C/375°F/ Gas 5. Lightly grease the cups of a muffin tin (pan), or line them with paper cases.

2 Sift the flour, baking powder, salt and cayenne into a mixing bowl. Stir in the barleycorn flour with the grated cheese until well combined.

3 In a small bowl, whisk the eggs, milk, buttermilk and mustard together. Mix in the melted butter.

4 Pour the liquid into the dry ingredients with the parsley. Fold in until half blended, then fold in the chopped walnuts.

5 Divide the batter equally between the paper cases and bake for 25 minutes, until golden on top and springy to the touch.

6 Leave in the tin for 5 minutes, then turn out on to a wire rack.

VARIATION
Use self-raising (self-rising) flour, in place of barleycorn flour.

Energy 291kcal/1216kJ; Protein 9g; Carbohydrate 26.4g, of which sugars 1.6g; Fat 16.9g, of which saturates 9.6g; Cholesterol 41mg; Calcium 233mg; Fibre 2.8g; Sodium 272mg.

Shallot, thyme and garlic cheese bakes

These light muffins are best served warm, fresh from the oven, when the cream cheese and the caramelized flavour complement each other perfectly. Spread them with soft cheese for an unusual, but tempting, addition to the afternoon tea table.

MAKES 10 TALL MUFFINS

225g/8oz shallots, peeled
25ml/1½ tbsp olive oil, for frying
15g/½oz/1 tbsp unsalted butter,
 for frying
10ml/2 tsp fresh thyme, plus a few
 sprigs for garnishing
225g/8oz/2 cups self-raising
 (self-rising) flour
pinch of salt
10ml/2 tsp baking powder
10ml/2 tsp caster (superfine) sugar
115g/4oz soft herb and garlic
 cream cheese
175ml/6fl oz/¾ cup milk
2 eggs
75g/3oz/6 tbsp butter, melted
salt and ground black pepper

1 Preheat the oven to 180°C/
350°F/Gas 4. Lightly grease and
line ten dariole moulds with
baking parchment.

2 Drop the peeled shallots into a
pan of boiling water and blanch
them for 2 minutes. Drain
thoroughly, then leave to stand on
kitchen paper. When the shallots are
cool enough to handle, slice them
into quarters.

3 In a frying pan, heat the oil and
butter over medium heat. Add the
shallots and sauté them, until
caramelized on all sides. Stir in the
thyme and seasoning. Leave to cool.

4 In a large bowl, sift together the
flour, salt, baking powder and sugar.

5 In another bowl, beat together the
cream cheese, milk, eggs and melted
butter. Pour into a well in the centre
of the dry ingredients and blend
until partly mixed.

6 Scrape the shallots and any liquid
into the batter (reserving a few of
them for garnishing) and stir lightly.

7 Divide the batter between the
moulds and dot with the reserved
shallots and a few thyme sprigs.

8 Bake for 25–30 minutes or until
the tops are firm to the touch. Leave
to cool slightly then invert on to a
floured tray. Serve warm.

Energy 236kcal/984kJ; Protein 4.5g; Carbohydrate 20.7g, of which sugars 3.5g; Fat 15.6g, of which saturates 9g; Cholesterol 71mg; Calcium 124mg; Fibre 1g; Sodium 207mg.

Broccoli and blue cheese muffins

Stilton, with its distinctive blue veins running through a round of cream-colour cheese, is perfect for these muffins, but you could use any sharp-tasting blue cheese. The creamy texture blends smoothly with the broccoli to add the most divine savoury flavour to these muffins. Serve fresh.

3 In a frying pan, heat the oil and butter over medium heat, add the broccoli and fry gently for 90 seconds, stirring. Scrape from the pan into a bowl and leave to cool.

4 Sift the flour and baking powder into a large bowl and set aside.

5 In a jug (pitcher), beat together the sour cream, melted butter, milk and eggs. Pour into the dry ingredients and partly combine.

MAKES 8 STANDARD MUFFINS

150g/5oz broccoli
30ml/2 tbsp olive oil, for frying
40g/1½oz/3 tbsp butter, for frying
250g/9oz/2¼ cups self-raising (self-rising) flour
12.5ml/2½ tsp baking powder
30ml/2 tbsp sour cream
75g/3oz/6 tbsp butter, melted
45ml/3 tbsp milk
2 eggs
20ml/4 tsp sweet chilli dipping sauce
150g/5oz Stilton, such as Colston Bassett, grated

1 Preheat the oven to 180°C/350°F/ Gas 4. Line the cups of a muffin tin (pan) with paper cases.

2 Cut the broccoli florets into tiny pieces. Discard the stems.

6 Stir in the broccoli, chilli sauce and Stilton, until just combined.

7 Spoon the batter into the paper cases. Bake for 25 minutes until golden and puffed up. Leave to stand in the tin for a few minutes, then transfer to a wire rack to cool.

Energy 346kcal/1441kJ; Protein 9.8g; Carbohydrate 24.4g, of which sugars 1.1g; Fat 23.6g, of which saturates 13.3g; Cholesterol 103mg; Calcium 199mg; Fibre 1.5g; Sodium 418mg.

Brioche with savoury pâté stuffing

Serve these savoury brioche-style muffins with cold cuts of meat, quiche and salad, or with a selection of toasted breads and pâté for a tasty tea-time buffet. These muffins take time to prepare but the results are well worthwhile. Eat fresh, either warm or cold, for the best taste.

MAKES 10 TALL MUFFINS

15g/½oz fresh yeast
4 eggs
350g/12oz/3 cups plain
  (all-purpose) flour
35g/1¼oz/3 tbsp caster (superfine)
  sugar
10g/¼oz salt
175g/6oz/¾ cup unsalted butter,
  softened
150g/5oz fairly coarse pâté
45ml/3 tbsp milk
1 small egg yolk

1 Crumble the yeast into the bottom of the bowl of a food processor, fitted with a dough hook, and mix with 10ml/2 tsp warm water until well blended.

2 Add the eggs, flour, sugar and salt. Beat together at a low speed for 6–7 minutes until a dough forms. Turn up to a moderate speed and gradually add the butter. Continue to knead for 12–15 minutes until the dough is smooth and shiny.

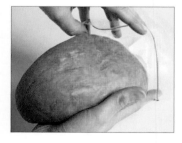

3 Seal the dough in a plastic bag and leave in the refrigerator for 24 hours, or overnight.

4 Line the cups of individual dariole moulds with paper cases.

5 Divide the pâté into ten pieces, and with lightly floured hands, form them into balls. Set aside.

6 Place the dough on a floured work surface. Form it into a sausage and cut it into ten equal pieces.

7 Add a ball of pâté to the centre of each piece of dough, then press the dough around the pâté to form a smooth ball. With the seal below, put the dough into the paper cases.

8 Preheat the oven to 220°C/425°F/ Gas 7. In a small bowl, mix the milk and egg yolk together to make an egg wash. Using a pastry brush, apply it thinly over the top of each dough ball. With a sharp knife slash the top of each muffin twice. Leave in a warm place to prove for 15 minutes.

9 Bake for 13–15 minutes, until well risen and golden. Turn out the muffins with a sharp shake on to a floured tray and leave them to cool.

Energy 347kcal/1449kJ; Protein 8.3g; Carbohydrate 31.2g, of which sugars 4.5g; Fat 21.9g, of which saturates 11.6g; Cholesterol 162mg; Calcium 75mg; Fibre 1.1g; Sodium 282mg.

Devils on horseback

The very moreish combination of salty bacon and sweet fresh dates makes an unusual and seductive addition to these light and delicious muffins. These are perfect for a savoury appetizer at tea time in place of sandwiches. Eat fresh for best results.

MAKES 10 STANDARD MUFFINS

225g/8oz/2 cups self-raising
  (self-rising) flour
10ml/2 tsp baking powder
10ml/2 tsp caster (superfine) sugar
12 rashers (strips) thin-cut
  smoked, streaky (fatty) bacon
24 fresh dates, pitted
30ml/2 tbsp olive oil, for frying
15g/½oz/1 tbsp butter, for frying
10ml/2 tsp fresh thyme or oregano,
  plus a few leaves for decoration
115g/4oz/1 cup soft herb and garlic
  cream cheese
175ml/6fl oz/¾ cup milk
75g/3oz/6 tbsp butter, melted
2 eggs
ground black pepper

1 Preheat the oven to 180°C/350°F/ Gas 5. Line the cups of a muffin tin (pan) with baking parchment.

2 Sift the flour, baking powder and sugar into a mixing bowl.

3 Using scissors, cut each bacon rasher in half and wrap one around each date.

4 In a frying pan, heat the oil and butter over medium heat, and when it is foaming, add the bacon rolls and sauté them, turning them in the juices until they are crisp and caramelized on all sides, 4 minutes. Stir in the thyme or oregano and season with the pepper. Leave to cool slightly in the warm juices.

5 When cool enough to handle, slice each of the bacon-wrapped dates into four discs. Return them to the pan and cover with foil.

6 Beat the cream cheese into the milk, with the butter and eggs. Pour into the dry ingredients and stir lightly until part blended. Scrape the bacon and date slices with any of the cooking juices into the batter and stir until evenly combined. Avoid overmixing.

7 Divide the batter between the paper cases and dot with a few extra thyme leaves. Bake for 25 minutes or until the tops are golden.

8 Leave the muffins to cool slightly then turn out on to a wire rack to cool. Serve warm or cold.

Energy 318kcal/1327kJ; Protein 8g; Carbohydrate 23.6g, of which sugars 6.9g; Fat 22g, of which saturates 11g; Cholesterol 85mg; Calcium 124mg; Fibre 1g; Sodium 491mg.

Wild mushroom and pine nut muffins

These light savoury muffins make attractive accompaniments to soft cheeses and sandwiches with tea. The pine nuts are decorative as well as adding texture and crunch, and a delicious warm nutty flavour. Serve them freshly baked and warm to enjoy them at their best.

MAKES 6–7 LARGE MUFFINS

250g/9oz/2¼ cups self-raising
(self-rising) flour
11.5ml/2¼ tsp baking powder
150g/5oz mixture of wild
mushrooms
90g/3½oz/scant ½ cup butter,
for frying
large pinch cayenne pepper
large pinch mace
50–75g/2–3oz/½–¾ cup pine nuts
30ml/2 tbsp olive oil
90ml/6 tbsp buttermilk
75g/3oz/6 tbsp butter, melted
2 eggs

1 Preheat the oven to 180°C/350°F/ Gas 4. Lightly grease the cups of a muffin tin (pan).

2 In a large bowl, sift the flour and baking powder and set aside.

3 Clean and slice the mushrooms. In a frying pan, heat 75g/3oz/6 tbsp of the butter over medium heat. When it is foaming, add the mushrooms. Season with cayenne pepper and mace. Fry gently, stirring, until just softened. Scrape into a bowl and set aside to cool.

4 Fry the pine nuts in the remaining butter and the olive oil for 30 seconds. Add to the mushrooms.

5 Beat together the buttermilk, melted butter and eggs in a bowl.

6 Stir into the dry ingredients with the mushrooms and pine nuts.

7 Spoon the batter into the muffin tins and bake for 25 minutes until the tops are golden and firm.

Energy 399kcal/1660kJ; Protein 6.9g; Carbohydrate 28g, of which sugars 1.4g; Fat 29.6g, of which saturates 14.2g; Cholesterol 109mg; Calcium 154mg; Fibre 1.5g; Sodium 334mg.

Teabreads and bakes

Teabreads are one of the oldest of family cakes, originally baked in a rectangular tin that fitted into the small side oven of a range cooker or wood-burning stove. These cakes are so simple and quick to make that it's a good idea to double up the mixture and bake two at a time, then keep one in the freezer until it's needed. Included in this winning collection are all the essential tea-time treats that will fill the home with sweet aromas as they bake. Who could resist lightly toasted Teacakes dripping with melted butter, or substantial fruit-filled Fat Rascals?

Left: Raspberry and Almond Teabread and Lemon and Walnut Teabread make a delicious addition to the tea table.

Crumpets

Made with a yeast batter and cooked quickly in metal rings on a griddle, crumpets are a particularly traditional English tea-time food with an unusual dense and spongy texture. Serve them freshly toasted and spread with butter and a drizzle of golden syrup or honey.

MAKES ABOUT 10

225g/8oz/2 cups plain (all-purpose) flour
pinch of salt
2.5ml/½ tsp bicarbonate of soda (baking soda)
5ml/1 tsp easy-blend (rapid-rise) dried yeast
150ml/¼ pint/⅔ cup milk
oil, for greasing

1 Sift the flour, salt and bicarbonate of soda into a bowl and stir in the yeast. Make a well in the centre.

2 Heat the milk with 200ml/7fl oz/ scant 1 cup water until lukewarm.

3 Pour the milk into the well and beat or whisk vigorously to make a thick, smooth batter.

4 Cover the bowl with a dish towel and leave in a warm place for about 1 hour until the mixture has a spongy texture.

5 Heat a griddle or heavy frying pan. Lightly oil the hot surface and the inside of three or four metal rings, each measuring about 8cm/3½in in diameter. Place the oiled rings on the hot surface and leave for 1–2 minutes until hot.

6 Spoon the batter into the rings to a depth of about 1cm/½in. Cook over medium-high heat for about 6 minutes until the top surface is set and bubbles have burst open to make holes.

7 When set, carefully lift off the metal rings and flip the crumpets over, cooking the second side for just 1 minute until lightly browned.

8 Lift off the griddle and leave to cool completely on a wire rack. Repeat with the remaining crumpet mixture until used up.

9 Just before serving, toast the crumpets on both sides so that the surface is quite hard. Butter the holey surface generously. Crumpets can be served with jam, curd, honey, peanut butter, cheese spread, or just with lashings of butter.

Energy 93kcal/393kJ; Protein 3g; Carbohydrate 16.5g, of which sugars 1g; Fat 2.1g, of which saturates 1g; Cholesterol 21mg; Calcium 48mg; Fibre 0.6g; Sodium 21mg.

English muffins

Unlike their American cousins, which are a type of small cake, English muffins are circles of bread cooked on a griddle, which are made for toasting. They have a bland flavour so are perfect served warm, split open and spread with butter.

MAKES 9

450g/1lb/4 cups unbleached strong
   white bread flour
7.5ml/1½ tsp salt
350–375ml/12–13fl oz/
   1½–1⅔ cups lukewarm milk
pinch of caster (superfine) sugar
15g/½oz fresh yeast
15ml/1 tbsp melted butter or
   olive oil
rice flour or semolina, for dusting

1 Generously flour a non-stick baking sheet and very lightly grease a griddle pan.

2 Sift the flour and salt together into a large bowl and make a well in the centre. Blend 150ml/¼ pint/⅔ cup of the milk, sugar and yeast together. Stir in the remaining milk and butter or oil.

3 Add the yeast mixture to the well and beat for 4–5 minutes until smooth and elastic. The dough will be soft but just hold its shape. Cover with lightly oiled clear film (plastic wrap) and leave to rise in a warm place for 45–60 minutes, or until doubled in bulk.

4 Turn out the dough on to a floured surface and knock back (punch down). Roll out to 1cm/½in thick. Stamp out 7.5cm/3in rounds.

5 Dust the dough rounds with rice flour or semolina and place on the prepared baking sheet. Cover and leave to rise, in a warm place, for about 20–30 minutes.

6 Warm the griddle over medium heat. Carefully transfer the muffins in batches to the griddle. Cook slowly for about 7 minutes on each side or until golden brown. Transfer to a wire rack to cool. When cold, toast like bread, and serve generously spread with butter.

Energy 201kcal/852kJ; Protein 6g; Carbohydrate 40.7g, of which sugars 2.6g; Fat 2.7g, of which saturates 1.4g; Cholesterol 6mg; Calcium 117mg; Fibre 1.6g; Sodium 356mg.

Drop scones

Variously known as girdle cakes, griddlecakes and Scotch pancakes, these make a quick and easy tea-time snack. Serve them warm with butter and drizzled with honey, maple syrup or golden syrup for a sweet and satisfying, warming treat.

4 Make a well in the centre of the flour mixture, then stir in the egg. Add the milk a little at a time, stirring well after each addition. Add enough milk to give a thick creamy consistency.

5 Cook the batter in batches. Drop three or four evenly sized spoonfuls of the mixture, spaced slightly apart, on the griddle or frying pan. Cook over medium heat for 2–3 minutes, until bubbles rise to the surface and burst.

MAKES 8–10

115g/4oz/1 cup plain
   (all-purpose) flour
5ml/1 tsp bicarbonate of soda
   (baking soda)
5ml/1 tsp cream of tartar
25g/1oz/2 tbsp butter, diced
1 egg, beaten
about 150ml/¼ pint/⅔ cup milk
butter and honey or maple syrup,
   to serve

1 Lightly grease a griddle pan or heavy frying pan, then preheat it over medium heat.

2 Meanwhile, sift the flour, bicarbonate of soda and cream of tartar together into a mixing bowl.

3 Add the diced butter and rub it into the flour with your fingertips until the mixture resembles fine, evenly sized breadcrumbs.

6 Turn the scones over and cook for a further 2–3 minutes, until golden underneath. Place the cooked scones between the folds of a clean dish towel while cooking the remaining batter. Serve warm, with butter and honey or maple syrup.

Energy 59kcal/249kJ; Protein 2g; Carbohydrate 10.9g, of which sugars 1.8g; Fat 1.1g, of which saturates 0.2g; Cholesterol 11mg; Calcium 65mg; Fibre 0.4g; Sodium 56mg.

Tinkers' cakes

These delicate little cakes can be rustled up in no time for eating hot off the stove. The quantities given are small because they must be eaten while really fresh. This is a classic Welsh recipe, but naturally finds a place on the English afternoon tea table.

MAKES 8–10

125g/4½oz/generous 1 cup self-raising (self-rising) flour, plus extra for dusting
pinch of salt
70g/2½oz/5 tbsp butter, diced
50g/2oz/4 tbsp demerara (raw) or light muscovado (brown) sugar
1 small cooking apple, weighing about 150g/5oz
about 30ml/2 tbsp milk
caster (superfine) sugar, for dusting

1 Preheat a heavy frying pan over low to medium heat.

2 Sift the flour and salt into a mixing bowl. Add the butter and, with your fingertips, rub it into the flour until the mixture resembles fine breadcrumbs. Stir in the sugar.

3 Peel and grate the apple, discarding the core. Stir the grated apple into the flour mixture with enough of the milk to make a mixture that can be gathered into a ball of soft, moist dough. Knead slightly to make sure the ingredients are thoroughly combined.

4 Transfer to a lightly floured surface and roll out the dough to about 5mm/¼in thick. With a 6–7.5cm/2½–3in cutter, stamp out rounds, gathering up the offcuts and re-rolling them to make more.

5 Smear a little butter on the hot griddle pan and cook the cakes, in batches, for about 4–5 minutes on each side or until golden brown and cooked through. Lift on to a wire rack and dust with caster sugar. Serve immediately.

VARIATIONS
• Add a good pinch of ground cinnamon or mixed (apple pie) spice to the sifted flour.
• Cut the rolled-out dough into squares or triangles for a change.

Energy 121kcal/508kJ; Protein 1.4g; Carbohydrate 16.5g, of which sugars 6.9g; Fat 6g, of which saturates 3.7g; Cholesterol 15mg; Calcium 26mg; Fibre 0.6g; Sodium 45mg.

Teacakes

These fruit-filled tea-time treats are thought to be a refinement of the original 'handbread': a shaped roll made on a flat tin. You can add 5ml/1 tsp allspice to the flour, if you like. Serve them split and buttered, either warm from the oven or toasted.

MAKES 8–10

450g/1lb/4 cups unbleached strong white bread flour
5ml/1 tsp salt
5ml/1 tsp easy-blend (rapid-rise) dried yeast
10fl oz/½ pint/1¼ cups milk, luke warm, plus extra, for glazing
40g/1½oz/3 tbsp caster (superfine) sugar
40g/1½oz/3 tbsp butter, diced
50g/2oz/¼ cup currants
50g/2oz/⅓ cup sultanas (golden raisins)

1 Sift the flour and salt into a bowl.

2 In a jug (pitcher) mix the yeast, 5ml/ 1 tsp of the sugar and the lukewarm milk and leave to stand for 5 minutes.

3 Add the remaining sugar to the flour and make a well in the centre. Pour in the milk a little at a time and mix well, adding just enough to make a dry dough. Add the butter and knead briefly.

4 Turn the dough out on to a lightly floured surface and knead vigorously for at least 15 minutes, until the dough is no longer sticky and full of little bubbles, adding a little extra milk if necessary.

5 Shape the dough into a ball, place in a clean bowl and cover with a dampened dish towel. Leave at room temperature for 1 hour, until it has doubled in bulk.

6 Grease two baking sheets.

7 Turn out the dough and knead in the dried fruit until it is evenly distributed. Divide the dough into eight to ten portions, and shape into balls. Flatten each one into a disc about 1cm/½in thick.

8 Place the discs on the baking sheets, 2.5cm/1in apart. Cover with oiled clear film (plastic wrap) and leave in a warm place for 30–45 minutes, or until they have almost doubled in size. Preheat the oven to 200°C/400°F/Gas 6.

9 Brush the top of each teacake with milk, then bake for 15–18 minutes, or until golden. Turn out on to a wire rack to cool slightly. To serve, split open while warm and spread with butter, or let the teacakes cool, then split and toast them.

Energy 239kcal/1011kJ; Protein 5.4g; Carbohydrate 47.4g, of which sugars 13.1g; Fat 4.4g, of which saturates 2.5g; Cholesterol 11mg; Calcium 107mg; Fibre 1.6g; Sodium 245mg.

Rock buns

These old-fashioned favourites are perfect fun in the kitchen and provide a great introduction to baking, as the mixture can be formed into little balls – great for hands-on kids' cooking. As rock buns are not a rich mixture, they are best eaten on the day they are baked.

4 Stir the sugar, fruit and grated rind into the dry mixture.

5 In a small bowl, beat the egg with the milk and add to the cake batter. Mix with a fork until the mixture leaves the sides of the bowl clean and is stiff but not sticky. If it is too dry add a little more milk, one teaspoon at a time.

6 Divide the mixture into 12 balls and put on to the baking tray, spacing well apart.

7 Flick the tops with a fork to roughen, then sprinkle each lightly with demerara sugar.

8 Bake for 15 minutes, or until firm and golden. Remove from the sheet and cool on a wire rack.

MAKES 12

225g/8oz/2 cups plain
  (all-purpose) flour
1.5ml/¼ tsp mixed (apple pie)
  spice
10ml/2 tsp baking powder
pinch of salt
65g/2½oz/generous ¼ cup
  butter, diced
65g/2½oz/generous ¼ cup golden
  caster (superfine) sugar
115g/4oz/⅔ cup mixed dried fruit
finely grated rind of ½ lemon or
  small orange
1 egg
about 30ml/2 tbsp milk
30ml/2 tbsp demerara (raw) sugar

1 Preheat the oven to 200°C/400°F/ Gas 6. Grease a large baking sheet.

2 Sift the flour, spice, baking powder and salt into a bowl. Add the butter.

3 Rub the butter into the flour until the mixture resembles crumbs.

Energy 206kcal/866kJ; Protein 2.7g; Carbohydrate 31.3g, of which sugars 17g; Fat 8.7g, of which saturates 5.2g; Cholesterol 36mg; Calcium 45mg; Fibre 0.8g; Sodium 71mg.

Fat rascals

These delicious cakes are a cross between a scone and a rock cake and are really simple to make.
Serve them warm or cold, just as they are or spread with butter at tea time.

MAKES 10

350g/12oz/3 cups self-raising
  (self-rising) flour
175g/6oz/³⁄₄ cup butter, diced
115g/4oz/generous ¹⁄₂ cup caster
  (superfine) sugar
75g/3oz/¹⁄₃ cup mixed currants,
  raisins and sultanas
  (golden raisins)
25g/1oz/1¹⁄₂ tbsp chopped
  mixed peel
50g/2oz/¹⁄₃ cup glacé
  (candied) cherries
50g/2oz/¹⁄₃ cup blanched almonds,
  roughly chopped
1 egg
about 75ml/5 tbsp milk

1 Preheat the oven to 200°C/400°F/
Gas 6. Line a baking sheet with
baking parchment.

2 Sift the flour into a large bowl.
Rub the butter into the flour until
the mixture resembles fine
breadcrumbs (alternatively whiz the
ingredients in a food processor).

3 Stir in the sugar, dried fruit, peel,
cherries and almonds.

4 In a small bowl, lightly beat the
egg and stir into the flour mixture a
spoonful at a time. Add sufficient
milk to gather the mixture into a
ball of dough, mopping up all the
dry ingredients. The dough should
have a soft texture, but not be
too wet.

5 With lightly floured hands, divide
the dough into ten balls, press them
into rough circles about 2cm/³⁄₄in
thick and arrange with plenty of
space between them on the prepared
baking sheet.

6 Cook for 15–20 minutes until
risen and golden brown. Transfer to
a wire rack to cool. Store in an
airtight container for 2–3 days.

Energy 375kcal/1574kJ; Protein 5.6g; Carbohydrate 50g, of which sugars 23.2g; Fat 18.4g, of which saturates 9.6g; Cholesterol 57mg; Calcium 93mg; Fibre 1.8g; Sodium 129mg.

Soul cakes

These simple cakes originated in the county of Shropshire, England, and were served on All Souls'
Day (2 November). They make an unpretentious addition to the tea table.

MAKES ABOUT 20

450g/1lb/4 cups self-raising
  (self-rising) flour
5ml/1 tsp ground mixed (apple
  pie) spice
pinch of ground ginger
175g/6oz/¾ cup butter, softened
175g/6oz/generous ¾ cup caster
  (superfine) sugar, plus extra
  for sprinkling
2 eggs, lightly beaten
50g/2oz/¼ cup currants, raisins or
  sultanas (golden raisins)
about 30ml/2 tbsp warm milk

1 Preheat the oven to 180°C/350°F/
Gas 4. Lightly grease two baking
sheets or line with baking
parchment. Sift the flour and spices
into a bowl, and set aside. In a large
bowl, beat the butter and sugar until
the mixture is light, pale and fluffy.

2 Gradually beat the eggs into the
butter mixture. Fold in the flour and
the dried fruit, then add sufficient
warm milk to bind the mixture and
gather it up into a ball of soft dough.

3 Transfer to a lightly floured surface
and roll out to 5mm/¼in thick. Cut
into 7.5cm/3in rounds.

4 Arrange the cakes on the prepared
baking sheets. Prick the surface of
the cakes lightly with a fork then,
with the back of a knife, mark a
deep cross on top of each.

5 Put the cakes into the hot oven
and cook for about 15 minutes until
risen and golden brown.

6 Sprinkle the cooked cakes with a
little caster sugar and then transfer
to a wire rack to cool.

COOK'S TIP
The original recipe for these
would have contained plain
(all-purpose) flour, but self-
raising produces a lighter result.

Energy 191kcal/803kJ; Protein 2.9g; Carbohydrate 28.4g, of which sugars 11.3g; Fat 8.1g, of which saturates 4.8g; Cholesterol 38mg; Calcium 45mg; Fibre 0.7g; Sodium 62mg.

Scones with jam and cream

The contrast of warm, buttered scone, homemade jam bursting with fruit, and thick clotted cream is the quintessential taste of English afternoon tea.

MAKES 12

450g/1lb/4 cups self-raising (self-rising) flour or 450g/1lb/4 cups plain (all-purpose) flour and 10ml/2 tsp baking powder
pinch of salt
50g/2oz/¼ cup butter, chilled and diced
15ml/1 tbsp lemon juice
about 400ml/14fl oz/1⅔ cups milk, plus extra to glaze
fruit jam and clotted cream, or whipped cream, to serve

1 Preheat the oven to 230°C/ 450°F/Gas 8.

2 Sift the flour, salt and baking powder, if using, into a mixing bowl. Rub in the butter with your fingertips until the mixture resembles fine breadcrumbs.

3 In a small bowl, whisk the lemon juice into the milk and leave for about 1 minute to thicken slightly, then pour into the flour mixture and mix quickly to form a soft dough.

4 Knead the dough lightly to form a ball, then roll it out on a floured surface to a thickness of about 2.5cm/1in.

5 Using a 5cm/2in cutter and dipping it into flour each time, stamp out 12 scones, and place them on a well-floured baking sheet. Re-roll any trimmings and cut out more if you can.

6 Brush the tops of the scones lightly with a little milk and then bake them for about 20 minutes, or until risen and golden brown.

7 Wrap the scones in a clean dish towel to keep them warm and soft until ready to serve. Eat with your favourite fruit jam and a generous dollop of clotted cream, or whipped cream if you prefer.

Energy 177kcal/749kJ; Protein 4.7g; Carbohydrate 30.7g, of which sugars 2.2g; Fat 4.8g, of which saturates 2.8g; Cholesterol 12mg; Calcium 93mg; Fibre 1.2g; Sodium 43mg.

Buttermilk scones

These deliciously light, not-too-sweet, scones are a favourite for afternoon tea, served fresh from the oven with butter and homemade jam.

MAKES 18 SMALL SCONES

450g/1lb/4 cups plain (all-purpose)
    flour
pinch of salt
5ml/1 tsp bicarbonate of soda
    (baking soda)
50g/2oz/¼ cup butter, at room
    temperature, diced
15ml/1 tbsp caster (superfine)
    sugar
1 small (US medium) egg,
    lightly beaten
about 300ml/½ pint/1¼ cups
    buttermilk

1 Preheat the oven to 220°C/425°F/
Gas 7. Grease two baking sheets.

2 Sift the flour, salt and bicarbonate
of soda into a mixing bowl. Rub
in the butter until the mixture
resembles fine breadcrumbs. Add
the sugar and mix well. Make a
well in the middle and add the egg
and enough buttermilk to mix
lightly into a soft dough.

VARIATION
Use half white and half
wholemeal (whole-wheat) flour.

3 Turn on to a floured surface and
knead lightly into shape. Roll out to
about 1cm/½in thick.

4 Stamp out 18 scones with a fluted
cutter, gathering the trimmings and
lightly re-rolling as necessary.
Arrange the scones on the baking
sheets, spacing well apart.

5 Bake in the preheated oven for
about 15–20 minutes, until the
scones are well risen and golden
brown, reversing the position of the
sheets halfway through cooking.
Cool on wire racks. Serve warm
with butter and jam.

Energy 120kcal/503kJ; Protein 2.7g; Carbohydrate 18.3g, of which sugars 1.1g; Fat 4.5g, of which saturates 2.7g; Cholesterol 11mg; Calcium 54mg; Fibre 0.7g; Sodium 235mg.

Coconut macaroons

Finely grated creamed coconut is combined with the desiccated variety to give these soft-centred cakes a rich creaminess. Made with minimal ingredients, these melt-in-the-mouth macaroons can be made in no time for an uplifting treat on a rainy afternoon.

MAKES 16–18

50g/2oz/1 cup creamed coconut
(US thick coconut milk), chilled
2 large (US extra large) egg whites
90g/3½oz/½ cup caster (superfine)
sugar
75g/3oz/1 cup desiccated (dry
unsweetened) coconut

VARIATIONS
• For a tangy flavour, add the grated rind of a lime in step 2.
• Baking the gooey mixture on baking parchment makes sure that the cookies are easily removed from the baking sheet.

1 Preheat the oven to 180°C/350°F/Gas 4. Line a large baking sheet with baking parchment. Finely grate the creamed coconut.

2 Using an electric beater, whisk the egg whites in a large bowl until stiff. Then whisk in the sugar, a little at a time, to make a stiff and glossy meringue. Fold in the grated, creamed and the desiccated coconut, using a large, metal spoon.

3 Place dessertspoonfuls of the mixture, spaced slightly apart, on the baking sheet. Bake for 15–20 minutes, until slightly risen and golden brown. Remove from the oven and leave to cool on the parchment, then transfer to an airtight container. The macaroons will keep for two to three days.

Energy 65kcal/270kJ; Protein 0.7g; Carbohydrate 5.7g, of which sugars 5.7g; Fat 4.5g, of which saturates 3.9g; Cholesterol 0mg; Calcium 4mg; Fibre 0.6g; Sodium 9mg.

Meringues

These pretty meringue nests make a stunning centrepiece to the finest of tea tables. They almost look too good to eat! The crystallized petal decoration is made with raw egg white, which is unsuitable for the elderly, young and pregnant. Replace them with fresh berries, if necessary.

MAKES ABOUT 14

4 egg whites
225g/8oz/2 cups icing
 (confectioners') sugar
10ml/2 tsp vanilla extract
300ml/½ pint/1¼ cups double
 (heavy) cream

For the crystallized petals
75–100 alpine pink or violet petals
1 egg white, lightly beaten
50g/2oz/¼ cup caster
 (superfine) sugar

1 Preheat the oven to 120°C/250°F/ Gas ½. Line two baking sheets with baking parchment.

2 Whisk the egg whites until stiff. Add the icing sugar, whisking in a tablespoonful at a time, until glossy. Whisk in the vanilla extract.

3 Place large spoonfuls of meringue, spaced well apart, on the baking sheets. Make an indent in the centre. Bake for 1–1¼ hours, until the meringues are crisp. Leave to cool for a few minutes before removing the baking parchment. Place on wire racks to go cold.

4 For the crystallized petals, gather clean, dry, perfect specimens. Remove the white heels at the bases. Place beaten egg white and caster sugar in separate saucers. Paint the front and back of each petal with the egg white.

5 Dredge both sides with caster sugar. Arrange the petals on baking parchment and leave them in a warm place until completely dry. These will last for up to two days.

6 Whip the cream and spoon into the nests. Sprinkle the crystallized petals over just before serving.

Energy 178kcal/744kJ; Protein 1.5g; Carbohydrate 21.1g, of which sugars 21.1; Fat 11.5g, of which saturates 6.4 g; Cholesterol 28mg; Calcium 21.7mg; Fibre 0g; Sodium 30.8mg.

Courgette and double ginger cake

Both fresh and preserved ginger are used to flavour this unusual teabread, which is made with oil rather than butter. Courgettes, like several other vegetables, bring moisture to a cake mix, making it soft and tasty. Keep for up to five days in an airtight container or freeze for two months.

4 Sift the flour, baking powder, cinnamon and salt over the batter and stir in.

5 Pour into the prepared tin and smooth level. Sprinkle the chopped ginger and demerara sugar on top.

SERVES 8–10

3 eggs
225g/8oz/generous 1 cup caster (superfine) sugar
250ml/8fl oz/1 cup sunflower oil
5ml/1 tsp vanilla extract
15ml/1 tbsp syrup from a jar of preserved stem ginger
225g/8oz courgettes (zucchini), grated, drained
2.5cm/1in piece fresh root ginger, peeled and grated
350g/12oz/3 cups plain (all-purpose) flour
5ml/1 tsp baking powder
5ml/1 tsp ground cinnamon
pinch of salt
2 pieces preserved stem ginger, chopped
15ml/1 tbsp demerara (raw) sugar

1 Preheat the oven to 190°C/ 325°F/Gas 5. Grease and line a 900g/2lb loaf tin (pan) with baking parchment.

2 In a large bowl, beat together the eggs and sugar until light and fluffy.

3 Slowly beat in the oil until a batter forms. Mix in the vanilla extract and ginger syrup, then stir in the courgettes and fresh ginger.

6 Bake for 1 hour, or until a skewer inserted into the centre comes out clean. Leave to cool for 20 minutes, then turn out to cool on a wire rack.

Energy 252kcal/1060kJ; Protein 5.6g; Carbohydrate 35.6g, of which sugars 8.8g; Fat 10.7g, of which saturates 1.6g; Cholesterol 57mg; Calcium 73mg; Fibre 1.3g; Sodium 82mg.

Pineapple and carrot cake

Universally loved, this is one of the most irresistible cakes there is. The poppy seeds and walnut pieces add crunch, and the pineapple and carrot give moisture. A tangy citrus mascarpone icing makes a delicious topping. Keep for up to four days in an airtight container.

SERVES 10–12

250g/9oz/2¼ cups plain
(all-purpose) flour
10ml/2 tsp baking powder
5ml/1 tsp bicarbonate of soda
(baking soda)
pinch of salt
5ml/1 tsp ground cinnamon
45ml/3 tbsp poppy seeds
225g/8oz/1 cup soft light
brown sugar
3 eggs, beaten
finely grated rind of 1 orange
225g/8oz raw carrots,
finely grated
75g/3oz fresh or canned pineapple,
drained and finely chopped
75g/3oz/¾ cup walnut pieces
115g/4oz/½ cup butter, melted
and cooled

For the icing
150g/5oz/scant ¾ cup
mascarpone
30ml/2 tbsp icing (confectioners')
sugar, sifted
finely grated rind of 1 orange

1 Preheat the oven to 180°C/
350°F/Gas 4. Grease and line a
900g/2lb loaf tin (pan) with
baking parchment.

2 Sift the flour, baking powder,
bicarbonate of soda, salt and
cinnamon into a bowl. Stir in the
poppy seeds.

3 In another large bowl, put the
sugar, eggs and orange rind. Beat
together until smooth and frothy.

4 Squeeze the excess moisture from
the carrots and stir into the egg
mixture with the pineapple and
walnut pieces.

5 Stir the flour into the egg mixture,
then gently fold in the butter. Spoon
the batter into the prepared tin and
smooth the top level.

6 Bake for 1–1¼ hours, or until
risen and golden. Leave to cool for
10 minutes, then turn out on a wire
rack. Remove the paper when cold.

7 To make the icing, beat the
mascarpone with the icing sugar and
orange rind. Spread thickly over the
cake top.

Energy 400kcal/1668kJ; Protein 4.2g; Carbohydrate 39.1g, of which sugars 29.9g; Fat 26.3g, of which saturates 7.2g; Cholesterol 55mg; Calcium 62mg; Fibre 1g; Sodium 67mg.

Date and walnut loaf

This fruit loaf is lower in sugar than some cakes but the dates and bananas add sweetness as well as a depth of flavour. As they also make the loaf very moist, it's great for keeping for an unexpected tea party. Keep for one week in an airtight container or freeze for up to two months.

SERVES 8–10

150g/5oz/scant 1 cup stoned
    (pitted), chopped, dried dates
finely grated rind and juice
    of 1 lemon
5ml/1 tsp bicarbonate of soda
    (baking soda)
75g/3oz/6 tbsp butter, softened
50g/2oz/¼ cup soft light
    brown sugar
150g/5oz/½ cup sweetened
    condensed milk
2 eggs, beaten
150g/5oz ripe bananas, peeled
    and mashed
225g/8oz/2 cups self-raising
    (self-rising) flour
5ml/1 tsp baking powder
75g/3oz/¾ cup walnuts, chopped
butter, to serve

1 Preheat the oven to 160°C/
325°F/Gas 3. Grease and line a
900g/2lb loaf tin (pan) with
baking parchment.

2 Put the dates in a bowl with the
lemon rind and juice, and 30ml/
2 tbsp boiling water. Stir in the
bicarbonate of soda. Leave to cool.

3 Put the butter, sugar and
condensed milk in a bowl and whisk
with an electric mixer until smooth.

4 Gradually whisk in the eggs. Stir
in the bananas and the date mixture.

5 Sift the flour and baking powder
into the bowl, then add the chopped
nuts and stir together until smooth.

6 Spoon the mixture into the tin
and smooth the top level. Bake for
about 1 hour 10–15 minutes, or
until a skewer inserted into the
middle comes out clean.

7 Leave to set for 10 minutes, then
turn out on to a wire rack to go
cold. Remove the lining paper. Serve
sliced and buttered.

Energy 266kcal/1124kJ; Protein 6.1g; Carbohydrate 42.9g, of which sugars 24.3g; Fat 9g, of which saturates 1.2g; Cholesterol 1.8mg; Calcium 64mg; Fibre 3.4g; Sodium 16mg.

Quick-and-easy teabread

This succulent, fruity teabread can be served just as it is, or spread with a little butter. It is a great cake to serve at afternoon tea. Make one for picnics or add a slice to a packed lunch. Keep for up to five days, tightly wrapped in foil, or freeze for up to two months.

SERVES 6–8

350g/12oz/2 cups luxury mixed
  dried fruit
75g/3oz/scant ⅓ cup demerara
  (raw) sugar, plus 15ml/1 tbsp
  for sprinkling
1 large (US extra large) egg
175g/6oz/1½ cups self-raising
  (self-rising) flour

1 Put the fruit in a large bowl. Add 150ml/¼ pint/⅔ cup boiling water and leave to stand for 30 minutes.

2 Preheat the oven to 180°C/350°F/ Gas 4. Grease and line a 450g/1lb loaf tin (pan) with baking parchment.

3 Stir the sugar into the fruit and then beat in the egg.

4 Sift the flour into the bowl and stir until combined.

5 Spoon into the prepared tin and level the surface. Sprinkle with the 15ml/1 tbsp remaining sugar.

6 Bake for 50 minutes, or until risen and firm to the touch; a skewer inserted into the centre will come out clean.

7 Leave the loaf in the tin for 10 minutes before turning out to cool on a wire rack.

Energy 236kcal/1004kJ; Protein 3.8g; Carbohydrate 56.1g, of which sugars 39.9g; Fat 1.1g, of which saturates 0.2g; Cholesterol 24mg; Calcium 117mg; Fibre 1.6g; Sodium 109mg.

Fruit malt loaf

Malt extract gives this traditional fruity loaf its wonderful chewy consistency, and wholemeal flour adds depth of flavour. Cut in slices and spread with butter, it's just right for giving to hungry guests with afternoon tea. Keep for up to five days in an airtight container.

2 Put the dry ingredients in a bowl.

3 Heat the malt extract and milk in a small pan, stirring until dissolved. Mix into the dry ingredients.

SERVES 8–10

250g/9oz/2¼ cups wholemeal
(whole-wheat) self-raising
(self-rising) flour
pinch of salt
2.5ml/½ tsp bicarbonate of soda
(baking soda)
175g/6oz/1 cup mixed dried fruit
15ml/1 tbsp malt extract
250ml/8fl oz/1 cup milk
butter, to serve

1 Preheat the oven to 160°C/
325°F/Gas 3. Grease and line a
900g/2lb loaf tin (pan) with
baking parchment.

4 Spoon into the tin. Bake for 45 minutes, or until a skewer inserted into the loaf comes out clean. Leave to stand for a few minutes, then turn out on to a wire rack to go cold. Remove the lining paper.

Energy 260kcal/1103kJ; Protein 5.3g; Carbohydrate 58.6g, of which sugars 25.3g; Fat 2.1g, of which saturates 0.3g; Cholesterol 1mg; Calcium 97mg; Fibre 1.8g; Sodium 38mg.

Marmalade teabread

Chunky orange marmalade adds a touch of citrus zest to this spicy teabread. It is so quick and easy to make and perfect for serving with a cup of tea. Keep for up to three days in an airtight container or freeze for up to two months wrapped in foil.

SERVES 6–8

200g/7oz/1¾ cups plain
  (all-purpose) flour
5ml/1 tsp baking powder
6.25ml/1¼ tsp ground cinnamon
100g/3¾oz/7 tbsp butter, diced
50g/2oz/¼ cup soft light
  brown sugar
1 egg, lightly beaten
60ml/4 tbsp chunky orange
  marmalade
about 45ml/3 tbsp milk
60ml/4 tbsp glacé icing,
  to decorate
shreds of orange and lemon rind,
  to decorate

1 Preheat the oven to 160°C/ 325°F/Gas 3. Grease and line a 450g/1lb loaf tin (pan) with baking parchment.

2 Sift the flour, baking powder and cinnamon into a mixing bowl. Add the butter and rub in with your fingertips until the mixture resembles fine crumbs. Stir in the sugar.

3 In a bowl, mix the egg with the marmalade and most of the milk.

4 Mix the milk mixture into the flour mixture, adding more milk if necessary to give a soft, dropping consistency.

5 Spoon into the prepared tin and smooth the top level. Bake for 1¼ hours, or until the cake is firm to the touch and cooked through.

6 Cool in the tin for 5 minutes, then turn out to cool on a wire rack. Peel off the lining paper.

7 Drizzle the glacé icing over the top of the cake and decorate with shreds of orange and lemon rind.

Energy 287kcal/1206kJ; Protein 8.3g; Carbohydrate 34.8g, of which sugars 9.3g; Fat 13.7g, of which saturates 8.1g; Cholesterol 63mg; Calcium 68mg; Fibre 1g; Sodium 554mg.

Gingerbread

Cinnamon as well as ginger gives gingerbread its familiar warm flavouring, which wouldn't be achieved by using ginger alone. Treacle and golden syrup are the essential ingredients to ensure the finished cake is soft and sticky. Store, foil-wrapped, for five days in an airtight container.

SERVES 8–10

115g/4oz/½ cup soft light
  brown sugar
75g/3oz/6 tbsp butter
75g/3oz/¼ cup golden (light corn)
  syrup
75g/3oz/¼ cup treacle (molasses)
105ml/7 tbsp milk
1 egg, beaten
175g/6oz/1½ cups plain
  (all-purpose) flour
50g/2oz/½ cup gram flour
pinch of salt
10ml/2 tsp ground ginger
5ml/1 tsp ground cinnamon
7.5ml/1½ tsp baking powder

1 Preheat the oven to 160°C/ 325°F/Gas 3. Grease and line a 900g/2lb loaf tin (pan) with baking parchment.

2 Put the sugar, butter, golden syrup and treacle in a pan and heat gently until melted, stirring occasionally.

3 Remove the pan and leave to cool slightly. Mix in the milk and egg.

4 Sift the flours, salt, spices and baking powder into a large bowl. Make a well in the centre and pour in the liquid mixture. Beat well.

5 Pour the batter into the tin. Bake for 1–1¼ hours, or until firm.

6 Turn out on to a wire rack to go cold. Peel off the lining.

Energy 191kcal/802kJ; Protein 1.6g; Carbohydrate 24.7g, of which sugars 24.6g; Fat 10.3g, of which saturates 6.3g; Cholesterol 45mg; Calcium 128mg; Fibre 0g; Sodium 116mg.

Banana bread

When you have some bananas that have become overripe in the fruit bowl, use them for this delicious tea-time cake. They need to be very ripe and will give the bread a lovely sweetness and fragrance as well as making it moist. Keep for up to five days in an airtight container.

SERVES 8–10

115g/4oz/½ cup butter
5ml/1 tsp bicarbonate of soda
   (baking soda)
225g/8oz/2 cups wholemeal
   (whole-wheat) flour
2 eggs, beaten
3 very ripe bananas
30–45ml/2–3 tbsp coconut milk

1 Preheat the oven to 180°C/
350°F/Gas 4. Grease and line a
900g/2lb loaf tin (pan) with
baking parchment.

2 In a large bowl, cream the butter
until it is fluffy.

3 Sift the bicarbonate of soda with
the flour, then add to the butter,
alternating with the eggs.

4 Peel the bananas and slice them
on to a plate. Mash them well, using
the back of a fork, then stir them
into the cake mixture. Mix in the
coconut milk and stir together.

5 Spoon the batter into the tin and
smooth the top level. Bake for
1¼ hours, or until firm to touch
and golden. Cool on a wire rack.
Remove the lining paper.

Energy 226kcal/954kJ; Protein 5.1g; Carbohydrate 37.2g, of which sugars 19.5g; Fat 73.g, of which saturates 3.8g; Cholesterol 51mg; Calcium 46mg; Fibre 1.8g; Sodium 55mg.

Lemon and walnut teabread

The unusual combination of earthy walnuts and fresh zesty lemons tastes so good in this teabread. Unusually for a teabread, whisked egg whites are added to the batter, making it light and airy. Keep for three days in an airtight container. Freeze for two months wrapped in foil.

SERVES 8–10

115g/4oz/½ cup butter, softened
100g/3¾oz/generous ½ cup caster
   (superfine) sugar
2 eggs, separated
grated rind of 2 lemons
30ml/2 tbsp lemon juice
200g/7oz/1¾ cups plain
   (all-purpose) flour
10ml/2 tsp baking powder
120ml/4fl oz/½ cup milk
50g/2oz/½ cup walnuts, chopped
pinch of salt

1 Preheat the oven to 180°C/
350°F/Gas 4. Grease and line a
900g/2lb loaf tin (pan) with
baking parchment.

2 Beat the butter with the sugar.
Beat in the egg yolks, lemon rind
and juice. Set aside.

3 Sift the flour and baking powder
over the butter mixture in batches,
and stir well, alternating with the
milk. Fold in the walnuts.

4 Put the egg whites into a clean,
grease-free bowl and whisk until
they form stiff peaks. Fold a large
tablespoon of the egg whites into the
walnut mixture to lighten it. Fold
in the remaining egg whites until
just blended.

5 Pour the batter into the tin and
smooth the top level. Bake for
45–50 minutes, or until a skewer
inserted into the centre comes
out clean.

6 Leave to stand in the tin for
5 minutes then turn out on to a wire
rack to go cold. Peel off the lining.

Energy 249kcal/1041kJ; Protein 4.5g; Carbohydrate 26.9g, of which sugars 10.4g; Fat 14.4g, of which saturates 6.7g; Cholesterol 63mg; Calcium 61mg; Fibre 0.8g; Sodium 90mg.

Coconut loaf

Sour cream and desiccated coconut make this quick-and-easy cake wonderfully moist and give it a full flavour that is lifted by a delicious lemony tang. Serve in thick slices as part of an afternoon tea party. This cake keeps for eight days in an airtight container.

SERVES 8–10

115g/4oz/½ cup butter,
   softened
115g/4oz/generous ½ cup caster
   (superfine) sugar
2 large (US extra large)
   eggs, beaten
115g/4oz/generous 1 cup
   desiccated (dry unsweetened)
   coconut
115g/4oz/1 cup self-raising
   (self-rising) flour
75ml/5 tbsp sour cream or natural
   (plain) yogurt
15ml/1 tbsp finely grated
   lemon rind

1 Preheat the oven to 180°C/350°F/ Gas 4. Grease and line a 900g/2lb loaf tin (pan) with baking parchment.

2 In a large bowl, beat the butter and sugar together until pale and fluffy, then add the eggs in batches, beating well after each addition.

3 Add the coconut, flour, sour cream or yogurt and lemon rind, and beat together until smooth.

4 Spoon into the tin. Bake for 50 minutes, or until a skewer inserted into the centre comes out clean.

5 Cool in the tin for 5 minutes, then turn out on to a wire rack to go cold. Peel off the lining paper.

COOK'S TIP
To freeze, wrap in foil and freeze for up to 3 months.

VARIATION
Add 75g/3oz/½ cup dried morello cherries at step 3.

Energy 221kcal/924kJ; Protein 3g; Carbohydrate 27.8g, of which sugars 22.1g; Fat 11.6g, of which saturates 8.2g; Cholesterol 61mg; Calcium 31mg; Fibre 1.6g; Sodium 51mg.

Raspberry and almond teabread

Fresh raspberries and almonds combine perfectly to flavour this mouthwatering loaf with its crunchy, toasted flaked-almond topping. Serve warm with a spoonful of crème fraîche as part of a tea table buffet. Eat this cake on the day of making.

3 Sift the flour into a large bowl or the bowl of a food processor. Add the butter and rub in, or process, until the mixture resembles fine breadcrumbs.

4 Stir in the sugar and ground almonds, then gradually mix in the eggs and milk, and beat until smooth.

5 Fold in the raspberries, being careful not to crush them.

6 Spoon into the prepared tin and sprinkle over the flaked almonds.

SERVES 6–8

175g/6oz/1½ cups self-raising (self-rising) flour
90g/3½oz/7 tbsp butter
90g/3½oz/½ cup caster (superfine) sugar
40g/1½oz/scant ½ cup ground almonds
2 eggs, beaten
30ml/2 tbsp milk
115g/4oz/1 cup fresh raspberries or partly thawed frozen raspberries
30ml/2 tbsp toasted flaked (sliced) almonds

1 Preheat the oven to 180°C/ 350°F/Gas 4.

2 Grease and line a 450g/1lb loaf tin (pan) with baking parchment.

7 Bake for about 55 minutes, or until a skewer inserted into the centre comes out clean. Cool in the tin for 5 minutes, then turn out on to a wire rack to go cold. Remove the lining paper.

Energy 215kcal/902kJ; Protein 4.3g; Carbohydrate 24.1g, of which sugars 10.5g; Fat 12g, of which saturates 5.3g; Cholesterol 44mg; Calcium 59mg; Fibre 1.4g; Sodium 79mg.

Peanut butter teabread

Crunchy peanut butter gives this teabread richness, as well as a distinctive flavour and texture. It makes a substantial tea-time treat. The topping of salted peanuts contrasts with the sweetness of the bread. This cake will keep for two days in an airtight container.

SERVES 10

225g/8oz/2 cups plain
(all-purpose) flour
7.5ml/1½ tsp baking powder
2.5ml/½ tsp bicarbonate of soda
(baking soda)
50g/2oz/¼ cup butter, softened
175g/6oz/½ cup crunchy
peanut butter
50g/2oz/¼ cup caster (superfine)
sugar
2 eggs, beaten
250ml/8fl oz/1 cup milk
25g/1oz/¼ cup roasted
salted peanuts

1 Preheat the oven to 180°C/350°F/Gas 4. Grease and line a 900g/2lb loaf tin (pan) with baking parchment.

2 Sift the flour, baking powder and bicarbonate of soda together into a large bowl.

3 Put the butter and peanut butter in a large bowl and beat together with a wooden spoon to soften. Beat in the caster sugar until light and fluffy and the sugar grains have disintegrated.

4 Gradually whisk in the eggs a little at a time, then beat in the milk with the sifted flour and mix until smooth.

5 Pour into the prepared tin and sprinkle the peanuts on top.

6 Bake for 1 hour or until a skewer inserted into the centre comes out clean. Cool in the tin for 5 minutes, then turn out on to a wire rack. Remove the lining paper.

COOK'S TIP
This teabread is tasty with soup or cold meats.

Energy 214kcal/904kJ; Protein 6.4g; Carbohydrate 33.5g, of which sugars 11.4g; Fat 6.9g, of which saturates 1.7g; Cholesterol 28mg; Calcium 70mg; Fibre 1.4g; Sodium 56mg.

Fruity treats

Contemporary additions to the afternoon tea table include muffins and cupcakes. This delicious selection includes treats perfect for any occasion. Blueberries, crunchy apples, sharp cranberries, sweet bananas, flavoursome peaches, dried cherries and exotic pineapple are all featured in this lavish recipe collection. Try Blackberry and Almond Cakes with a hint of sloe gin and rose water, or Apple and Calvados Muffins with Quince for a mid-morning treat. Orange Poppy Seed Cakes drizzled with icing, or subtle Apricot and Maple Syrup Muffins, make appealing accompaniments to a cup of tea.

Left: Raspberry buns are packed with fruit and nutritional goodness – these little cakes make perfect fare for little people joining in with afternoon tea, though adults will love them too.

Blackberry and almond cakes

Sloe gin and rose water add depth of flavour to these muffins, helping them to stand out from the crowded tea table. Autumnal blackberries are perfectly complemented by the mild flavour and crunch of blanched almonds. Store in an airtight container for up to three days.

MAKES 12 STANDARD MUFFINS

100g/3¹/₂oz/scant 1 cup fresh
  blackberries
300g/11oz/2¾ cups plain
  (all-purpose) flour
50g/2oz/¼ cup soft light
  brown sugar
20ml/4 tsp baking powder
60g/2¹/₄oz/¹/₃ cup blanched
  almonds, chopped
2 eggs
100ml/3¹/₂fl oz/scant ½ cup milk
50g/2oz/¼ cup butter, melted
15ml/1 tbsp sloe gin
15ml/1 tbsp rose water

1 Preheat the oven to 200°C/400°F/ Gas 6. Line the cups of a muffin tin (pan) with paper cases.

2 Rinse the blackberries in a colander and pat dry.

3 Sift the flour, sugar and baking powder into a large bowl.

4 Stir in the almonds and black-berries, mixing them well to coat with the flour mixture. Make a well in the centre of the dry ingredients.

5 In another bowl, whisk the eggs with the milk, then mix in the butter, sloe gin and rose water. Add to the dry ingredients and stir in.

6 Spoon the batter into the prepared paper cases and bake for 20–25 minutes or until golden. Leave to stand for 5 minutes before turning out on to a wire rack to cool. Serve with butter, if you like.

Energy 181kcal/761kJ; Protein 4.8g; Carbohydrate 25g, of which sugars 5.8g; Fat 7.6g, of which saturates 2.9g; Cholesterol 42mg; Calcium 68mg; Fibre 1.4g; Sodium 49mg.

Rhubarb muffins with ginger

The shiny candied strips of scarlet rhubarb and paper-thin slices of stem ginger add a sweet, colourful topping to these muffins. Extra slices of stem ginger add a decorative flourish – perfect for a special tea party. Serve fresh for the best flavour, or store for up to three days.

MAKES 9–10 TALL MUFFINS

275g/10oz rhubarb, cleaned
30ml/2 tbsp syrup from a jar
  of preserved stem ginger
1 piece preserved stem
  ginger, chopped
50g/2oz/4 tbsp demerara
  (raw) sugar
150g/5oz/1¼ cups plain
  (all-purpose) flour
75g/3oz/⅔ cup wholemeal
  (whole-wheat) or spelt flour
50g/2oz/¼ cup caster
  (superfine) sugar
10ml/2 tsp baking powder
2.5ml/½ tsp bicarbonate of soda
  (baking soda)
5ml/1 tsp ground ginger
120ml/4fl oz/½ cup low-fat natural
  (plain) yogurt
1 egg, lightly beaten

For the topping
15g/½oz/1 tbsp butter
15ml/1 tbsp ginger syrup
15ml/1 tbsp caster (superfine) sugar
1 piece stem ginger, finely sliced

2 Bring to the boil, stirring. Lower the heat and simmer until soft, about 2–3 minutes. Set aside.

3 Preheat the oven to 180°C/350°F/ Gas 4. Line the dariole moulds with tall paper cases. Sift the dry ingredients into a bowl.

5 To make the topping, heat the butter, ginger syrup, 15ml/1 tbsp water and sugar in a small frying pan over medium heat and stir until the sugar dissolves.

1 Slice 175g/6oz rhubarb and put in a pan with 30ml/2 tbsp water, the ginger syrup, stem ginger and demerara sugar.

4 In another bowl, beat the yogurt and egg together. Stir in the cooked rhubarb and juices and mix into the dry ingredients. Divide the batter between the paper cases.

6 Cut the rest of the rhubarb into short fine strips and lightly stir them in the syrup. Leave to soften for 2 minutes, then add the stem ginger slices until warmed through. Remove from the heat. Add in small piles to the centre of the muffin tops and bake for 20 minutes until golden.

Energy 152kcal/646kJ; Protein 3.9g; Carbohydrate 31.1g, of which sugars 15g; Fat 2.3g, of which saturates 1.1g; Cholesterol 23mg; Calcium 82mg; Fibre 1.5g; Sodium 42mg.

Cranberry and orange buns

These delicious muffins are a real energy boost for the middle of the afternoon. Use fresh or frozen cranberries; both will work equally well for these tea-table delights. The orange rind adds to the tangy flavour of the cranberries.

4 Pour the egg mixture into the dry ingredients. Stir with a wooden spoon until just blended to a smooth batter.

5 Gently fold in the orange rind and cranberries with a metal spoon.

MAKES 10 STANDARD MUFFINS

350g/12oz/3 cups plain
 (all-purpose) flour, sifted
15ml/1 tsp baking powder
pinch of salt
115g/4oz/generous ½ cup caster
 (superfine) sugar
2 eggs
150ml/¼ pint/⅔ cup milk
50ml/2fl oz/¼ cup corn oil
finely grated rind of 1 orange
150g/5oz/1¼ cups cranberries,
 thawed if frozen

1 Preheat the oven to 190°C/375°F/ Gas 5. Lightly grease the cups of a muffin tin (pan) or line them with paper cases.

2 Sift together the flour, baking powder and salt into a large bowl. Add the sugar and stir to mix. Make a well in the centre.

3 Using a fork, lightly beat the eggs with the milk and corn oil in another bowl, until they are thoroughly combined.

6 Fill the paper cases and bake for about 25 minutes, until risen and golden. Leave to stand for 5 minutes before transferring to a wire rack. Serve warm or cold. Store in an airtight container for up to 3 days.

COOK'S TIP
The tart flavour of cranberries is not to everyone's taste, but for those who enjoy a less sweet treat, these muffins are ideal.

Energy 221kcal/936kJ; Protein 5.1g; Carbohydrate 41.3g, of which sugars 14.6g; Fat 5.1g, of which saturates 1g; Cholesterol 39mg; Calcium 79mg; Fibre 1.3g; Sodium 24mg.

Apple and Calvados muffins with quince

A simple apple muffin is transformed into something suitable for the grandest tea table with the addition of luxurious apple brandy and the aromatic flavour of quince. Quince glaze adds an appetizing shine to these autumnal muffins. Store in an airtight container for up to three days.

MAKES 10 STANDARD MUFFINS

250g/9oz peeled and cored cooking
   apple flesh
30–45ml/2–3 tbsp quince paste
75g/3oz/6 tbsp butter
15ml/1 tbsp Calvados
225g/8oz/2 cups plain
   (all-purpose) flour
12.5ml/2½ tsp baking powder
75g/3oz/scant ½ cup caster
   (superfine) sugar
1 egg, lightly beaten
60ml/4 tbsp buttermilk
grated rind of 1 lemon

For the quince glaze
45ml/3 tbsp quince paste
5ml/1 tsp lemon juice
30ml/2 tbsp Calvados

1 Preheat the oven to 180°C/350°F/
Gas 4. Line the cups of a muffin tin
(pan) with paper cases.

2 Chop most of the apples into
cubes, and set aside. Cut a few into
crescents and put in lemon water.

3 Put the quince paste and butter in
a pan and stir until melted. Remove
from the heat. Add the Calvados.

4 Sift the flour, baking powder and
sugar into a large bowl and form a
well in the centre. Blend the egg and
buttermilk. Pour into the dry
ingredients with the lemon rind,
Calvados mixture and apple. Stir
until just blended.

5 Spoon the batter into the paper
cases. Drain and slice the reserved
apple segments into thin pieces and
lightly press several on each muffin.

6 Bake for 25–30 minutes until
golden and springy to the touch.
Leave to stand for a few minutes
then transfer to a wire rack.

7 To make the quince glaze, add the
quince paste, lemon juice and 15ml/
1 tbsp water to a small pan. Boil
rapidly to make a thin syrup. Stir
in the Calvados and simmer for
1 minute. Brush thickly over the
surface of the warm muffins.

Energy 213kcal/899kJ; Protein 3.1g; Carbohydrate 34.1g, of which sugars 16.9g; Fat 7.1g, of which saturates 4.3g; Cholesterol 37mg; Calcium 50mg; Fibre 1.1g; Sodium 70mg.

Blueberry and cinnamon bakes

The traditional blueberry muffin is given a twist with the addition of warming cinnamon.
This sweet spice complements the fresh and juicy flavour of the berries. Eat while warm and fresh
from the oven, or enjoy them cold. Store in an airtight container for up to three days.

MAKES 8 STANDARD MUFFINS

115g/4oz/1 cup plain
  (all-purpose) flour
15ml/1 tbsp baking powder
65g/2¹/₂oz/5 tbsp soft light
  brown sugar
10ml/2 tsp ground cinnamon
1 egg
175ml/6fl oz/³/₄ cup milk
45ml/3 tbsp vegetable oil
115g/4oz/1 cup blueberries

VARIATION
Peel and dice one apple and use
it in place of the blueberries.

1 Preheat the oven to 190°C/375°F/
Gas 5. Line the cups of a muffin tin
(pan) with paper cases.

2 Sift the flour, baking powder,
sugar and cinnamon into a bowl.
Add the egg, milk and vegetable oil
and whisk together until smooth.

3 Fold in the blueberries.

4 Spoon the batter into the muffin
cups, filling them two-thirds full.
Bake until a skewer inserted into the
centre of a muffin comes out clean,
about 25 minutes.

5 Leave to cool in the tin for
10 minutes, then turn out on to a
wire rack to go completely cold.

COOK'S TIP
Fresh blueberries are available
year round in supermarkets, but
they are naturally in season in
late summer, so this is the best
time to buy them – they are
likely to be sweeter and have a
better flavour.

Energy 141kcal/593kJ; Protein 3.1g; Carbohydrate 21.4g, of which sugars 10.5g; Fat 5.4g, of which saturates 0.9g; Cholesterol 25mg; Calcium 60mg; Fibre 0.9g; Sodium 19mg.

Raspberry buns

Wholemeal flour makes these muffins a filling treat for hungry tea-time guests, and with so little added sugar, they are healthier than most cakes. Raspberries are slightly acidic and bursting with goodness and flavour, and you can use frozen berries to make this recipe.

MAKES 10–12 STANDARD MUFFINS

115g/4oz/1 cup self-raising (self-rising) flour
115g/4oz/1 cup self-raising wholemeal (self-rising whole-wheat) flour
45ml/3 tbsp caster (superfine) sugar
2 eggs, beaten
200ml/7fl oz/scant 1 cup milk
50g/2oz/¹/₄ cup butter, melted
175g/6oz/1¹/₂ cups raspberries, fresh or frozen (defrosted for less than 30 minutes)

1 Preheat the oven to 190°C/375°F/ Gas 5. Lightly grease the cups of a muffin tin (pan) or line them with paper cases.

2 Sift the dry ingredients together, then turn in the wholemeal flakes from the sieve (strainer). Make a well in the centre.

3 Beat the eggs, milk and melted butter together in a small bowl until thoroughly combined, then pour into the dry ingredients and mix to a smooth batter.

4 Add the raspberries and gently stir them in. (If you are using frozen raspberries, work quickly so that the cold berries remain solid.) If you mix too much, the raspberries will disintegrate.

5 Spoon the batter into the prepared paper cases. Bake for 30 minutes, until well risen and just firm. Leave to stand, then turn out on to a wire rack. Serve warm or cold. Store in an airtight container for up to 3 days.

Energy 132kcal/555kJ; Protein 4g; Carbohydrate 19g, of which sugars 5.7g; Fat 5g, of which saturates 2.7g; Cholesterol 42mg; Calcium 48mg; Fibre 1.5g; Sodium 45mg.

Orange poppy seed cakes

These muffins look attractive on the tea table when baked in large muffin cups and without paper cases so the poppy-seed flecked sides are visible. To serve, break open and spread with butter and marmalade. Store without icing in an airtight container for three days.

4 Pour over the dry ingredients. Fold in until just mixed. Leave for 1 hour.

5 Preheat the oven to 180°C/350°F/ Gas 4.

6 Fold the reserved flour into the batter but leave it lumpy.

7 Fill the muffin cups three-quarters full. Bake for 25 minutes, until risen and golden.

8 Leave to stand in the tin for a few minutes, then turn out on to a wire rack to go cold.

9 To make the icing, mix the icing sugar and orange juice in a bowl. Add a small quantity of water, if needed, to make a runny consistency. Drizzle over the cakes.

MAKES 8 LARGE MUFFINS

275g/10oz/2½ cups plain (all-purpose) flour
150g/5oz/¾ cup caster (superfine) sugar
15ml/1 tbsp baking powder
2 eggs
75g/3oz/6 tbsp butter, melted
75ml/5 tbsp vegetable oil
25ml/1½ tbsp poppy seeds
30ml/2 tbsp orange juice, plus grated rind of 1½ oranges
5ml/1 tsp lemon juice, plus grated rind of 1 lemon

For the icing
25g/1oz/¼ cup icing (confectioners') sugar
15ml/1 tbsp orange juice

1 Lightly grease the cups of a muffin tin (pan) with melted butter or line them with paper cases.

2 Set aside 40g/1½oz of flour. Place the remaining flour with the dry ingredients in a mixing bowl. Make a well in the centre.

3 Mix the eggs, butter, oil, poppy seeds, citrus juices and rinds.

Energy 377kcal/1583kJ; Protein 5.7g; Carbohydrate 50.7g, of which sugars 24.5g; Fat 18.3g, of which saturates 7.5g; Cholesterol 89mg; Calcium 85mg; Fibre 1.2g; Sodium 107mg.

Apple and sour cream crumble muffins

Two-thirds of the cooking apples in this recipe are chopped and baked in the muffin batter. The remaining apples are sliced and coated in a sweet almond crumble, which makes a delicious crunchy texture for the muffin top. Store in an airtight container for up to three days.

MAKES 8 STANDARD MUFFINS

3 small cooking apples, peeled
  and cored
115g/4oz/½ cup caster (superfine)
  sugar, plus 10ml/2 tsp for coating
5ml/1 tsp ground cinnamon
250g/9oz/2¼ cups plain
  (all-purpose) flour
15ml/1 tbsp baking powder
75g/3oz/6 tbsp butter, melted
2 eggs, beaten
30ml/2 tbsp sour cream

For the cinnamon crumble
30ml/2 tbsp plain (all-purpose) flour
45ml/3 tbsp demerara (raw) sugar
30ml/2 tbsp ground almonds
pinch of ground cinnamon

1 Preheat the oven to 190°C/375°F/ Gas 5. Line the cups of a muffin tin (pan) with paper cases.

2 To make the crumble, mix all the ingredients together in a bowl. Cut one apple into thin crescents, and toss in the crumble. Set aside.

3 Dice the remaining apples. Sift 10ml/2 tsp sugar and the cinnamon over the top. Set aside.

4 Sift the flour, baking powder and sugar into a bowl. Stir in the melted butter, eggs and sour cream.

5 Add the apple chunks and lightly fold them into the batter.

6 Fill the paper cases with the batter, then arrange the crumble-coated apple on top.

7 Bake for 25 minutes until risen and golden. Cool on a wire rack.

Energy 272kcal/1144kJ; Protein 4.8g; Carbohydrate 42.8g, of which sugars 19g; Fat 10.2g, of which saturates 6g; Cholesterol 71mg; Calcium 65mg; Fibre 1.6g; Sodium 92mg.

Apricot and maple syrup muffins

Spelt flour has a nutty flavour and is slightly sweet. If you have trouble locating it, substitute plain wholegrain flour instead. Healthy and low in fat, serve these dense tall apricot muffins for afternoon tea – they're quite filling.

MAKES 8 TALL MUFFINS

175g/6oz/⅔ cup ready-to-eat
   dried apricots
40g/1½oz/3 tbsp caster
   (superfine) sugar
150g/5oz/1¼ cups plain
   (all-purpose) flour
75g/3oz/⅔ cup spelt flour
10ml/2 tsp baking powder
2.5ml/½ tsp bicarbonate of soda
   (baking soda)
120ml/4fl oz/½ cup low-fat natural
   (plain) yogurt
1 egg, lightly beaten
60ml/4 tbsp maple syrup

1 Preheat the oven to 180°C/350°F/ Gas 4. Grease and line the dariole moulds with baking parchment.

2 Put the apricots in a pan with 30ml/2 tbsp water and the sugar. Bring the liquid slowly to the boil, stirring, then cover and leave to simmer for 4 minutes.

3 Mix the flours, baking powder and bicarbonate of soda in a large bowl and set aside.

4 Drain the apricots, reserving the syrup. Cut the apricots into quarters.

5 In a small bowl, mix the yogurt, egg, maple syrup and reserved syrup and pour them over the dry ingredients. Fold lightly in with the chopped apricot until just combined.

6 Spoon into the lined moulds and bake for 18 minutes. Leave to stand then transfer to a wire rack to cool completely. Store in an airtight container for up to 3 days.

COOK'S TIP
If you don't have dariole moulds, use a standard muffin tin (pan) lined with paper cases and bake for 22–24 minutes.

Energy 187kcal/796kJ; Protein 5.4g; Carbohydrate 40.8g, of which sugars 20.7g; Fat 1.4g, of which saturates 0.3g; Cholesterol 24mg; Calcium 83mg; Fibre 2.8g; Sodium 46mg.

Blueberry and vanilla muffins

Vanilla extract has a sweet aroma and intense, easily identifiable flavour. In this recipe it is used to enhance the natural taste of the juicy blueberries. These muffins are perfect for a mid-afternoon treat with a cup of tea. Store in an airtight container for up to three days.

MAKES 12 STANDARD MUFFINS

350g/12oz/3 cups plain
  (all-purpose) flour
10ml/2 tsp baking powder
115g/4oz/½ cup caster
  (superfine) sugar
2 eggs, beaten
300ml/½ pint/1¼ cups milk
115g/4oz/ ½ cup butter, melted
5ml/1 tsp vanilla extract
175g/6oz/1½ cups blueberries

1 Preheat the oven to 200°C/400°F/
Gas 6. Line the cups of a muffin tin
(pan) with paper cases.

2 Sift the flour and baking powder
into a bowl. Stir in the sugar.

3 In another bowl, whisk together
the eggs, milk, butter and vanilla.

4 Fold the egg mixture into the dry
ingredients with a metal spoon, then
gently stir in the blueberries.

5 Spoon the batter into the prepared
paper cases, filling them until just
below the top. Fill any empty cups
half full with water to prevent
burning. Bake for 20–25 minutes,
until the muffins are well risen and
lightly browned.

6 Leave the muffins in the tin for
5 minutes and then turn them out
on to a wire rack to cool. Serve
warm or cold with a spoonful of
berry preserve.

Energy 243kcal/1021kJ; Protein 4.9g; Carbohydrate 35.9g, of which sugars 13.1g; Fat 9.9g, of which saturates 6g; Cholesterol 56mg; Calcium 82mg; Fibre 1.2g; Sodium 102mg.

Banana and pecan muffins

The rich, buttery flavour of pecan nuts complements the sweetness of banana in these deliciously moreish muffins. Pecans are a healthy treat, and can be frozen for convenience. Serve these muffins warm and freshly baked, or store in an airtight container for up to three days.

3 In a large bowl, beat together the butter and sugar until light and fluffy.

4 Add the egg and vanilla and beat until smooth. Mix in the bananas.

MAKES 8 STANDARD MUFFINS

150g/5oz/1¼ cups plain
  (all-purpose) flour
7.5ml/1½ tsp baking powder
50g/2oz/¼ cup butter, softened
150g/5oz/¾ cup caster
  (superfine) sugar
1 egg
5ml/1 tsp vanilla extract
3 bananas, mashed
75ml/5 tbsp milk
50g/2oz/⅓ cup pecans, chopped,
  plus extra for decorating
  (optional)

1 Preheat the oven to 190°C/375°F/ Gas 5. Line the cups of a muffin tin (pan) with paper cases.

2 Sift the flour and baking powder into a small bowl. Set aside.

5 With the mixer on low speed, beat in the flour mixture, alternating it with the milk. Add the pecans.

6 Spoon the batter into the paper cases, filling them two-thirds full. Bake until golden brown and a skewer inserted into the centre comes out clean, about 20–25 minutes. Decorate with extra pecans.

7 Leave to cool in the tin for 10 minutes, then transfer to a wire rack. Leave for 10 minutes longer before serving.

Energy 277kcal/1164kJ; Protein 4g; Carbohydrate 43.7g, of which sugars 28.5g; Fat 10.7g, of which saturates 4g; Cholesterol 38mg; Calcium 58mg; Fibre 1.3g; Sodium 53mg.

Coconut and rum portions

Malibu is an intoxicating mix of pineapple juice, coconut milk and white rum. If it's your favourite tipple, then you'll love these muffins, because the same indulgent ingredient combination is used. Make these for a special occasion tea. Store in an airtight container for up to three days.

MAKES 8 STANDARD MUFFINS

175g/6oz fresh pineapple, plus
    extra for decoration
115g/4oz/½ cup natural glacé
    (candied) cherries, halved, plus
    extra for decoration
45ml/3 tbsp white rum
225g/8oz/2 cups plain
    (all-purpose) flour
10ml/2 tsp baking powder
175g/6oz/¾ cup butter, softened
175g/6oz/¾ cup soft light
    brown sugar
2 eggs
7.5ml/1½ tsp vanilla extract
75ml/2½fl oz/⅓ cup coconut milk
icing (confectioners') sugar,
    for dusting

1 Cut the pineapple into segments, then into thin slices. Put in a small bowl with the glacé cherries. Pour over the rum and leave to marinate for 30–60 minutes.

2 Preheat the oven to 180°C/350°F/ Gas 4. Line the cups of a muffin tin (pan) with paper cases.

3 Sift the flour and the baking powder into a large bowl. Set aside.

4 In a bowl, beat the butter and sugar until light and creamy, then gradually beat in the eggs, one at a time. Stir in the vanilla and coconut milk and mix well.

5 Add the rum-soaked fruit in small amounts with the flour and baking powder mixture until just combined.

6 Divide the batter between the paper cases and decorate the tops with extra thin pieces of pineapple and cherry halves.

7 Bake for 20–25 minutes until golden on top and springy to touch.

8 Leave to cool slightly then turn out on to a wire rack to go cold. Serve warm.

Energy 420kcal/1764kJ; Protein 4.6g; Carbohydrate 56.9g, of which sugars 35.4g; Fat 19.7g, of which saturates 12.3g; Cholesterol 98mg; Calcium 76mg; Fibre 1.3g; Sodium 197mg.

Lemon and elderflower poppy seed muffins

Poppy seeds add an unexpectedly light and crunchy texture to the cake crumb, which traditionally is soaked in a sweet lemon syrup. For a variation, omit the syrup, break open the freshly baked muffin and spread it with butter and fresh lemon curd instead.

4 Pour the liquid into the flour mix and stir until just combined.

5 Fill the lined moulds three-quarters full and bake for 25 minutes. Leave to stand for a few minutes, then transfer to a wire rack to go cold.

MAKES 8 TALL MUFFINS

225g/8oz/2 cups self-raising (self-rising) flour
200g/7oz/1 cup caster (superfine) sugar
40g/1½oz ground almonds
2 eggs, beaten
75g/3oz/6 tbsp butter, melted
50ml/2fl oz/¼ cup vegetable oil
25ml/1½ tbsp poppy seeds
30ml/2 tbsp lemon juice
grated rind of 1 lemon
grated rind of 1 clementine

For the syrup
115g/4oz/generous ½ cup caster (superfine) sugar
50ml/2fl oz /¼ cup lemon juice
15ml/1 tbsp elderflower cordial
lemon segments, to decorate

1 Preheat the oven to 180°C/350°F/Gas 4. Grease and line 8 dariole moulds with baking parchment.

2 Sift the flour and sugar into a bowl. Stir in the ground almonds. Make a well in the centre.

3 In a jug (pitcher) mix together the eggs, butter, oil, poppy seeds, lemon juice and the grated fruit rinds.

6 To make the syrup, put the sugar, 120ml/4fl oz/½ cup water and the lemon juice in a pan and heat gently, stirring frequently until dissolved.

7 Leave to boil without stirring for 5–6 minutes until syrupy. Remove from the heat. Stir in the cordial.

8 Prick holes in the top of each muffin using a skewer. Pour over the warm syrup. Store for up to 1 week. Decorate the muffin tops with thin segments of lemon, before serving.

Energy 408kcal/1717kJ; Protein 5.9g; Carbohydrate 63.9g, of which sugars 42.4g; Fat 16.1g, of which saturates 6.2g; Cholesterol 69mg; Calcium 94mg; Fibre 1.4g; Sodium 92mg.

Peach and almond bakes

Ripe peaches with their soft, juicy flesh, velvety coat and distinctive scent are synonymous with late summer. These luxurious fruits make a delightful addition to these tea-time muffins. Use them when they are in season and fully mature for the best flavour. Eat fresh.

MAKES 8 STANDARD MUFFINS

2 large ripe peaches
225g/8oz/2 cups plain
  (all-purpose) flour
15ml/1 tbsp baking powder
150g/5oz/¾ cup caster
  (superfine) sugar
40g/1½oz ground almonds
2 eggs
75g/3oz/6 tbsp butter, melted
50ml/2fl oz/¼ cup sunflower oil
20ml/4 tsp sour cream
15ml/1 tbsp flaked (sliced)
  almonds, for decorating
icing (confectioners') sugar,
  for dusting
passion fruit and lime curd,
  to serve

1 Preheat the oven to 180°C/350°F/
Gas 4. Line the cups of a muffin tin
(pan) with paper cases.

2 Cut one peach into small chunks
to add to the batter. Cut the other
peach into thin crescents and set
aside for the topping.

3 Sift the flour, baking powder and
sugar into a bowl. Stir in the ground
almonds. Form a well in the centre.

4 In a jug (pitcher), whisk together
the eggs, melted butter, oil and sour
cream until combined. Pour into the
dry ingredients and partly fold in.
Add the chopped peaches and fold
in until just combined.

5 Divide the batter between the
paper cases.

6 Decorate the top of each with
sliced fruit crescents. Sprinkle over
the flaked almonds.

7 Bake for 25–30 minutes. Leave to
stand in the tin for a few minutes,
then transfer to a wire rack to cool.
Dust with icing sugar and serve with
passion fruit and lime curd.

Energy 326kcal/1369kJ; Protein 5.7g; Carbohydrate 43.8g, of which sugars 22.2g; Fat 15.5g, of which saturates 6.4g; Cholesterol 71mg; Calcium 74mg; Fibre 1.6g; Sodium 92mg.

Pastries

This winning collection of sweet and delicate pastries, individual treats and filled choux buns is a delectable feast to behold. All the classics are included here, from traditional fruit-filled English Eccles Cakes, luxurious Jam Tarts that are the perfect treat for children, and deep Apple Pie, packed with seasonal fruits. This recipe selection includes fabulous traybakes too, with their complex layers of flavours and crunchy toppings. Try moreish Almond Slices, crunchy Grated Berry Bake, light and airy Chocolate Whirls or decadent Coffee Cream Profiteroles.

Left: Bakewell tart is a traditional English dessert that is perfect for serving cold and sliced at afternoon tea.

Apple pie

The rich sweet pastry of this indulgent apple pie has the texture and taste of cake. Serve it with a generous dollop of whipped cream for a slice of apple heaven.

SERVES 6–8

215g/7½oz/scant 2 cups plain (all-purpose) flour, plus extra for dusting
5ml/1 tsp baking powder
pinch of salt
115g/4oz/½ cup cold unsalted butter, cubed
finely grated rind of ½ lemon
75g/3oz/scant ½ cup caster (superfine) sugar, plus extra for sprinkling
2 small (US medium) eggs
3 eating apples, peeled, cored and diced
ground cinnamon, for sprinkling
whipped cream, to serve

1 Sift the flour, baking powder and salt into a food processor. Add the butter and grated lemon rind and process briefly, then add the sugar, 1 whole egg and 1 yolk to the mixture and process to make a soft dough.

2 Divide the dough into two pieces, one portion nearly double the size of the other. Pat the dough into two flat cakes. Wrap tightly in clear film (plastic wrap) and chill for at least 2 hours until firm.

3 Preheat the oven to 180°C/350°F/Gas 4. Place a baking sheet in the oven and grease a 20cm/8in loose-based flan tin (pan).

4 Place the large ball of dough between two lightly floured sheets of clear film. Roll out a 25cm/10in round. Discard the top layer of film and lift the dough on the lower piece. Place it face down in the tin. Peel off the film. Press into the tin so that it stands just clear of the top.

5 Pack with the apples and sprinkle with cinnamon. Roll out the second piece of dough in the same way, to the same size as the tin. Lay the dough on top of the apples and fold the edges of the bottom piece of dough inward, pressing to seal.

6 Prick the dough, brush with egg white and sprinkle with sugar. Place on the hot baking sheet and bake for 20 minutes. Reduce the oven temperature to 160°C/325°F/Gas 3 and bake for 25–30 minutes.

Energy 362kcal/1519kJ; Protein 5.8g; Carbohydrate 47g, of which sugars 19.7g; Fat 18.1g, of which saturates 10.6g; Cholesterol 104mg; Calcium 72mg; Fibre 2.2g; Sodium 143mg.

Curd tart

The distinguishing characteristic of curd tart is the unmistakable flavour of allspice. The result tastes superb and is not too sweet. Serve with a spoonful of cream for a tea-time treat.

SERVES 6–8

225g/8oz/2 cups plain
   (all-purpose) flour
115g/4oz/½ cup butter, diced
1 egg yolk
15–30ml/1–2 tbsp chilled water

For the filling
90g/3½oz/scant ½ cup soft light
   brown sugar
large pinch of ground allspice
3 eggs, beaten
grated rind and juice of 1 lemon
40g/1½oz/3 tbsp butter, melted
450g/1lb/2 cups soft white curd
   (farmer's) cheese
75g/3oz/scant ½ cup raisins

1 To make the pastry, place the flour in a large mixing bowl and rub in the butter until the mixture resembles fine breadcrumbs. Stir the egg yolk into the flour and add just enough of the water to bind the mixture together to form a dough.

2 Place the dough on a lightly floured surface, knead lightly and briefly, then form into a ball. Roll out the pastry to 3mm/⅛in thick and use to line a 20cm/8in fluted loose-based flan tin (pan). Cover with clear film (plastic wrap) and chill for 15 minutes.

VARIATION
Although it is not traditional, mixed (apple pie) spice would make a good substitute for the ground allspice.

3 Preheat the oven to 190°C/375°F/Gas 5. Mix the brown sugar with the ground allspice in a bowl, then stir in the beaten eggs, lemon rind and juice, butter, curd cheese and raisins. Mix thoroughly with a wire whisk.

4 Pour the filling into the pastry case (pie shell), then bake for 40 minutes, or until the pastry is cooked and the filling is lightly set and golden brown. Cool slightly, remove from the tin and serve warm or cold.

Energy 480kcal/2005kJ; Protein 16.2g; Carbohydrate 48.2g, of which sugars 23.7g; Fat 27g, of which saturates 15.8g; Cholesterol 173mg; Calcium 153mg; Fibre 1.2g; Sodium 451mg.

Custard tarts

These luxurious little tarts are an indulgent treat. The silky texture of the custard combined with the rich vanilla-flavoured pastry is truly unsurpassable. The nutmeg-dusted delights are perfect served still warm with tea, but can be cooled and kept in the refrigerator for up to two days.

MAKES ABOUT 8

175g/6oz/1½ cups plain
 (all-purpose) flour
pinch of salt
75g/3oz/6 tbsp unsalted butter, at
 room temperature
75g/3oz/scant ½ cup caster
 (superfine) sugar
3 egg yolks, at room temperature
a few drops vanilla extract

For the filling
600ml/1 pint/2½ cups full cream
 (whole) milk
6 egg yolks
75g/3oz/scant ½ cup caster
 (superfine) sugar
freshly grated nutmeg

1 To make the pastry, sift the flour and salt into a bowl.

2 Put the butter, sugar, egg yolks and vanilla extract in a food processor and process until the mixture resembles scrambled eggs. Add the flour and blend briefly.

3 Transfer the dough to a lightly floured surface and knead gently until smooth. Form into a ball, flatten and wrap in clear film (plastic wrap). Chill for at least 30 minutes. Bring back to room temperature before rolling out.

4 Roll out the pastry and use to line eight individual 10cm/4in loose-bottomed tartlet tins (pans). Place on a baking sheet and chill for 30 minutes.

5 Preheat the oven to 200°C/400°F/ Gas 6. To make the custard filling, gently heat the milk in a pan until just warmed but not yet boiling.

6 In a bowl, vigorously beat the egg yolks and sugar together until they become pale and creamy in texture.

7 Pour the milk on to the yolks and stir well to mix. Do not whisk as this will produce too many bubbles.

8 Strain the milk mixture into a jug (pitcher), then carefully pour the liquid into the tart cases.

9 Liberally grate fresh nutmeg over the surface of the tartlets.

10 Bake for about 10 minutes, then lower the heat to 180°C/350°F/ Gas 4 and bake for another 10 minutes, or until the filling has set and is just turning golden. The tartlets should be a bit wobbly when they come out of the oven.

11 Remove from the oven and lift the tarts out of the tins. Serve warm or cold.

Energy 336kcal/1409kJ; Protein 7.9g; Carbohydrate 40g, of which sugars 23.4g; Fat 17.1g, of which saturates 8.6g; Cholesterol 257mg; Calcium 157mg; Fibre 0.7g; Sodium 101mg.

Jam tarts

These nostalgic jam tarts are the perfect treat for afternoon tea, especially when children are present. Fill them with your favourite jams, homemade if possible.

2 Preheat the oven to 220°C/425°F/ Gas 7. Lightly grease a 12-hole (or two 6-hole) tartlet tins (muffin pans).

3 Roll out the pastry on a lightly floured surface to about 3mm/⅛in thick and, using a 7.5cm/3in cutter, stamp out 12 circles. Gather the trimmings, re-roll and cut out more.

4 Press the pastry circles into the prepared tartlet tin. Place a heaped teaspoonful of jam into the centre of each one.

MAKES 12

175g/6oz/1½ cups plain
  (all-purpose) flour
pinch of salt
30ml/2 tbsp caster
  (superfine) sugar
75g/3oz/6 tbsp butter, diced
1 egg, lightly beaten
60–75ml/4–5 tbsp jam

VARIATION
Replace the jam with orange, lemon or lime curd, or you could try chocolate spread.

1 Sift the flour, salt and sugar into a bowl. Rub in the butter until the mixture resembles fine crumbs. Stir in the egg and gather into a smooth dough ball. Wrap in clear film (plastic wrap) and chill for 30 minutes.

5 Put the tartlet tin into the hot oven and bake for 15–20 minutes until the pastry is cooked through and light golden brown in colour. Carefully lift the tarts out of the tin on to a wire rack and leave to cool before serving.

Energy 114kcal/479kJ; Protein 1.1g; Carbohydrate 18.8g, of which sugars 12.5g; Fat 4.3g, of which saturates 2.6g; Cholesterol 18mg; Calcium 16mg; Fibre 0.3g; Sodium 39mg.

Bakewell tart

This is a classic old-fashioned English tart that has a very popular appeal. The frangipane topping of ground almonds, sugar and butter is not too sweet and contrasts perfectly with the jam.

SERVES 6–8

225g/8oz puff pastry dough
30ml/2 tbsp raspberry or
   apricot jam
2 eggs, plus 2 egg yolks
115g/4oz/generous ½ cup caster
   (superfine) sugar
115g/4oz/½ cup butter, melted
50g/2oz/½ cup ground almonds
a few drops almond extract
icing (confectioners') sugar,
   for dusting

1 Preheat the oven to 200°C/400°F/
Gas 6.

2 Roll out the pastry on a lightly
floured surface and use to line an
18cm/7in tart tin (pan). Trim the
edges with a sharp knife.

3 Prick the pastry case (pie shell) all
over, then spread jam over the base.

COOK'S TIP
Although the pastry base is
made of puff pastry, you could
substitute a sweet, rich
shortcrust pastry instead,
if you prefer.

4 Whisk the eggs, egg yolks and
sugar together in a bowl until thick
and pale. Stir the melted butter,
ground almonds and almond extract
into the whisked egg mixture.

5 Pour the mixture into the pastry
case and bake for 30 minutes, or
until the filling is just set and lightly
browned. Dust with icing sugar
before serving hot, warm or cold.

Energy 350kcal/1460kJ; Protein 5.4g; Carbohydrate 28.6g, of which sugars 18.5g; Fat 25g, of which saturates 8.7g; Cholesterol 129mg; Calcium 55mg; Fibre 0.5g; Sodium 197mg.

Treacle tart

Traditional shortcrust pastry is perfect for this old-fashioned tea-time favourite, with its sticky lemon and syrup filling and twisted lattice topping. It's delicious warm or cold with cream.

3 Put a baking sheet in the oven and preheat to 200°C/400°F/Gas 6. To make the filling, warm the syrup in a pan until it melts.

4 Remove the syrup from the heat and stir in the breadcrumbs and lemon rind. Leave to stand for 10 minutes, then add more breadcrumbs if it is too runny. Stir in the lemon juice, then spread evenly in the pastry case.

SERVES 4–6

150g/5oz/1¼ cups plain
   (all-purpose) flour
pinch of salt
130g/4½oz/9 tbsp chilled
   butter, diced
45–60ml/3–4 tbsp chilled water

For the filling
260g/9½oz/generous ¾ cup golden
   (light corn) syrup
about 75g/3oz/1½ cups fresh
   white breadcrumbs
grated rind of 1 lemon
30ml/2 tbsp lemon juice
cream or custard, to serve

1 To make the pastry, combine the flour and salt in a bowl. Rub in the butter until the mixture resembles coarse crumbs. With a fork, stir in enough water to bind the dough. Gather into a ball, knead lightly for a few seconds until smooth then wrap in clear film (plastic wrap) and chill for 20 minutes.

2 On a lightly floured surface, roll out the pastry to a thickness of 3mm/⅛in. Use to line a 20cm/8in fluted flan tin (pan) and trim off the overhang. Chill the pastry case (pie shell) for 20 minutes. Reserve the pastry trimmings.

5 Roll out the pastry trimmings and cut into 10–12 thin strips. Twist the strips and arrange half on the filling and the rest at right angles to form a lattice. Press the ends on to the rim.

6 Place the tart on the hot baking sheet and bake for 10 minutes. Lower the oven temperature to 190°C/375°F/Gas 5. Bake for 15 minutes more, until golden.

Energy 420kcal/1764kJ; Protein 4.1g; Carbohydrate 63.5g, of which sugars 35.1g; Fat 18.4g, of which saturates 11.3g; Cholesterol 46mg; Calcium 62mg; Fibre 1.1g; Sodium 344mg.

Border tart

This rich and sweet fruity tart comes from the border region of England and Scotland – two great tea-drinking nations. It is good served hot or cold with a spoonful of cream on the side.

SERVES 4

150g/5oz/10 tbsp butter
50g/2oz/¼ cup caster
  (superfine) sugar
225g/8oz/2 cups plain
  (all-purpose) flour
1 egg, beaten

For the filling
1 egg, beaten
75g/3oz/scant ½ cup soft light
  brown sugar
50g/2oz/¼ cup butter, melted
10ml/2 tsp white wine vinegar
115g/4oz/½ cup currants
25g/1oz/¼ cup chopped walnuts
double (heavy) cream, to serve

1 Make the pastry: cream the butter with the sugar in a large bowl. Add the flour and egg. Mix until just combined. Wrap in clear film (plastic wrap) and chill for 1 hour.

2 Roll out the pastry and use to line a 20cm/8in flan tin (pan). Trim the edges neatly.

3 Preheat the oven to 190°C/375°F/ Gas 5. To make the filling, in a large bowl, mix together the egg, sugar and butter.

4 Stir the vinegar, currants and walnuts into the egg mixture.

VARIATION
The white wine vinegar can be replaced with lemon juice if you prefer a citrus flavour.

5 Pour the mixture into the pastry case (pie shell) and bake in the preheated oven for 30 minutes.

6 Leave to stand for a few minutes, then remove from the tin and leave to cool on a wire rack for at least 30 minutes. Serve with a dollop of fresh cream.

Energy 312kcal/1307kJ; Protein 3.4g; Carbohydrate 41.1g, of which sugars 41g; Fat 16.1g, of which saturates 7.3g; Cholesterol 74mg; Calcium 54mg; Fibre 0.8g; Sodium 99mg.

Summer berry tart

A simple crisp pastry case is all that is needed to set off this classic filling of vanilla-flavoured custard, topped with luscious berry fruits and drizzled with syrup. Use whatever fruits are available locally for a colourful tart that is ideal to serve at a summer tea table.

SERVES 6–8

190g/6½oz/1⅔ cups plain
   (all-purpose) flour
pinch of salt
115g/4oz/½ cup butter, diced
1 egg yolk
30ml/2 tbsp chilled water

For the filling
3 egg yolks
50g/2oz/¼ cup caster
   (superfine) sugar
30ml/2 tbsp cornflour (cornstarch)
30ml/2 tbsp plain
   (all-purpose) flour
5ml/1 tsp vanilla extract
300ml/½ pint/1¼ cups milk
150ml/¼ pint/⅔ cup double
   (heavy) cream
800g/1¾lb/7 cups mixed
   summer berries
60ml/4 tbsp redcurrant jelly
30ml/2 tbsp raspberry liqueur

1 To make the pastry, sift the flour and salt into a mixing bowl. Rub in the butter until the mixture resembles fine breadcrumbs. Mix the egg yolk with the chilled water and sprinkle over the dry ingredients. Mix to a firm dough.

2 Knead the dough on a lightly floured surface for a few seconds, until smooth. Wrap in clear film (plastic wrap) and chill for 30 minutes.

3 Roll out the pastry and use to line a 23cm/9in round flan tin (pan). Wrap in clear film and chill.

4 Preheat the oven to 200°C/400°F/ Gas 6. Prick the base of the pastry, line it with baking parchment, fill with baking beans and bake on a tray for 15 minutes. Remove the baking parchment and beans and bake for 10 minutes more. Leave to cool.

COOK'S TIP
Dust the tart with icing (confectioners') sugar, if you like.

5 To make the filling, beat the egg yolks, sugar, cornflour, flour and vanilla together in a large bowl.

6 Pour the milk into a pan, and heat gently until almost boiling. Slowly pour the milk on to the egg mixture, whisking all the time.

7 Pour the custard back from the bowl into the pan and stir constantly over low heat, until it has thickened. Work quickly or lumps will form. Return to a clean mixing bowl, cover the surface with a piece of clear film and set aside to cool.

8 Whip the cream until thick, then fold into the cooled custard. Spoon the custard into the pastry case (pie shell) and spread out evenly.

9 Wash and dry the fruit, then arrange it on top of the custard.

10 In a small pan, gently heat the redcurrant jelly and liqueur together until melted. Allow to cool, then brush liberally over the surface of the fruit. Serve the tart within 3 hours of assembling. Serve with cream for a decadent treat.

Energy 432kcal/1807kJ; Protein 6.7g; Carbohydrate 47.6g, of which sugars 21.8g; Fat 25.7g, of which saturates 14.6g; Cholesterol 160mg; Calcium 130mg; Fibre 2g; Sodium 150mg.

Almond slices

A light pastry base is spread with raspberry jam, topped with almond cake and a layer of flaked almonds to make elegant old-fashioned pastry slices. They are the quintessential summer tea-party cake. These cakes keep for up to three days in an airtight container.

MAKES 16

225g/8oz shortcrust or sweet
  shortcrust pastry, thawed
  if frozen
flour, for dusting
60ml/4 tbsp raspberry jam
4 egg whites
175g/6oz/1½ cups ground
  almonds
175g/6oz/scant 1 cup golden caster
  (superfine) sugar
a few drops of almond extract
75g/3oz/¾ cup flaked
  (sliced) almonds
15ml/1 tbsp icing (confectioners')
  sugar, for dusting

1 Preheat the oven to 180°C/350°F/
Gas 4. Grease a 28 × 18cm/11 × 7in
shallow tin (pan).

2 Roll out the pastry on a lightly
floured surface to a rectangle large
enough to line the base and sides
of the tin.

3 Lower the pastry into the tin,
using a rolling pin. Press into all the
corners, then trim the edges.

4 Spread the jam over the pastry.

5 Put the egg whites into a clean,
grease-free bowl and whisk until
they form stiff peaks.

6 Fold in the ground almonds, sugar
and almond extract. Spoon into the
tin, then spread the top level.
Sprinkle over the flaked almonds.

7 Bake for 30–35 minutes, or until
the pastry is crisp and the topping is
golden and firm to the touch. Leave
to cool completely in the tin.

8 Mark into 16 slices, then cut these
out with a sharp knife. Serve with a
light dusting of icing sugar.

Energy 204kcal/850kJ; Protein 4.7g; Carbohydrate 18.7g, of which sugars 12.2g; Fat 12.7g, of which saturates 0.7g; Cholesterol 0mg; Calcium 50mg; Fibre 1.4g; Sodium 41mg.

Grated berry bake

Pastry layers envelop a delicious and sticky fruit filling for this tea-time traybake. If your pastry skills are zero, however, never fear, as the pastry is grated into the tin, so you'll still be able to make this a success. Serve with a spoonful of cream. Keep for two days in an airtight container.

MAKES 12 BARS

275g/10oz/2½ cups plain
   (all-purpose) flour
2.5ml/½ tsp ground cinnamon
175g/6oz/¾ cup butter, diced
115g/4oz/generous ½ cup golden
   caster (superfine) sugar
1 egg, beaten
icing (confectioners') sugar,
   for dusting

For the filling
350g/12oz/3 cups fresh or
   frozen fruits of the forest
   (mixed blackcurrants,
   redcurrants, raspberries,
   blackberries)
150g/5oz/¾ cup sugar

1 Sift the flour and cinnamon into a bowl or food processor, add the butter, then rub together.

2 Stir in the sugar and beaten egg, and mix together to form a firm dough. Put in a plastic bag and chill for 2 hours or freeze for 20 minutes, or until the pastry forms a firm block.

3 To make the filling, put the fruit in a pan with 30ml/2 tbsp water and simmer for 5 minutes to soften. Add the sugar and stir until it dissolves, then boil for 5 minutes, or until syrupy and thick. Leave to cool.

COOK'S TIP
Freeze baked or unbaked in the tin, foil-wrapped, for 2 months.

4 Preheat the oven to 200°C/400°F/ Gas 6. Grease and line a 28 × 18cm/ 11 × 7in shallow tin (pan) with baking parchment.

5 Cut the chilled dough in half and, using a coarse grater, grate one half into the tin. Spread out evenly and press down lightly.

6 Spoon the cooled fruit over the pastry. Coarsely grate the rest of the pastry over the fruit to cover completely, but do not flatten it.

7 Bake for 35 minutes, or until golden brown and firm. When cool, remove the lining paper and cut into 12 bars. Dust with icing sugar.

Energy 286kcal/1203kJ; Protein 3.3g; Carbohydrate 42.2g, of which sugars 24.8g; Fat 12.8g, of which saturates 8.1g; Cholesterol 49mg; Calcium 56mg; Fibre 1.4g; Sodium 118mg.

Chocolate éclairs

These crisp choux pastry fingers are filled with fresh cream, and make an indulgent treat with afternoon tea. The finishing touch to the éclairs is a thick, glossy coat of dark chocolate.

MAKES 12

65g/2½oz/9 tbsp plain
  (all-purpose) flour
pinch of salt
50g/2oz/¼ cup butter, diced
150ml/¼ pint/⅔ cup water
2 eggs, lightly beaten

For the filling and topping
300ml/½ pint/1¼ cups double
  (heavy) cream
10ml/2 tsp icing (confectioners')
  sugar, sifted
1.5ml/¼ tsp vanilla extract
115g/4oz plain (semisweet)
  chocolate
30ml/2 tbsp water
25g/1oz/2 tbsp butter

1 Preheat the oven to 200°C/400°F/ Gas 6. Grease a large baking sheet and line it with baking parchment.

2 To make the pastry, sift the flour and salt on to a small sheet of baking parchment.

3 Heat the butter and water in a pan very gently until the butter melts. Increase the heat and bring to a rolling boil. Remove the pan from the heat and add all the flour. Beat vigorously with a wooden spoon until the flour is incorporated.

> **COOK'S TIP**
> When melting the chocolate, ensure that the bowl does not touch the hot water and keep the heat low.

4 Return the pan to low heat, then beat the mixture until it leaves the sides of the pan and forms a ball. Set the pan aside and allow to cool for 2–3 minutes.

5 Add the beaten eggs a little at a time, beating well after each addition, until you have a smooth, shiny paste, which is thick enough to hold its shape.

6 Spoon the choux pastry into a piping (pastry) bag fitted with a 2.5cm/1in plain nozzle. Pipe 10cm/4in lengths on to the prepared baking sheet. Use a wet knife to cut off the pastry at the nozzle.

7 Bake for 25–30 minutes, or until the pastry fingers are well risen and golden brown in colour. Remove from the oven.

8 Make a neat slit along the side of each to release the steam. Lower the oven temperature to 180°C/350°F/ Gas 4 and bake for a further 5 minutes. Cool on a wire rack.

9 To make the filling, whip the cream with the icing sugar and vanilla extract until it just holds its shape. Spoon into a piping bag fitted with a 1cm/½in plain nozzle and use to fill the éclairs.

10 Place the chocolate and water in a heatproof bowl set over a pan of simmering water until melted. Remove from the heat and gradually stir in the butter. Dip the top of each éclair in the melted chocolate, then place on a rack. Leave in a cool place until the chocolate is set. Best served within 2 hours of making, but can be chilled for 24 hours if required.

Energy 253kcal/1046kJ; Protein 2.7g; Carbohydrate 10.8g, of which sugars 6.5g; Fat 22.4g, of which saturates 13.5g; Cholesterol 86mg; Calcium 30mg; Fibre 0.4g; Sodium 58mg.

Coffee cream profiteroles

Crisp-textured coffee choux pastry puffs are filled with cream and drizzled with a white chocolate sauce. For tea drinkers with a sweet tooth, there is plenty of extra sauce.

SERVES 6

65g/2½oz/9 tbsp plain
  (all-purpose) flour
pinch of salt
50g/2oz/¼ cup butter, diced
150ml/¼ pint/⅔ cup brewed coffee
2 eggs, lightly beaten

For the topping and filling
50g/2oz/¼ cup caster
  (superfine) sugar
100ml/3½fl oz/scant ½ cup water
150g/5oz good quality white
  chocolate, broken into pieces
25g/1oz/2 tbsp unsalted butter
45ml/3 tbsp double (heavy) cream
30ml/2 tbsp coffee liqueur
250ml/8fl oz/1 cup double
  (heavy) cream

1 Preheat the oven to 220°C/425°F/
Gas 7.

2 Sift the flour and salt into a
medium mixing bowl.

3 Put the butter into a small pan
with the coffee. Melt the butter
gently, then bring the liquid to a
rolling boil. Remove from the heat
and tip in all the flour. Mix together
quickly with a wooden spoon.

4 Beat quickly until the mixture
leaves the sides of the pan and there
are no lumps. Leave to cool for
2 minutes.

5 Gradually add the eggs, beating
well between each addition. Spoon
the mixture into a piping (pastry) bag
fitted with a 1cm/½in plain nozzle.

6 Pipe about 24 small buns on to a
dampened baking sheet. Bake for 20
minutes, until well risen and crisp.

7 Remove the buns from the oven
and pierce the side of each with a
sharp knife to let out the steam.

8 To make the sauce, put the sugar
and water in a heavy pan and heat
gently until dissolved. Bring to the
boil and simmer for 3 minutes.

9 Remove from the heat. Add the
chocolate and butter, stirring until
smooth. Stir in the smaller amount
of cream and the liqueur.

10 To assemble, whip the remaining
cream until soft peaks form. Part-fill
a piping bag fitted with a plain
nozzle. Fill the choux buns through
the slits in the sides.

11 Arrange on plates and pour a
little of the sauce over. Serve the
remaining sauce separately.

Energy 579kcal/2401kJ; Protein 6g; Carbohydrate 32.6g, of which sugars 24.4g; Fat 46.8g, of which saturates 28.4g; Cholesterol 159mg; Calcium 123mg; Fibre 0.3g; Sodium 138mg.

English Eccles cakes

These traditional dried fruit-filled pastry rounds taste fabulous when homemade. Make your own pastry instead of using bought and you'll notice the difference in its light and flaky texture and rich flavour. Inside is a warmly spiced fruit filling. These cakes keep for 1–2 days in an airtight tin.

MAKES 16

225g/8oz/2 cups plain (all-purpose)
  flour, plus extra for dusting
pinch of salt
200g/7oz/scant 1 cup butter, diced
5ml/1 tsp lemon juice
100ml/3½fl oz/scant ½ cup
  iced water

For the filling
2.5ml/½ tsp mixed (apple pie)
  spice
50g/2oz/¼ cup muscovado
  (molasses) sugar
175g/6oz/¾ cup currants
50g/2oz/⅓ cup mixed chopped
  (candied) peel
5ml/1 tsp lemon juice
finely grated rind of 1 lemon

For the glaze
1 egg, beaten
caster (superfine) sugar,
  for dusting

1 To make the pastry, sift the flour and salt into a bowl. Add the butter, lemon juice and iced water. Mix to a soft dough using a flat-bladed knife. Add 5–10ml/1–2 tsp extra water if it is too dry.

2 Flour your work surface and your hands, then gently knead and shape the pastry into a rectangle 28 × 13cm/11 × 5in. (The pastry will just hold together and will contain noticeable pieces of diced butter.)

3 Fold up the lower third of pastry and bring the top third down over it. Turn with the fold on the left, and press three times with the rolling pin to flatten.

4 Roll out into a rectangle and fold and roll as before. Wrap in a plastic bag and chill for 20 minutes, or freeze for 5 minutes.

5 Repeat the rolling, folding and chilling four more times. Wrap and chill for 20 minutes, or until needed.

6 Preheat the oven to 220°C/425°F/Gas 7 and lightly grease two baking sheets.

7 Put all the filling ingredients in a bowl and stir together.

8 Roll the pastry to 5mm/¼in thick. Using a 10cm/4in round pastry (cookie) cutter, stamp out 16 rounds and place a heaped teaspoonful of the filling in the centre of each.

9 Dampen the edges with water, gather up the pastry over the filling and press to seal. Turn the pastries so the seal is underneath and roll each gently. Put on a baking sheet. Cut three slits across the top of each. Brush with beaten egg and sprinkle with sugar. Bake for 20 minutes, then cool on a wire rack.

Energy 201kcal/842kJ; Protein 1.7g; Carbohydrate 23.5g, of which sugars 12.8g; Fat 11.8g, of which saturates 7.4g; Cholesterol 30mg; Calcium 38mg; Fibre 0.8g; Sodium 96mg.

Chocolate whirls

These pastry cookies are so easy to make that you don't even have to make any dough – and because they are quick to make are perfect for times when guests drop in unexpectedly. They're made with ready-made puff pastry rolled up with chocolate filling.

MAKES 20

75g/3oz/scant ½ cup golden caster (superfine) sugar
40g/1½oz/6 tbsp unsweetened cocoa powder
2 eggs
500g/1¼lb puff pastry
25g/1oz/2 tbsp butter, softened
75g/3oz/scant ½ cup sultanas (golden raisins)
90g/3½oz milk chocolate

1 Preheat the oven to 220°C/ 425°F/Gas 7. Put the sugar, cocoa powder and eggs in a bowl and mix to a paste.

2 Roll out the pastry on a lightly floured surface to make a 30cm/12in square. Trim off any rough edges.

3 Dot the pastry all over with the butter, then spread with the chocolate paste. Sprinkle sultanas over the top.

4 Roll the pastry into a sausage shape, then cut the roll into 1cm/ ½in slices. Place the slices on the baking sheets, spacing them apart.

5 Bake for 10 minutes until risen and pale golden. Transfer to a wire rack and leave to cool.

6 Break the chocolate into pieces and put in a heatproof bowl set over a pan of simmering water. Heat, stirring until melted and smooth.

7 Spoon lines of melted chocolate over the cookies.

> **COOK'S TIP**
> Use a sharp knife to cut the cookie slices from the pastry roll.

Energy 165kcal/689kJ; Protein 2.9g; Carbohydrate 18.6g, of which sugars 9.4g; Fat 9.5g, of which saturates 1.9g; Cholesterol 23mg; Calcium 34mg; Fibre 0.4g; Sodium 117mg.

Chocolate and strawberry-filled palmiers

Who could resist sweet and crisp puff pastry, with layers of chocolate, whipped cream and fresh strawberries, as a summer treat? These traditional little pastries, formed into rounded swirls, may look complicated but are actually easy to make, and they look delightful on the tea table.

MAKES 8

15g/½oz/2 tbsp unsweetened
   cocoa powder
375g/13oz puff pastry, thawed,
   if frozen
25g/1oz/2 tbsp golden caster
   (superfine) sugar

For the filling
300ml/½ pint/1¼ cups whipping
   cream, whipped
45ml/3 tbsp dark (bittersweet)
   chocolate spread
175g/6oz/1¼ cups sliced
   strawberries
icing (confectioners') sugar,
   for dusting

1 Preheat the oven to 220°C/
425°F/Gas 7. Grease two large
baking sheets.

2 Dust a clean, dry working
surface lightly with 15ml/1 tbsp
cocoa powder.

3 Keeping the long side of pastry
towards you, roll it out on the cocoa
powder to a rectangle 35 × 23cm/
14 × 9in. Lightly brush the top of
the pastry with cold water, then
sprinkle over the caster sugar and
remaining cocoa.

4 Measure and with a sharp knife
mark the centre of the pastry. Roll
up each of the short sides like a
Swiss roll (jelly roll) so that they
both meet in the centre. Brush the
join with a little water and press the
rolls together to secure.

5 With a sharp knife, mark out and
then cut the doubled pastry roll
into 16 slices.

6 Arrange on the baking sheets,
using a metal spatula, spacing them
well apart. Bake for 8–10 minutes,
or until risen, puffy and golden
brown. Remove from the baking
sheets and cool on a wire rack.

7 To make the filling, put the cream
in a piping (pastry) bag fitted with a
small plain nozzle. Lightly spread
half the pastries with the chocolate
spread. Pipe the cream on to the
remaining pastries and top with a
few strawberry slices. Sandwich the
chocolate base with the cream and
strawberry layer. Dust lightly with
icing sugar and serve immediately.

Energy 368kcal/1533kJ; Protein 4.2g; Carbohydrate 27g, of which sugars 9.7g; Fat 28.3g, of which saturates 10.4g; Cholesterol 40mg; Calcium 60mg; Fibre 0.5g; Sodium 180mg.

Biscuits
and bars

A small treat for any time of day, biscuits and bars are packed with flavour and sweetness. Eaten with tea following a savoury sandwich, they will stave off hunger pangs in the late afternoon. Try fragrant Tea Fingers, or spicy Ginger Thins, or traditional Brandy Snaps with Cream. If you like soft-centred treats, Sticky Treacle Squares or a Mincemeat and Marzipan Traybake are just the thing, or for the ultimate filling finale try Millionaire's Shortbread – a thick layer of crunchy shortbread topped with soft and chewy caramel, and coated with lavish melted chocolate.

Left: Indulgent Chocolate Brownies and chewy Flapjacks are two perennial favourites that will disappear quickly from the tea table.

Tea fingers

The unusual ingredient in these cookies is Lady Grey tea – similar to Earl Grey but with the addition of Seville orange and lemon peel, which imparts a subtle citrus flavour.

3 Using your hands, roll the dough on a lightly floured surface into a log, about 23cm/9in long.

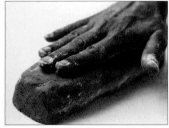

4 Gently press down on the top of the log with the palm of your hand to flatten slightly. Wrap the dough in clear film (plastic wrap) and chill for about 1 hour until the dough is firm enough to slice.

5 Using a sharp knife, cut the dough log widthways into 5mm/¼in slices and place, slightly apart, on the prepared baking sheets.

6 Sprinkle the cookies with a little demerara sugar, then bake for 10–15 minutes until lightly browned. Using a metal spatula, transfer the cookies to a wire rack and leave to cool.

MAKES ABOUT 36

150g/5oz/10 tbsp unsalted butter, diced and softened
115g/4oz/½ cup light muscovado (brown) sugar
15–30ml/1–2 tbsp Lady Grey tea leaves
1 egg, beaten
200g/7oz/1¾ cups plain (all-purpose) flour
demerara (raw) sugar, for sprinkling

1 Preheat the oven to 190°C/375°F/ Gas 5. Line two or three baking sheets with baking parchment.

2 In a large bowl, beat the butter with the sugar until light and creamy. Stir in the tea leaves until well combined. Add the beaten egg, then carefully fold in the flour using a metal spoon.

VARIATION
You could use other exotic types of tea for making these cookies. Try Earl Grey, flavoured with bergamot, Rose Congou, or aromatic flower or fruit teas, such as jasmine, passion fruit, chrysanthemum or strawberry.

Energy 65kcal/270kJ; Protein 0.7g; Carbohydrate 7.7g, of which sugars 3.4g; Fat 3.7g, of which saturates 2.2g; Cholesterol 14mg; Calcium 11mg; Fibre 0.2g; Sodium 28mg.

Shortbread

This easy recipe makes a very light, crisp shortbread with an excellent flavour that is delicious with a cup of tea. The lemon rind and almonds are delicious additions, but not traditional.

MAKES ABOUT 48

275g/10oz/2½ cups plain
(all-purpose) flour
25g/1oz/¼ cup ground almonds
225g/8oz/1 cup butter, softened
75g/3oz/scant ½ cup caster
(superfine) sugar
grated rind of ½ lemon

1 Preheat the oven to 180°C/350°F/ Gas 4 and grease a large Swiss roll tin (jelly roll pan).

3 Place the dough in the tin and flatten out. Bake for 20 minutes, or until pale golden brown.

COOK'S TIP
Use a food processor for speed.

4 Remove from the oven and immediately cut the shortbread into fingers or squares while the mixture is soft. Allow to cool a little, and then transfer to a wire rack and leave until cold. If stored in an airtight container, the shortbread should keep for up to two weeks.

2 Sift the flour and almonds into a bowl. In another bowl, beat the butter, sugar and lemon rind together until the mixture is soft and light. Add the flour and almonds to the butter mixture, then work it together first using a wooden spoon and then your fingers to make a smooth dough.

VARIATIONS
• Replace the lemon rind with the grated rind of two oranges.
• Use a flat decorative mould and make one large shortcake for an attractive, professional-looking result.

Energy 57kcal/239kJ; Protein 0.8g; Carbohydrate 5.6g, of which sugars 1.2g; Fat 3.7g, of which saturates 2g; Cholesterol 8mg; Calcium 12mg; Fibre 0.3g; Sodium 22mg.

Melting moments

As the name suggests, these crisp biscuits really do melt in the mouth. They have a texture like shortbread but are covered in rolled oats to give a crunchy surface and extra flavour, and are traditionally topped with a piece of cherry. They look especially attractive on the tea table.

2 Sift the flour over the mixture and stir to make a soft dough. Gather up the dough, divide into 16–20 pieces and roll into small balls.

3 Spread rolled oats on a sheet of baking parchment and toss the balls in them until evenly coated.

4 Space the dough balls slightly apart, on two baking sheets. Flatten each ball a little with your thumb.

5 Cut the cherries into quarters and place a piece on top of each flat ball. Bake for 15–20 minutes, until they are lightly browned.

6 Allow the biscuits to cool for a few minutes on the baking sheets before transferring them to a wire rack to cool completely.

MAKES 16–20

40g/1½oz/3 tbsp butter, at
 room temperature
65g/2½oz/5 tbsp lard
75g/3oz/scant ½ cup caster
 (superfine) sugar
1 egg yolk, beaten
few drops of vanilla or
 almond extract
150g/5oz/1¼ cups self-raising
 (self-rising) flour
rolled oats, for coating
4–5 glacé (candied) cherries

1 Preheat the oven to 180°C/350°F/ Gas 4. Beat together the butter, lard and sugar, then beat in the egg yolk and vanilla or almond extract.

Energy 88kcal/370kJ; Protein 0.7g; Carbohydrate 10.9g, of which sugars 5.4g; Fat 5g, of which saturates 2.4g; Cholesterol 7mg; Calcium 30mg; Fibre 0.3g; Sodium 40mg.

Oat biscuits

These crisp and crunchy biscuits are wonderfully quick and easy to make, as well as being utterly delicious. They are homely and comforting at any time of day, and are filling enough to keep hunger pangs at bay. Perfect with a cup of tea.

MAKES ABOUT 18

115g/4oz/½ cup butter
115g/4oz/½ cup soft light
   brown sugar
115g/4oz/⅓ cup golden (light corn)
   syrup
150g/5oz/1¼ cups self-raising
   (self-rising) flour
150g/5oz rolled oats

1 Preheat the oven to 180°C/350°F/Gas 4. Lightly grease or line two or three baking sheets with baking parchment.

2 Gently heat the butter, sugar and golden syrup in a heavy pan until the butter has melted and the sugar has dissolved, taking care not to let it get too hot as the mixture will easily burn. Remove from the heat and leave to cool slightly.

3 Sift the flour and stir into the mixture in the pan, together with the oats, to make a soft dough.

4 Roll the dough into small balls and arrange them on the prepared baking sheets, leaving plenty of room for them to spread out.

5 Flatten each ball with a spatula. Bake for 12–15 minutes until golden brown, longer if more than one tray is in the oven.

6 Leave to cool on the baking sheet briefly, then transfer to a wire rack to crisp up and cool completely.

VARIATION
Add 25g/1oz/¼ cup finely chopped toasted almonds or walnuts, or a small handful of dried fruit (raisins or currants) to the mixture in step 3.

Energy 151kcal/637kJ; Protein 1.8g; Carbohydrate 23.9g, of which sugars 11.9g; Fat 6g, of which saturates 3.3g; Cholesterol 14mg; Calcium 22mg; Fibre 0.8g; Sodium 59mg.

Jam sandwich biscuits

These buttery cookies are an absolute classic. Sandwiched with buttercream and a generous dollop of strawberry jam, they make a perfect treat for afternoon tea.

MAKES 20

225g/8oz/2 cups plain
(all-purpose) flour
175g/6oz/³⁄₄ cup unsalted butter,
chilled and diced
130g/4¹⁄₂oz/²⁄₃ cup caster
(superfine) sugar
1 egg yolk

For the filling
50g/2oz/¹⁄₄ cup unsalted butter, at
room temperature, diced
130g/4¹⁄₂oz/generous 1 cup icing
(confectioners') sugar
60–75ml/4–5 tbsp strawberry jam

1 Put the flour and butter in a food processor and process until the mixture resembles breadcrumbs.

2 Add the sugar and egg yolk and process until the mixture starts to form a dough.

3 Turn out on to a floured surface and knead until smooth. Shape into a ball, wrap in clear film (plastic wrap) and chill for at least 30 minutes.

4 Preheat the oven to 180°C/ 350°F/Gas 4. Lightly grease two baking sheets.

5 Roll out the dough thinly on a lightly floured surface and stamp out rounds using a 6cm/2¹⁄₂in cookie cutter. Re-roll the trimmings and cut out more rounds until you have 40 or an even number.

6 Place half the cookie rounds on a prepared baking sheet. Using a small heart-shaped cutter, about 2cm/³⁄₄in in diameter, cut out the centres of the remaining rounds. Place these rounds on the second baking sheet.

7 Bake the cookies for 12 minutes until pale golden, then transfer to a wire rack and leave to go completely cold.

8 To make the buttercream filling, beat together the butter and icing sugar until smooth and creamy.

9 Using a metal spatula, spread a little buttercream on to each whole cookie. Spoon a little jam on to the buttercream, then gently press the cut-out cookies on top, so that the jam fills the heart-shaped hole.

Energy 166kcal/695kJ; Protein 1.2g; Carbohydrate 22.4g, of which sugars 13.8g; Fat 8.6g, of which saturates 5.4g; Cholesterol 22mg; Calcium 24mg; Fibre 0.4g; Sodium 65mg.

Ginger thins

These warming ginger biscuits have a wonderful crispness to them, giving a satisfying 'snap' when broken in half. You can use any shape of cookie cutter you wish.

MAKES ABOUT 50

150g/5oz/10 tbsp butter
400g/14oz/2 cups sugar
50ml/2fl oz/¼ cup golden
  (light corn) syrup
15ml/1 tbsp black treacle
  (molasses)
15ml/1 tbsp ground ginger
30ml/2 tbsp ground cinnamon
15ml/1 tbsp ground cloves
5ml/1 tsp ground cardamom
5ml/1 tsp bicarbonate of soda
  (baking soda)
250ml/8fl oz/1 cup water
150g/5oz/1¼ cups plain
  (all-purpose) flour

1 Put the butter, sugar, syrup, treacle, ginger, cinnamon, cloves and cardamom in a heavy pan and heat gently until the butter has melted. Stir thoroughly to combine.

2 Put the bicarbonate of soda and water in a large heatproof bowl. Pour in the warm spice mixture and mix well together, then add the flour and stir until well blended.

3 Cover with clear film (plastic wrap) and chill overnight.

4 Preheat the oven to 220°C/425°F/ Gas 7. Line several baking sheets with baking parchment. Knead the dough, then roll out on a lightly floured surface as thinly as possible without the dough breaking.

5 Stamp out shapes of your choice and place on the baking sheets. Bake for about 5 minutes until golden brown, cooking in batches until all the dough is used. Transfer to wire racks to go completely cold.

Energy 57kcal/239kJ; Protein 0.6g; Carbohydrate 10.3g, of which sugars 6.8g; Fat 1.7g, of which saturates 1g; Cholesterol 7mg; Calcium 16mg; Fibre 0.1g; Sodium 15mg.

Almond cookies

Crystallized petals of alpine pinks, rose petals, primroses or violets make these delicious almond cookies a fragrant and attractive treat to grace the most elegant of tea tables.

3 Add the ground almonds, egg yolk, vanilla and flour. Knead the mixture until blended.

4 Roll the dough into 2.5cm/1in balls, then place on a baking sheet. Brush with lightly beaten egg white and bake for 15 minutes, until golden. Cool on a wire rack.

MAKES ABOUT 24

115g/4oz/½ cup butter
115g/4oz/ generous ½ cup caster (superfine) sugar
115g/4oz/1 cup ground almonds
1 egg, separated
5ml/1 tsp vanilla extract
115g/4oz/1 cup plain (all-purpose) flour, sifted
50g/2oz/½ cup icing (confectioners') sugar

For the crystallized petals
75–100 alpine pink or violet petals
1 egg white, lightly beaten
50g/2oz/½ cup caster (superfine) sugar

1 Preheat the oven to 180°C/ 350°F/Gas 4. Lightly grease two baking sheets.

2 In a large bowl, beat together the butter and caster sugar until light and fluffy. Use a food processor or electric beater for speed, if you like.

CAUTION
Raw eggs should not be consumed by pregnant women, the young and elderly.

5 For the crystallized petals, remove the white heels at the base of each petal. Paint the front and back of each with the egg white. Dredge both sides with caster sugar. Arrange on baking parchment and leave to dry in a warm place. These will last for up to 2 days.

6 To decorate the cookies, mix the icing sugar with 7.5ml/1½ tsp water and spoon on to each cookie, then fix a few petals on top of each one.

Energy 115kcal/481kJ; Protein 1.5g; Carbohydrate 15g, of which sugars 10.1g; Fat 5.8g, of which saturates 2.4g; Cholesterol 9mg; Calcium 24mg; Fibre 0.5g; Sodium 27mg.

Dark chocolate fingers

With their understated elegance and distinctly grown-up flavour, these moreishly decadent chocolate fingers are perfect for a stylish afternoon tea.

MAKES ABOUT 26

115g/4oz/1 cup plain
  (all-purpose) flour
pinch of baking powder
30ml/2 tbsp unsweetened
  cocoa powder
50g/2oz/¼ cup caster
  (superfine) sugar
50g/2oz/¼ cup unsalted butter,
  softened
20ml/4 tsp golden (light corn)
  syrup
150g/5oz dark (bittersweet)
  chocolate
chocolate mini flakes,
  for sprinkling

1 Preheat the oven to 160°C/325°F/ Gas 3. Line two baking sheets with baking parchment.

2 Sift the dry ingredients into a bowl. Add the butter and golden syrup and work the ingredients together with your hands to form a dough.

> **VARIATION**
> Use plain (semisweet) or milk chocolate, if you like.

3 Roll the dough out between sheets of baking parchment to an 18 x 24cm/7 x 9in rectangle. Remove the top sheet. Cut in half lengthways, then cut each half into 13 slices. Place on the baking sheets.

4 Bake for about 15 minutes. Transfer to a wire rack to cool.

> **COOK'S TIP**
> Do not allow the bars to brown or they will taste bitter.

5 Melt the chocolate in a heatproof bowl set over a pan of simmering water. Half-dip the cookies, place on baking parchment, sprinkle with chocolate flakes, then leave to set.

Energy 72kcal/303kJ; Protein 0.9g; Carbohydrate 9.9g, of which sugars 6.3g; Fat 3.5g, of which saturates 2.1g; Cholesterol 4mg; Calcium 11mg; Fibre 0.4g; Sodium 25mg.

Double ginger cookies

These are a supreme treat for ginger lovers – richly spiced cookies packed with chunks of succulent preserved stem ginger as well as ground ginger. They are perfect for a sophisticated afternoon tea party.

5 Pour the butter mixture over the dry ingredients, then add the egg and two-thirds of the ginger. Mix thoroughly, then use your hands to bring the dough together.

6 Shape the dough into 20 large balls, depending on the size you require. Place them, spaced well apart, on the baking sheets.

7 Gently flatten the balls, then press a few pieces of the remaining preserved stem ginger into the top of each of the cookies.

MAKES 20

350g/12oz/3 cups self-raising (self-rising) flour
pinch of salt
200g/7oz/1 cup golden caster (superfine) sugar
15ml/1 tbsp ground ginger
5ml/1 tsp bicarbonate of soda (baking soda)
115g/4oz/½ cup unsalted butter
90g/3½oz/generous ¼ cup golden (light corn) syrup
1 large (US extra large) egg, beaten
150g/5oz preserved stem ginger in syrup, drained and coarsely chopped

1 Preheat the oven to 160°C/ 325°F/Gas 3.

2 Line three baking sheets with baking parchment.

3 Sift the flour into a large mixing bowl, add the salt, caster sugar, ground ginger and bicarbonate of soda and stir to combine.

4 Dice the butter and put it in a small, heavy pan with the syrup. Heat gently, stirring, until the butter has melted. Remove from the heat and set aside to cool until just warm.

8 Bake for about 12–15 minutes, depending on the size of your cookies, until light golden in colour. Remove from the oven and leave to cool for 1 minute on the baking sheets to firm up.

Energy 114kcal/479kJ; Protein 1.4g; Carbohydrate 20.4g, of which sugars 11.5g; Fat 3.5g, of which saturates 2.1g; Cholesterol 15mg; Calcium 23mg; Fibre 0.4g; Sodium 42mg.

Butter cookies

Rich and buttery, with a melt-in-the-mouth texture, these cookies are lavish creations for the most discerning palates. Quick to make from everyday ingredients, they are sure to disappear quickly when served for afternoon tea.

MAKES 18

6 egg yolks, lightly beaten
15ml/1 tbsp milk
250g/9oz/2¼ cups plain
  (all-purpose) flour
175g/6oz/generous ¾ cup caster
  (superfine) sugar
200g/7oz/scant 1 cup butter at
  room temperature, diced

1 Preheat the oven to 180°C/350°F/ Gas 4. Lightly grease two heavy baking sheets.

2 Mix 15ml/1 tbsp of the egg yolks with the milk to make a glaze and set aside.

3 Sift the flour into a large bowl and make a well in the centre. Add sugar, egg yolks and butter. Using your fingertips, work them together until smooth and creamy.

4 Gradually add a little flour at a time from the edge of the well, working it to form a smooth and slightly sticky dough.

5 Using floured hands, pat out the dough to about 1cm/½in thick and cut out rounds using a 7.5cm/3in cookie cutter.

6 Transfer the rounds to a baking sheet, brush each with a little egg glaze, then using the back of a knife, score with lines to create a lattice pattern.

7 Bake for 12–15 minutes until golden. Allow to set for 5 minutes. Transfer to a wire rack to go cold.

COOK'S TIP
To make one large Butter Cookie, pat the dough into a well-greased 23cm/9in loose-based cake tin (pan).

Energy 170kcal/711kJ; Protein 2.2g; Carbohydrate 19g, of which sugars 9.4g; Fat 10g, of which saturates 5.7g; Cholesterol 82mg; Calcium 32mg; Fibre 0.4g; Sodium 65mg.

Brandy snaps with cream

Records show that brandy snaps were sold at fairs in the north of England in the 19th century. Brandy snaps were once considered a special treat for high days and holidays and so make the ideal treat for afternoon tea.

4 Put small spoonfuls of the mixture on the lined baking sheets, space them about 10cm/4in apart to allow for spreading. Put into the hot oven and cook for 7–8 minutes or until bubbling and golden. Meanwhile grease the handles of several wooden spoons.

MAKES 12

50g/2oz/¼ cup butter
50g/2oz/¼ cup caster
  (superfine) sugar
30ml/2 tbsp golden
  (light corn) syrup
50g/2oz/½ cup plain
  (all-purpose) flour
2.5ml/½ tsp ground ginger
5ml/1 tsp brandy
150ml/¼ pint/⅔ cup double
  (heavy) or whipping cream

1 Preheat the oven to 180°C/ 350°F/Gas 4. Line two or three baking sheets with baking parchment.

2 Put the butter, sugar and golden syrup in a small pan set over gentle heat. Stir until the butter has melted and the sugar dissolved.

3 Remove the pan from the heat. Sift the flour and ginger and stir into the mixture with the brandy.

5 Allow the wafers to cool on the sheet for about 1 minute then loosen with a metal spatula and quickly roll around the spoon handles. The wafers will set quickly. Leave to set for 1 minute, before sliding them off the handles and cooling completely on a wire rack.

6 Just before serving, whip the cream until soft peaks form. Spoon into a pastry bag and pipe a little into both ends of each brandy snap.

Energy 121kcal/505kJ; Protein 0.6g; Carbohydrate 11.7g, of which sugars 10g; Fat 7.9g, of which saturates 5g; Cholesterol 21mg; Calcium 16mg; Fibre 0.1g; Sodium 24mg.

Black and white ginger florentines

Florentines are special occasion cookies packed with luxurious ingredients and topped with a thick coating of melted chocolate. Traditionally they are made for Christmas and would make a perfect centrepiece for a seasonal afternoon tea.

MAKES 30

120ml/4fl oz/½ cup double
  (heavy) cream
50g/2oz/¼ cup butter
50g/2oz/¼ cup granulated
  (white) sugar
30ml/2 tbsp honey
150g/5oz/1¼ cups flaked
  (slivered) almonds
40g/1½oz/⅓ cup plain (all-
  purpose) flour
2.5ml/½ tsp ground ginger
50g/2oz/⅓ cup diced candied
  orange peel
75g/3oz/½ cup diced stem ginger
50g/2oz milk chocolate chopped
  into small pieces
150g/5oz plain (semisweet)
  chocolate, chopped into
  small pieces
150g/5oz white chocolate, chopped
  into small pieces

1 Preheat the oven to 180°C/350°F/
Gas 4. Lightly grease two large
baking sheets.

2 In a small pan over medium heat,
stir the cream, butter, sugar and
honey until the sugar dissolves.
Bring the mixture to the boil, stirring.

3 Remove the pan from the heat
and stir in the almonds, flour and
ground ginger. Stir in the candied
peel, ginger and milk chocolate.

4 Drop teaspoons of the mixture on
to the baking sheets at least 7.5cm/
3in apart. Spread each round thinly
with the back of a spoon.

5 Bake for 8–10 minutes or until
the edges are golden brown and the
cookies are bubbling. Allow to
cool on the baking sheets for
10 minutes, then transfer to a wire
rack to go cold.

6 Melt the plain chocolate in a
heatproof bowl over a pan of gently
simmering water. Melt the white
chocolate in a separate bowl in the
same way.

7 Using a small metal spatula,
spread half the florentines with the
plain chocolate and half with the
white chocolate. Place on a wire
rack, chocolate side up. Chill for
10–15 minutes to set completely.

Energy 71kcal/298kJ; Protein 0.9g; Carbohydrate 8.6g, of which sugars 7.8g; Fat 3.9g, of which saturates 1.3g; Cholesterol 2mg; Calcium 16mg; Fibre 0.3g; Sodium 11mg.

Rich peanut crunch cookies

These delicious sweet and nutty cookies are so easy to make. They puff up into lovely domed rounds during baking, giving them a very appealing look. If you prefer cookies with a slightly less 'nutty' texture, use smooth peanut butter rather than the crunchy variety.

MAKES 25

150g/5oz/1¼ cups self-raising
   (self-rising) flour
2.5ml/½ tsp baking powder
115g/4oz/½ cup unsalted
   butter, at room temperature,
   diced
115g/4oz/½ cup light muscovado
   (brown) sugar
1 egg
150g/5oz/generous ½ cup crunchy
   peanut butter
icing (confectioners') sugar,
   for dusting

1 Preheat the oven to 190°C/
375°F/Gas 5. Lightly grease two
baking sheets.

2 Sift the flour and baking powder together into a bowl.

3 Put the butter and sugar in a mixing bowl and beat until pale and creamy.

4 Beat in the egg, then add the sifted flour mixture and the peanut butter.

5 Beat together until the ingredients are thoroughly mixed.

6 Place heaped teaspoonfuls of the mixture on to the baking sheets; space well apart to allow the cookies to spread while baking. (Work in batches, if necessary.)

7 Bake the cookies for about 20 minutes until risen; they will still be quite soft to the touch.

8 Leave the cookies on the baking sheets to set for about 5 minutes, then using a metal spatula carefully transfer them to a wire rack and leave to cool completely.

9 To serve, lightly dust with icing sugar. Store in an airtight container for 2–3 days.

Energy 112kcal/466kJ; Protein 2.1g; Carbohydrate 10.3g, of which sugars 5.3g; Fat 7.2g, of which saturates 3.2g; Cholesterol 18mg; Calcium 15mg; Fibre 0.5g; Sodium 50mg.

Malted oat cookies

These cookies are packed with oats, which produce a crisp, chewy cookie and a filling snack to add to the tea table. Flavoured with malt and the caramelized taste of muscovado sugar, they are hard to resist.

MAKES 18

175g/6oz/1½ cups rolled oats
75g/3oz/scant ½ cup light
  muscovado (brown) sugar
1 egg
60ml/4 tbsp sunflower or
  vegetable oil
30ml/2 tbsp malt extract

1 Preheat the oven to 190°C/ 375°F/Gas 5. Lightly grease two baking sheets.

2 Mix the rolled oats and brown sugar in a bowl, breaking up any lumps in the sugar.

3 Beat the egg in a small bowl and add it together with the oil and malt extract to the oats and sugar mixture. Set the mixture aside to soak for 15 minutes, then beat together to combine thoroughly.

VARIATION
Replace 25g/1oz/¼ cup of the rolled oats with Brazil nuts. This makes a cookie with a slightly different taste and texture.

4 Place small heaps of the mixture well apart to allow room for spreading on the prepared baking sheets. Flatten them slightly.

5 Press the heaps into 7.5cm/3in rounds with the back of a dampened fork.

6 Bake the cookies in the oven for 10–15 minutes, until golden brown. Leave on the baking sheets for 1 minute to cool slightly.

7 With a metal spatula, transfer the cookies to a wire rack and leave to cool completely.

Energy 86kcal/364kJ; Protein 1.6g; Carbohydrate 12.8g, of which sugars 5.7g; Fat 3.6g, of which saturates 0.4g; Cholesterol 11mg; Calcium 9mg; Fibre 0.7g; Sodium 12mg.

Fruity chocolate cookie cakes

The combination of spongy cookie, fruity preserve and dark chocolate makes irresistible eating at tea time. As cookies go, these are a little fiddly to make, but they are well worth the effort, with bags more flavour than the bought varieties.

MAKES 18

90g/3½oz/½ cup caster
  (superfine) sugar
2 eggs
50g/2oz/½ cup plain
  (all-purpose) flour
75g/3oz/6 tbsp orange marmalade
  or apricot jam
125g/4¼oz plain (semisweet)
  chocolate

1 Preheat the oven to 190°C/375°F/ Gas 5. Lightly grease 18 patty tins (muffin pans), preferably non-stick.

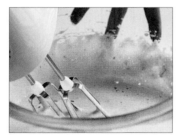

2 Stand a mixing bowl in very hot water for a couple of minutes to heat through, keeping the inside of the bowl dry. Put the sugar and eggs in the bowl and whisk with a hand-held electric mixer until light and frothy and the beaters leave a ribbon trail when lifted.

3 Sift the flour over the mixture and stir in gently using a large metal spoon.

4 Divide the sponge mixture among the patty tins. Bake for 10 minutes, until just firm and pale golden around the edges. Leave to set for a few minutes, then using a metal spatula transfer the sponges to a wire rack to go cold.

5 Press the marmalade or jam through a sieve (strainer) to remove any rind or fruit pieces. Spoon a little of the smooth jam on to the centre of each sponge.

6 Break the chocolate into pieces and place in a heatproof bowl set over a pan of gently simmering water. Heat, stirring frequently, until melted and smooth.

7 Spoon a little chocolate on to the top of each cookie and spread to the edges, covering the jam completely. Once the chocolate has just started to set, very gently press it with the back of a fork to give a textured surface. Leave to set for at least 1 hour.

Energy 84kcal/353kJ; Protein 1.3g; Carbohydrate 14.7g, of which sugars 12.5g; Fat 2.6g, of which saturates 1.3g; Cholesterol 22mg; Calcium 12mg; Fibre 0.3g; Sodium 11mg.

Sticky treacle squares

This three-layered treat of buttery cookie base, covered with a sticky dried fruit filling, followed by an oaty flapjack-style topping is utterly delicious. It's perfect to serve for afternoon tea, with its complex flavours, sticky texture and filling combination.

MAKES 14

175g/6oz/1½ cups plain (all-purpose) flour
90g/3½oz/7 tbsp unsalted butter, diced
50g/2oz/¼ cup caster (superfine) sugar

For the filling
250g/9oz/generous 1 cup mixed dried fruit, such as prunes, apricots, peaches, pears and apples
300ml/½ pint/1¼ cups apple or orange juice

For the topping
225g/8oz/⅔ cup golden (light corn) syrup
finely grated rind of 1 small orange, plus 45ml/3 tbsp juice
90g/3½oz/1 cup rolled oats

1 Preheat the oven to 180°C/350°F/ Gas 4. Lightly grease a 28 x 18cm/ 11 x 7in shallow baking tin (pan).

2 Put the flour and butter in a food processor and process until the mixture begins to resemble fine breadcrumbs. Add the sugar and mix until the dough starts to cling together in a ball.

3 Transfer the mixture to the baking tin and press down in an even layer with the back of a fork. Bake for about 15 minutes, until the surface just begins to colour.

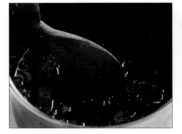

4 Meanwhile prepare the filling. Remove the stones (pits) from any of the dried fruits. Chop the fruit fairly finely and put in a pan with the fruit juice.

5 Bring to the boil, reduce the heat and cover with a lid. Simmer gently for about 15 minutes, or until all the juice has been absorbed.

6 Leaving the base in the tin, add the dried fruit filling on top and spread out in an even layer with the back of a spoon.

7 Put the golden syrup in a bowl with the orange rind and juice and oats and mix together. Spoon over the fruits, spreading it out evenly. Return to the oven for 25 minutes.

Energy 213kcal/898kJ; Protein 2.6g; Carbohydrate 39.3g, of which sugars 25.1g; Fat 6.1g, of which saturates 3.4g; Cholesterol 14mg; Calcium 35mg; Fibre 1.8g; Sodium 88mg.

Blueberry cakes

Coffee cakes were probably first made in Europe during the 17th century to accompany the newly imported coffee drink. This cake is studded with blueberries, giving it a lovely fruity flavour and texture. Keep for up to two days in an airtight container.

MAKES 12 SLICES

225g/8oz/2 cups plain
(all-purpose) flour
15ml/1 tbsp baking powder
5ml/1 tsp salt
65g/2½oz/5 tbsp butter, at room
temperature
150g/5oz/¾ cup caster
(superfine) sugar
1 egg
250ml/8fl oz/1 cup milk
2.5ml/½ tsp grated
lemon rind
225g/8oz/2 cups fresh or frozen
blueberries, well drained
115g/4oz/1 cup icing
(confectioners') sugar
30ml/2 tbsp fresh lemon juice

1 Preheat the oven to 180°C/350°F/ Gas 4. Grease and line a 33 × 9cm/ 13 × 9in shallow tin (pan).

2 Sift the flour with the baking powder and salt.

3 In a large bowl, beat the butter and sugar until light and fluffy. Beat in the egg and milk. Fold in the flour mixture, then mix in the lemon rind.

4 Scrape half of the batter into the cake tin, spreading it to the edges.

5 Sprinkle with half the blueberries. Top with the remaining batter and then the remaining blueberries.

6 Bake for 35–45 minutes, or until golden brown and a skewer inserted into the centre comes out clean.

7 Allow to stand for 5 minutes in the tin, then turn out on to a wire rack to go cold. Remove the lining.

8 To make the topping, mix the icing sugar with the lemon juice to make a smooth glaze with a pouring consistency.

9 Drizzle the glaze over the top of the warm cake. Allow to set before cutting into slices and serving.

Energy 217kcal/918kJ; Protein 3.3g; Carbohydrate 41.3g, of which sugars 26.3g; Fat 5.5g, of which saturates 3.3g; Cholesterol 30mg; Calcium 66mg; Fibre 1g; Sodium 60mg.

Florentine slices

If you're looking for a popular cake for afternoon tea, you'll find the colourful jewel-like topping on these fruity slices makes them a real winner – and they'll also be snapped up by guests in no time. These cakes keep in an airtight container for up to four days.

MAKES 12 SLICES

150g/5oz/10 tbsp butter
150g/5oz/¾ cup golden caster
(superfine) sugar
3 eggs
175g/6oz/1½ cups self-raising
(self-rising) flour
275g/10oz/1⅔ cups mixed
dried fruit
90g/3½oz/generous ½ cup
glacé (candied) cherries, halved
a few drops of almond extract

For the topping
100g/3¾oz/½ cup glacé (candied)
cherries, chopped
15ml/1 tbsp golden
(light corn) syrup
50g/2oz/½ cup flaked
(sliced) almonds
25g/1oz/2 tbsp angelica,
chopped

1 Preheat the oven to 190°C/375°F/
Gas 5. Grease and line a 28 × 18cm/
11 × 7in shallow cake tin (pan) with
baking parchment.

2 Whisk the butter and sugar
together until light and fluffy. Whisk
in the eggs one at a time.

3 Fold in the flour, then set aside
30ml/2 tbsp of the mixture in a bowl.

4 Fold the dried fruit, cherries and
almond extract into the remaining
cake mixture, then spoon into the
tin and smooth the top level.

5 Bake for 20 minutes, reduce the
heat to 180°C/350°F/Gas 4. Bake for
a further 15 minutes, until just set.

6 To make the topping, stir the
chopped cherries into the reserved
cake mixture with the syrup,
almonds and angelica, and mix well.

7 Spread evenly over the cake top
using a wetted spoon. Bake for
15 minutes. Leave to cool in the tin.

8 Loosen the lining papers. Cut into
12 fingers when cold.

Energy 340kcal/1429kJ; Protein 4.6g; Carbohydrate 51.7g, of which sugars 40.8g; Fat 14.2g, of which saturates 7.4g; Cholesterol 76mg; Calcium 101mg; Fibre 1.4g; Sodium 177mg.

Mincemeat and marzipan traybake

This easy dark fruit cake is mixed all in one go and then has a crunchy almond-paste topping. It is ideal for tea parties or to make for cake sales at Christmas. Home-made almond paste adds an edge when it comes to flavour. Keep for up to five days in an airtight container.

MAKES 15 SQUARES

115g/4oz/½ cup butter, softened
225g/8oz/2 cups self-raising
  (self-rising) flour
400g/14oz jar fruit mincemeat
115g/4oz/⅔ cup mixed dried fruit
115g/4oz/½ cup muscovado
  (molasses) sugar
finely grated rind of ½ lemon
5ml/1 tsp mixed (apple pie) spice
2 eggs, beaten

For the topping and icing
250g/9oz almond paste
115g/4oz/1 cup icing
  (confectioners') sugar
15ml/1 tbsp lemon juice

1 Preheat the oven to 160°C/
325°F/Gas 3. Grease and line a
28 × 18cm/11 × 7in shallow tin
(pan) with baking parchment.

2 Put all the cake ingredients in a
mixing bowl and beat for about
3 minutes, or until smooth. Spoon
into the prepared tin and smooth
the top level. Bake for 50 minutes,
or until golden.

3 To make the topping, grate the
almond paste using a coarse grater.

4 Sprinkle the almond paste on top
of the hot cake in an even layer.
Return to the oven and bake for
10 minutes, or until the almond
paste is light golden. Cool in the tin
for 5 minutes, then turn out on to a
wire rack to go cold. Remove the
lining paper.

5 To make the icing, mix the icing
sugar with the lemon juice and
5–10ml/1–2 tsp water to make a
drizzling consistency.

6 Fill a small paper piping (icing)
bag with icing, snip off the end,
then drizzle lines over the cooled
cake in a random pattern. When set,
cut into 15 squares.

Energy 290kcal/1230kJ; Protein 3.6g; Carbohydrate 60.8g, of which sugars 49.4g; Fat 5g, of which saturates 1.6g; Cholesterol 29mg; Calcium 57mg; Fibre 1.3g; Sodium 60mg.

Cornflake crunch-nut traybake

These squares have a moist, cranberry sponge base topped with a fruity and crunchy layer made with cornflakes. The combination of contrasting textures in one cake makes them hard to resist. These cakes keep for up to two days in an airtight container.

MAKES 15 SQUARES

175g/6oz/1½ cups self-raising
  (self-rising) flour
5ml/1 tsp baking powder
175g/6oz/¾ cup butter, softened
175g/6oz/scant 1 cup caster
  (superfine) sugar
3 eggs, beaten
75ml/5 tbsp cranberry sauce

For the topping
45ml/3 tbsp golden (light corn)
  syrup
75g/3oz/¾ cup dried cranberries
115g/4oz/4 cups cornflakes

1 Preheat the oven to 180°C/350°F/
Gas 4. Grease and line a 28 × 18cm/
11 × 7in shallow tin (pan) with
baking parchment.

2 Sift the flour and baking powder
into a bowl and add the remaining
ingredients, then beat until smooth.

COOK'S TIP
The cakes are not suitable
for freezing.

3 Spoon into the tin and smooth the
top level. Bake for 30 minutes, or
until golden and firm in the centre.

4 To make the topping, heat the
syrup and cranberries in a large pan
over low heat, then simmer for
2 minutes.

5 Add the cornflakes and gently fold
in. Spoon over the cake layer and
return to the oven. Bake for
10 minutes, or until lightly brown.

6 Cool in the tin for 5 minutes, then
turn out on a wire rack to go cold.
Remove the lining paper.

Energy 237kcal/994kJ; Protein 3.2g; Carbohydrate 33.7g, of which sugars 18.8g; Fat 10.9g, of which saturates 6.6g; Cholesterol 65mg; Calcium 35mg; Fibre 0.5g; Sodium 197mg.

Flapjacks

The wholesome and satisfying combination of rolled oats and golden syrup makes flapjacks popular with adults and children alike. They are sweet, dense and filling, with a soft, chewy consistency. With so few ingredients, flapjacks are quick to make and guaranteed to please.

MAKES 12

175g/6oz/¾ cup unsalted butter
50g/2oz/¼ cup caster (superfine) sugar
150g/5oz/scant ⅓ cup golden (light corn) syrup
250g/9oz/1½ cups rolled oats

COOK'S TIP
Store the flapjacks in an airtight container for up to one week.

1 Preheat the oven to 180°C/350°F/ Gas 4. Grease and line a shallow 20cm/8in square baking tin (pan).

2 Place the butter, sugar and syrup in a pan and heat gently until the butter has melted.

3 Add the oats and stir until all the ingredients are combined.

4 Transfer the mixture into the tin and level the surface. Bake for 15–20 minutes, until turning golden. Leave to cool slightly, then cut into fingers and cool on a wire rack.

Energy 241kcal/1007kJ; Protein 2.7g; Carbohydrate 29.5g, of which sugars 14.3g; Fat 13.2g, of which saturates 7.2g; Cholesterol 30mg; Calcium 18mg; Fibre 1.4g; Sodium 125mg.

Luscious lemon bars

A crisp shortbread cookie base is drenched with a light and tangy lemon topping to make a sweet citrus confection. These bars make a wonderful addition to the summer tea table. Try exchanging the lemon for orange to give a new twist to this recipe.

MAKES 12

150g/5oz/1¼ cups plain
  (all-purpose) flour
90g/3½oz/7 tbsp unsalted butter,
  chilled and diced
50g/2oz/½ cup icing
  (confectioners') sugar, sifted,
  plus extra for dusting

For the topping
2 eggs
175g/6oz/scant 1 cup caster
  (superfine) sugar
finely grated rind and juice of
  1 large lemon
15ml/1 tbsp plain (all-purpose)
  flour
2.5ml/½ tsp bicarbonate of soda
  (baking soda)

1 Preheat the oven to 180°C/350°F/
Gas 4. Grease and line a 20cm/8in
square shallow cake tin (pan) with
baking parchment.

2 Blend the flour, butter and icing sugar in a food processor until the mixture comes together as a firm dough. Press into the base of the tin and spread smooth using the back of a spoon. Bake for 12–15 minutes.

3 To make the topping, whisk the eggs in a bowl until frothy. Add the caster sugar, a little at a time, whisking between each addition. Whisk in the lemon rind and juice, flour and bicarbonate of soda.

4 Pour over the cookie base. Bake for 20–25 minutes, until set and golden. Leave to cool slightly. Cut into bars and dust with icing sugar. Cool on a wire rack. Store in an airtight container for 2–3 days.

Energy 189kcal/795kJ; Protein 2.5g; Carbohydrate 30.3g, of which sugars 19.8g; Fat 7.3g, of which saturates 4.2g; Cholesterol 48mg; Calcium 35mg; Fibre 0.4g; Sodium 59mg.

Walnut and date bars

These wonderfully rich, moist cake bars are perfect for afternoon tea. The dates are first soaked before being added to the batter giving this sweet treat a lovely texture.

MAKES 24 BARS

225g/8oz/1⅓ cups chopped dates
250ml/8fl oz/1 cup boiling water
5ml/1 tsp bicarbonate of soda
  (baking soda)
225g/8oz/generous 1 cup caster
  (superfine) sugar

1 egg, beaten
275g/10oz/2½ cups plain
  (all-purpose) flour
pinch of salt
75g/3oz/6 tbsp butter, softened
5ml/1 tsp vanilla extract
5ml/1 tsp baking powder
50g/2oz/½ cup chopped walnuts

1 Put the chopped dates into a warm bowl and pour the boiling water over the top; it should just cover the dates. Add the bicarbonate of soda and mix well. Leave to stand for 5–10 minutes.

2 Preheat the oven to 180°C/350°F/ Gas 4. Lightly grease a 23 x 30cm/ 9 x 12in cake tin (pan) and line with baking parchment.

3 Combine all the remaining ingredients in a separate mixing bowl. Mix in the dates, along with the soaking water until you have a thick batter. You may find it necessary to add a little more boiling water to help the consistency.

4 Pour the batter into the tin and bake for 45 minutes until firm. Cool on a wire rack and cut into bars.

Energy 111kcal/468kJ; Protein 2.5g; Carbohydrate 17.9g, of which sugars 10.2g; Fat 3.75g, of which saturates 0.5g; Cholesterol 0.75mg; Calcium 27mg; Fibre 1.45g; Sodium 6.8mg.

Chocolate brownies

This classic American recipe is popular with lovers of all things sweet and chocolatey. The double dose of chocolate makes them a rich and intense indulgence at tea time.

MAKES 15 BARS

75g/3oz dark (bittersweet)
  chocolate
115g/4oz/½ cup butter, plus extra
  for greasing
4 eggs, beaten
10ml/2 tsp vanilla extract
400g/14oz/2 cups caster
  (superfine) sugar
115g/4oz/1 cup plain
  (all-purpose) flour
25g/1oz/¼ cup unsweetened
  cocoa powder
115g/4oz dark (bittersweet)
  chocolate chips
115g/4oz/1 cup chopped walnuts

1 Preheat the oven to 190°C/375°F/
Gas 5. Liberally grease an
18 x 28cm/7 x 11in shallow baking
tin (pan) and line the base with
baking parchment.

2 Break the dark chocolate into
pieces and put it in a heatproof
bowl with the butter. Place the bowl
over a pan of barely simmering
water and leave until the chocolate
and butter have melted. Remove
from the heat and stir in the beaten
eggs, vanilla and sugar. Mix all the
ingredients well together.

3 Sift the flour with the cocoa
powder into the chocolate mixture.
Gently stir in with the chocolate
chips and walnuts. Pour the mixture
into the tin and level the surface.

4 Bake for about 35 minutes.
To test if the brownies are fully
cooked, gently shake the tin. The
cakes should be set but moist. Leave
to cool in the tin. Cut into bars
when cold.

VARIATION
For almond brownies, add a few
drops of almond extract, 75g/
3oz/¾ cup chopped almonds
and reduce the chocolate chips
to 75g/3oz/½ cup.

Energy 285kcal/1190kJ; Protein 3.1g; Carbohydrate 29.6g, of which sugars 25.9g; Fat 18g, of which saturates 10.7g; Cholesterol 61mg; Calcium 37mg; Fibre 0.9g; Sodium 98mg.

Tea-time treats

This delicious selection of tea-time treats rings the changes on basic sponge cake recipes, and offers plenty of variety to inspire you, from luscious chocolate and spice cakes to summery fresh berry muffins and tangy citrus confections. Ingredients such as crunchy nuts, chocolate chips and fresh fruit mean that these little cakes don't need icing, though some are drizzled with simple glazes.

Left: Little Madeira Cakes are quick to make, and offer a perfect solution when feeding lots of people.

Espresso cupcakes with maple syrup

Strong dark coffee and maple syrup give a bitter edge to the sweetness of these little cakes. Drizzle more maple syrup over them while they are still warm. This recipe uses freshly made espresso, but you could use your own favourite coffee made at double strength.

MAKES 12

250g/9oz/2¼ cups plain
  (all-purpose) flour
10ml/2 tsp baking powder
pinch of cinnamon
50g/2oz/¼ cup golden caster
  (superfine) sugar
75g/3oz/6 tbsp butter
1 egg
105ml/7 tbsp pure maple syrup,
  plus extra for drizzling
105ml/7 tbsp strong coffee
45ml/3 tbsp buttermilk

1 Preheat the oven to 180°C/350°F/ Gas 4. Line a bun tin (pan) with paper cases. Sift the flour, baking powder and cinnamon into a large bowl and mix in the sugar.

2 Melt the butter, pour it into another mixing bowl and leave to cool. Beat the egg and stir it into the butter. Add the maple syrup, coffee and buttermilk.

3 Fold the egg mixture lightly into the dry ingredients until just combined. Spoon the mixture into the cases and bake for about 25 minutes. Serve with extra maple syrup drizzled over the top.

167kcal/703kJ; Protein 2.7g; Carbohydrate 27.6g, of which sugars 11.8g; Fat 5.9g, of which saturates 3.6g; Cholesterol 30mg; Calcium 42mg; Fibre 0.7g; Sodium 79mg.

Honey and spice cakes

These little golden cakes are fragrant with honey and cinnamon and are ideal for an autumnal afternoon tea. Though their appearance is more traditional when they are cooked directly in a bun tin, they tend to rise higher and are therefore lighter when baked in paper cases.

MAKES 18

250g/9oz/2¼ cups plain (all-
  purpose) flour
5ml/1 tsp ground cinnamon
5ml/1 tsp bicarbonate of soda
  (baking soda)
125g/4½oz/generous ½ cup butter,
  softened
125g/4½oz/generous ½ cup soft
  dark brown sugar
1 egg, separated
125g/4½oz/10 tbsp clear honey
60ml/4 tbsp milk

1 Preheat the oven to 200°C/400°F/
Gas 6. Grease the cups of two bun
tins (pans) or line them with paper
cake cases.

2 Sift the flour into a large mixing
bowl, together with the ground
cinnamon and the bicarbonate
of soda.

3 Beat the butter with the sugar in
another large mixing bowl using an
electric mixer until the mixture is
very light and fluffy.

4 Beat in the egg yolk, then
gradually add the honey.

5 Lightly fold the flour, spice and
bicarbonate of soda into the mixture
until just combined.

6 Add sufficient milk from the
measured amount to make a soft
mixture that will just drop off the
spoon. Do not make the mixture too
wet or the cakes will be heavy.

7 In a separate bowl, whisk the
separated egg white until stiff peaks
form. Using a large metal spoon,
fold the egg white gently into the
cake mixture.

8 Divide the mixture among the tins
or cases. Bake for about 25 minutes,
until lightly coloured. Leave to stand
for 5 minutes before transferring to a
wire rack to cool.

Energy 152kcal/639kJ; Protein 1.9g; Carbohydrate 23.6g, of which sugars 13g; Fat 6.3g, of which saturates 3.8g; Cholesterol 26mg; Calcium 30mg; Fibre 0.4g; Sodium 49mg.

Chocolate chip cakes

Nothing could be easier – or nicer – than these classic cakes. The cake mixture is plain, but has a surprise layer of chocolate chips inside. Sprinkle a few chocolate chips on top of the cakes to make them look irresistible. They are delicious eaten warm with your favourite tea.

3 Sift the flour and baking powder together twice. Fold into the butter mixture, alternating with the milk.

4 Divide half the mixture among the paper cases. Sprinkle with half the chocolate chips, then cover with the remaining mixture and the rest of the chocolate chips. Bake for about 25 minutes, until golden. Leave to stand for 5 minutes then transfer to a wire rack to cool.

MAKES 10

115g/4oz/½ cup butter, softened
75g/3oz/scant ½ cup caster (superfine) sugar
30ml/2 tbsp soft dark brown sugar
2 eggs
175g/6oz/1½ cups plain (all-purpose) flour
5ml/1 tsp baking powder
120ml/4fl oz/½ cup milk
175g/6oz/1 cup plain (semisweet) chocolate chips

1 Preheat the oven to 190°C/375°F/ Gas 5. Arrange ten paper cases in a muffin tin (pan).

2 In a large bowl, beat the butter until it is pale and light. Add the caster and dark brown sugars and beat until the mixture is light and fluffy. Beat in the eggs, one at a time, beating thoroughly after each addition.

Energy 296kcal/1241kJ; Protein 4.2g; Carbohydrate 36.5g, of which sugars 22.3g; Fat 15.9g, of which saturates 9.5g; Cholesterol 67mg; Calcium 59mg; Fibre 0.5g; Sodium 110mg.

Chunky chocolate and banana cupcakes

Luxurious but not overly sweet, these cakes are simple and quick to make for afternoon tea. They taste best if served while still warm, when the chocolate is soft and gooey, but including bananas gives a moist result. The cakes will keep for a couple of days.

MAKES 12

90ml/6 tbsp semi-skimmed
  (low-fat) milk
2 eggs
150g/5oz/⅔ cup butter, melted
225g/8oz/2 cups plain
  (all-purpose) flour
5ml/1 tsp baking powder
150g/5oz/¾ cup golden caster
  (superfine) sugar
150g/5oz plain (semisweet)
  chocolate, cut into chunks
2 small bananas, mashed

3 Sift together the flour and baking powder into a separate bowl. Add the sugar, chocolate and bananas to the flour mixture.

4 Stir gently to combine, gradually stirring in the milk and egg mixture, but do not beat it. Spoon the mixture into the paper cases. Bake for about 20 minutes until the cakes are risen and golden. Allow to stand for 5 minutes, then turn out and leave to cool on a wire rack.

COOK'S TIP
Choose bananas that are fully ripe and can be mashed easily.

1 Preheat the oven to 200°C/400°F/ Gas 6. Arrange 12 paper cases in a muffin tin (pan).

2 In a small bowl, whisk the milk, eggs and melted butter together until combined.

Energy 303kcal/1268kJ; Protein 4g; Carbohydrate 40g, of which sugars 24.6g; Fat 15.2g, of which saturates 9.3g; Cholesterol 62mg; Calcium 54mg; Fibre 0.8g; Sodium 112mg.

Fresh raspberry and fig cakes

Beautiful purple figs, with their luscious red flesh, nestle with fresh raspberries in this delicious cake batter, which puffs up around them in a golden dome as it bakes. Cakes made with fresh summer fruit are a seasonal treat and best eaten while still warm from the oven.

MAKES 8–9

150g/5oz/1¼ cups fresh raspberries
15ml/1 tbsp caster
  (superfine) sugar
3 fresh figs
225g/8oz/2 cups plain
  (all-purpose) flour
10ml/2 tsp baking powder
150g/5oz/¾ cup golden (superfine)
  caster sugar
90g/3½oz/7 tbsp butter, melted
1 egg, beaten
300ml/½ pint/1¼ cups buttermilk
grated rind of ½ small orange

1 Preheat the oven to 180°C/350°F/ Gas 4. Grease the cups of a large muffin tin (pan) or line with paper muffin cases.

2 Arrange the fresh raspberries in a single layer on a large plate and sprinkle them evenly with the 15ml/ 1 tbsp caster sugar. Slice the figs vertically into eighths and set them aside with the raspberries.

3 Sift the flour and baking powder into a large mixing bowl and mix in the sugar. Make a well in the centre of the dry ingredients.

4 In another bowl, mix the cooled melted butter with the egg, butter-milk and grated orange rind. Pour this mixture into the dry ingredients and fold in gently until just blended. Do not overwork the mixture.

5 Set aside a small quantity of the raspberries and figs. Sprinkle the remaining fruit over the surface of the batter and fold in lightly. Spoon the mixture into the tin or the paper cases, filling each not more than two-thirds full.

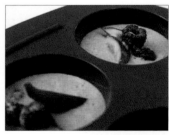

6 Lightly press the reserved fruit into the top of the batter. Bake for 22–25 minutes until the muffins are risen and golden. Leave in the tin for 5 minutes, then turn out on to a wire rack to cool, or serve while still warm as a dessert.

Energy 260kcal/1098kJ; Protein 4.7g; Carbohydrate 43.2g, of which sugars 24.2g; Fat 8.9g, of which saturates 5.4g; Cholesterol 44mg; Calcium 107mg; Fibre 1.7g; Sodium 102mg.

Little frosted fruit cupcakes

These tasty cakes are simple to make using a basic cupcake recipe. Dust your choice of seasonal fruits with a sugar frosting, then mound them up on top of the cakes just before serving, for an elegant tea-time treat. Serve with fresh cream, if you like.

MAKES 8

175g/6oz/¾ cup butter, softened
175g/6oz/¾ cup caster
  (superfine) sugar
5ml/1 tsp vanilla extract, or
  5ml/1 tsp finely grated lemon rind
4 eggs, lightly beaten
175g/6oz/1½ cups self-raising
  (self-rising) flour, sifted

For the frosted fruit
seasonal soft fruits, rinsed
a few leaves, for decoration
1 egg white, lightly beaten
caster (superfine) sugar, for dusting
icing (confectioners') sugar,
  for dusting

1 Preheat the oven to 180°C/350°F/ Gas 4. Set 8 oblong silicone cake cases on a baking sheet.

2 In a bowl, beat together the butter and sugar until creamy. Add the vanilla or lemon rind, then the eggs, beating well after each addition.

3 Fold in the flour. Divide the batter among the cake cases. Bake for 20 minutes until the cakes are golden and firm to the touch.

4 Leave to go cold on a wire rack. Remove the cases.

5 Rinse the fruit and leaves, then pat them dry with kitchen paper.

6 Brush each fruit, stem and leaf, with the beaten egg white.

7 Dredge each item with caster sugar while the egg white is wet, then leave to dry on baking parchment in a warm place.

8 Arrange the sugar-frosted pieces on top of each cake. Dust with a light sprinkling of icing sugar.

Energy 317kcal/1326kJ; Protein 35g; Carbohydrate 20.6g, of which sugars 18.6g; Fat 11.2g, of which saturates 7.5g; Cholesterol 129mg; Calcium 94mg; Fibre 0.6g; Sodium 248mg.

Citrus syrup cupcakes

These moist, syrupy cakes, with a very intense tangy citrus flavour, are made without flour, which makes them entirely safe to eat for anyone who has a wheat allergy. To make a luscious dessert add your choice of berries and a scoop of vanilla ice cream.

3 Remove the fruit from the water and leave to cool. Split open and discard the pips (seeds). Liquidize the fruit into a purée. Set aside.

4 Whisk the eggs and sugar together until foamy, then stir in the ground almonds and the fruit purée. Pour the mixture into the prepared cases and bake for 30 minutes.

5 To make the citrus syrup. Dissolve the sugar in 250ml/9fl oz water over medium heat. Add the strips of rind and the lemon juice and bring to the boil. Reduce the heat and simmer for 2–3 minutes, until the liquid coats the back of a spoon.

MAKES 12

3 clementines
6 eggs
225g/8oz/generous 1 cup caster
  (superfine) sugar
225g/8oz/2 cups ground almonds
icing (confectioners') sugar, to dust

For the citrus syrup
350g/12oz/1¾ cups caster
  (superfine) sugar
rind of 1 clementine, pith removed,
  cut into very fine strips
juice of ¾ lemon

1 Put the whole, unpeeled clementines into a pan and cover generously with boiling water. Bring to the boil, then simmer for about 2 hours. This will soften the fruit and remove some of the bitterness from the skin. Keep a check on the water level and top up as necessary with boiling water.

2 Meanwhile, preheat the oven to 160°C/325°F/Gas 3. Set 12 oblong silicone cake cases on a baking sheet, or line a 12-hole bun tin (pan) with paper cake cases.

6 Allow the cakes to cool in the cases, then drizzle the warm syrup over, a spoonful at a time.

Energy 344kcal/1449kJ; Protein 7.4g; Carbohydrate 52.2g, of which sugars 51.7g; Fat 13.3g, of which saturates 1.7g; Cholesterol 95mg; Calcium 88mg; Fibre 1.5g; Sodium 41mg.

Orange cupcakes with orange glaze

These delicious cakes are ideal as a snack with a cup of tea or frothy cappuccino. They are finished with a slightly sour orange glaze that perfectly complements the sweetness of the cakes. If Seville oranges are not available you can use a mixture of sweet orange and lemon.

MAKES 9–10

75g/3oz/6 tbsp butter
1 egg, lightly beaten
175ml/6fl oz/¾ cup buttermilk
juice of 1½ Seville (Temple)
    oranges, plus grated rind of
    2 Seville oranges
225g/8oz/2 cups plain
    (all-purpose) flour
10ml/2 tsp baking powder
150g/5oz/¾ golden caster
    (superfine) sugar
15ml/1 tbsp Seville orange
    marmalade

For the orange glaze
juice and finely grated rind of
    ½ Seville (Temple) orange
75–90ml/5–6 tbsp icing
    (confectioners') sugar, sifted
5ml/1 tsp Seville orange
    marmalade

1 Preheat the oven to 180°C/350°F/ Gas 4. Lightly grease a muffin tin (pan). Melt the butter in a pan over low heat, set aside to cool slightly.

2 In a bowl mix together the egg, buttermilk, orange juice and grated rind and the cooled, melted butter.

3 Add the flour, baking powder and sugar. Fold in gently, with the marmalade, until just blended.

4 Spoon the mixture into the tin, filling almost to the top. Bake for 25 minutes until golden. Leave to stand then turn on to a wire rack to cool.

5 To make the orange glaze, put the juice in a bowl and beat in the sugar, grated rind and marmalade. The mixture should cover the back of a spoon, but be thin and fluid. Drizzle the glaze in a loose zigzag over the tops of the cakes just before serving.

Energy 242kcal/1020kJ; Protein 3.5g; Carbohydrate 43.9g, of which sugars 26.8g; Fat 7g, of which saturates 4.3g; Cholesterol 37mg; Calcium 70mg; Fibre 0.7g; Sodium 76mg.

Blueberry buns

Light and fruity, these popular American cakes are delicious at any time of day. Serve them warm for breakfast or brunch, or as a tea-time treat. Blueberries have a sweet but tangy flavour and are perfect for baking because they hold their shape during cooking.

MAKES 12

2 eggs
50g/2oz/¼ cup butter, melted
175ml/6fl oz/¾ cup milk
5ml/1 tsp vanilla extract
5ml/1 tsp grated lemon rind

175g/6oz/1½ cups plain
  (all-purpose) flour
50g/2oz/¼ cup caster (superfine)
  sugar
10ml/2 tsp baking powder
175g/6oz/1½ cups blueberries

1 Preheat the oven to 200°C/400°F/ Gas 6. Arrange 12 paper cases in a muffin tin (pan) or grease the tin.

2 Whisk the eggs until blended and stir in the melted butter, milk, vanilla and lemon rind.

3 Sift the flour, sugar and baking powder into another large bowl. Make a well in the centre and add the egg mixture. Stir in lightly with a metal spoon.

4 Fold in the blueberries gently, then spoon the batter into the muffin tin or paper cases.

5 Bake for 20–25 minutes, until the tops spring back when touched lightly. Leave in the tin for 5 minutes before turning out on to a wire rack.

Energy 236kcal/992kJ; Protein 4.9g; Carbohydrate 34.7g, of which sugars 12.4g; Fat 9.6g, of which saturates 5.6g; Cholesterol 54mg; Calcium 88mg; Fibre 1.4g; Sodium 82mg.

Apple and Calvados cakes

The subtle bouquet of Calvados (Normandy apple brandy) and the earthy, fruity flavour of quince add depth to tea-time cakes. Quince paste is always available, but when the fruit is in season replace a third of the chopped apple with finely grated fresh quince to add extra flavour.

MAKES 10

250g/9oz cooking apple, peeled
  and cored
grated rind of 1 lemon
45ml/3 tbsp quince paste
75g/3oz/6 tbsp butter, melted
15ml/1 tbsp Calvados
225g/8oz/2 cups plain
  (all-purpose) flour
10ml/2 tsp baking powder
75g/3oz/scant ½ cup caster
  (superfine) sugar
1 egg, lightly beaten
60ml/4 tbsp buttermilk

For the quince glaze
45ml/3 tbsp quince or apple jelly
15ml/1 tbsp water
5ml/1 tsp lemon juice
30ml/2 tbsp Calvados

1 Preheat the oven to 180°C/350°F/ Gas 4. Grease the cups of a large muffin tin (pan) or line them with paper muffin cases.

2 Slice one quarter of the apple very thinly and reserve in a bowl of water acidulated with a squeeze of lemon. Roughly dice the rest of the apple and set aside in another bowl of acidulated water.

3 In a small pan, gently melt the quince paste with the butter over low heat, mashing the paste with a wooden spoon to break up any little lumps.

4 Remove the pan from the heat. Stir in the Calvados and set aside.

5 Sift the dry ingredients into a large bowl. In another bowl, stir the egg and the buttermilk together and add the grated lemon rind.

6 Pour the egg mixture into the dry ingredients, with the butter, quince paste and Calvados and the chopped apple. Stir until just combined, then spoon into the prepared muffin tin.

7 Press a few slices of apple into the top of each cake. Bake for 25–30 minutes until golden.

8 To make the glaze, put the jelly, water and lemon juice in a small pan, and boil rapidly until slightly thickened. Add the Calvados and simmer for about 1 minute. Brush over the cakes while still warm.

Energy 213kcal/899kJ; Protein 3.1g; Carbohydrate 34.1g, of which sugars 16.9g; Fat 7.1g, of which saturates 4.3g; Cholesterol 37mg; Calcium 50mg; Fibre 1.1g; Sodium 70mg.

Nutty cakes with walnut liqueur

These spicy little cakes have a crunchy topping and moist crumb studded with chopped walnuts: chop the nuts very coarsely to give the cakes plenty of texture. The walnut liqueur brings out their flavour and adds a little punch and warmth of its own.

2 Sift the flour, baking powder and mixed spice into a large bowl. Stir in the sugar and the chopped walnuts, reserving about 15ml/ 1 tbsp of each to sprinkle over the top of the cakes. Make a well in the centre.

3 Pour the butter mixture into the dry ingredients and stir for just long enough to combine the ingredients. Do not overmix: the nuts mean that the batter will be lumpy.

4 Fill the paper muffin cases two-thirds full, then top with a sprinkling of the reserved sugar and walnuts. Bake for about 15 minutes until the cakes have risen and are golden brown. Leave to stand for about 5 minutes, then turn out on to a wire rack to cool.

MAKES 12

50g/2oz/¼ cup butter, melted
2 eggs, beaten
175ml/6fl oz/¾ cup milk
30ml/2 tbsp walnut liqueur
225g/8oz/2 cups plain
   (all-purpose) flour
20ml/4 tsp baking powder
2.5ml/½ tsp mixed (apple
   pie) spice
115g/4oz/½ cup soft light
   brown sugar
75g/3oz/¾ cup chopped walnuts

1 Preheat the oven to 200°C/400°F/ Gas 6. Line a muffin tin (pan) with paper cases. In a jug (pitcher) mix the butter, eggs, milk and liqueur.

Energy 201kcal/844kJ; Protein 4.3g; Carbohydrate 26.3g, of which sugars 12g; Fat 9.1g, of which saturates 3g; Cholesterol 42mg; Calcium 60mg; Fibre 0.8g; Sodium 53mg.

Gooey butterscotch cakes

If you like, you can make up the two mixtures for these cakes the night before a tea party and stir them together first thing next day for an irresistible mid-afternoon treat. Instead of butterscotch, you could try adding chocolate chips, marshmallows or blueberries.

MAKES 9–12

150g/5oz butterscotch sweets
 (candies)
225g/8oz/2 cups plain
 (all purpose) flour
90g/3½oz/½ cup golden caster
 (superfine) sugar
10ml/2 tsp baking powder
pinch of salt
1 egg, beaten
150ml/¼ pint/⅔ cup milk
50ml/2fl oz/¼ cup sunflower oil or
 melted butter
75g/3oz/¾ cup chopped hazelnuts

1 Preheat the oven to 200°C/400°F/ Gas 6. Arrange 9–12 paper cases in a muffin tin (pan).

2 With floured fingers, break the butterscotch sweets into small chunks. Toss them in a little flour, if necessary, to prevent them from sticking together.

3 Sift together the flour, sugar, baking powder and salt into a large mixing bowl.

4 Whisk together the egg, milk and oil or melted butter, then stir the mixture into the dry ingredients with the sweets and nuts. Stir together only lightly – the mixture should be lumpy.

5 Spoon the batter evenly into the paper cases, filling about half full. Bake for 20 minutes, until risen and golden. They should spring back when pressed lightly in the centre.

6 Leave the muffins in the tin for 5 minutes, then remove and transfer to a wire rack to cool.

COOK'S TIP
Try drizzling these cakes with the Spanish treat dulce de leche – a thick caramelized syrup.

Energy 224kcal/941kJ; Protein 3.9g; Carbohydrate 31.7g, of which sugars 14.6g; Fat 10g, of which saturates 2.1g; Cholesterol 19mg; Calcium 66mg; Fibre 1g; Sodium 55mg.

Lemon meringue cakes

This recipe is a delightful amalgam of a traditional fairy cake with the classic lemon meringue pie – soft lemon sponge cake is topped with crisp meringue. The little cakes are lovely with tea, but can also be served hot as a dessert, accompanied by cream or ice cream.

MAKES 18

115g/4oz/½ cup butter, softened
200g/7oz/1 cup caster
  (superfine) sugar
2 eggs
115g/4oz/1 cup self-raising
  (self-rising) flour
5ml/1 tsp baking powder
grated rind of 2 lemons
30ml/2 tbsp lemon juice
2 egg whites

1 Preheat the oven to 190°C/375°F/ Gas 5. Arrange 18 paper cases in muffin tins (pans).

2 Put the butter in a bowl and beat until soft. Add 115g/4oz/generous ½ cup of the caster sugar and continue to beat until the mixture is light and creamy. Add the eggs, one at a time, beating thoroughly after each addition until the mixture is smooth.

3 Sift together the flour and baking powder over the creamed mixture, add half the lemon rind and all the lemon juice and beat well until thoroughly combined.

4 Divide the mixture among the paper cases, filling each case about two-thirds full.

5 To make the meringue, whisk the egg whites in a clean grease-free bowl until they stand in soft peaks. Stir in the remaining caster sugar and lemon rind.

6 Put a spoonful of the meringue mixture on top of each cake. Cook for 20–25 minutes, until the meringue is crisp and brown. Serve the cakes hot or turn out on to a wire rack to cool.

Energy 123kcal/514kJ; Protein 1.7g; Carbohydrate 16.6g, of which sugars 11.7g; Fat 6g, of which saturates 3.5g; Cholesterol 35mg; Calcium 19mg; Fibre 0.2g; Sodium 54mg.

Mandarin syrup cupcakes

For this recipe, mandarins are boiled to soften them and remove some of the bitterness, then puréed to add an intense citrus flavour to the finished cakes, which are then saturated in a citrus syrup. Serve as cakes with tea or as a sumptuous dessert with a compote of fresh fruit.

MAKES 12

3 mandarins
225g/8oz/generous 1 cup caster
 (superfine) sugar
6 eggs
225g/8oz ground almonds

For the syrup
350g/12oz/1⅔ cups caster
 (superfine) sugar
rind of 2 mandarins cut into very
 fine strips
juice of ¾ lemon

1 Preheat the oven to 160°C/325°F/ Gas 3. Line a 12-hole muffin tin (pan) with paper cases.

2 Put the whole unpeeled mandarins into a pan and cover with boiling water. Bring to the boil then simmer for about 2 hours. Check the water level and top up if necessary.

3 Remove the mandarins. When the fruit is cool, split open and remove the pips. Liquidize them into a smooth orange purée and set aside.

4 Whisk the eggs and sugar until well combined.

5 Stir in the ground almonds and the puréed fruit.

6 Spoon the mixture into the prepared cases and bake for 30 minutes until golden.

7 To make the syrup, dissolve the sugar over medium heat in 250ml/ 9fl oz water. Add the strips of fruit rind and the lemon juice and bring to the boil. Simmer for 2–3 minutes. Spoon on to the surface of the cakes.

Energy 344kcal/1449kJ; Protein 7.4g; Carbohydrate 52.2g, of which sugars 51.7g; Fat 13.3g, of which saturates 1.7g; Cholesterol 95mg; Calcium 88mg; Fibre 1.5g; Sodium 41mg.

Chocolate and sour cherry cakes

Sour cherries have an intense, tangy flavour, a contrast to the sweetness of white chocolate. These cakes, made with pure extracts of chocolate and vanilla, are topped with a vibrantly fruity sour cherry and white chocolate icing.

1 Preheat the oven to 180°C/350°F/ Gas 4. Grease the cups of a large muffin tin (pan). Sift the flour, baking powder and salt into a large mixing bowl and mix in the sugar. Set aside.

2 In a pan melt the butter, then remove it from the heat. Break half the chocolate into the melted butter and stir until melted. Grate the remaining chocolate and set aside.

3 In a bowl, whisk together the egg, milk, vanilla and chocolate extracts. Stir into the dry ingredients with the melted chocolate butter and the grated chocolate. Fold the ingredients lightly together.

4 Divide the batter among the muffin cups, filling three-quarters full. Bake for 25 minutes until golden. Turn on to a rack to cool.

MAKES 10

225g/8oz/2 cups plain
  (all-purpose) flour
10ml/2 tsp baking powder
pinch of salt
75g/3oz/scant ½ cup golden caster
  (superfine) sugar
75g/3oz/6 tbsp butter
130g/4½oz milk chocolate
1 small (US medium) egg,
  lightly beaten

90ml/6 tbsp milk
5ml/1 tsp vanilla extract
5ml/1 tsp pure chocolate extract

**For the white chocolate and sour
  cherry icing**
100g/3¾oz vanilla white chocolate
50g/2oz/½ cup icing
  (confectioners') sugar, sifted
40g/1½oz butter
40g/1½oz dried sour cherries,
  roughly chopped

5 To make the icing, melt the white chocolate in a bowl set over a pan of gently simmering water. Stir in the icing sugar and the butter. Add 15ml/1 tbsp warm water and mix until smooth. Add the dried fruit. Coat the tops of the cooled cakes.

Energy 369kcal/1546kJ; Protein 5.1g; Carbohydrate 47.2g, of which sugars 29.7g; Fat 19.1g, of which saturates 11.7g; Cholesterol 55mg; Calcium 112mg; Fibre 0.7g; Sodium 142mg.

Blueberry and chocolate cupcakes

Blueberries are one of the many fruits that combine deliciously with the richness of chocolate in cakes, while still retaining their own distinctive flavour. These cakes are best served on the day they are made, preferably while still warm with a cup of your favourite tea.

MAKES 12

115g/4oz/½ cup butter
75g/3oz plain (semisweet)
  chocolate, chopped
200g/7oz/1 cup sugar
1 egg, lightly beaten
250ml/8fl oz/1 cup buttermilk
10ml/2 tsp vanilla extract
275g/10oz/2½ cups plain (all-
  purpose) flour
5ml/1 tsp bicarbonate of soda
  (baking soda)
175g/6oz/1½ cups fresh or thawed
  frozen blueberries
25g/1oz plain (semisweet)
  chocolate, melted, to decorate

1 Preheat the oven to 190°C/375°F/
Gas 5. Arrange 12 paper cases in a
muffin tin (pan).

2 Melt the butter and chocolate in a
pan over medium heat, stirring
frequently, until smooth. Remove
from the heat and leave the mixture
to cool slightly.

3 Put the sugar in a mixing bowl,
add the egg, buttermilk and vanilla
extract, and pour in the chocolate
mixture. Stir until smooth.

4 Sift the flour and bicarbonate of
soda over the mixture, then gently
fold in until just blended. (The
mixture should be slightly lumpy.)

5 Gently fold in the blueberries.
Spoon the batter into the paper
cases. Bake for 25–30 minutes, until
a skewer inserted in the centre
comes out with just a few crumbs
attached. Remove from the oven and
leave in the tin for 5 minutes, then
turn the cupcakes out on to a wire
rack to cool.

6 If serving warm, drizzle melted
chocolate over the top of each, then
serve. Otherwise, leave until cold
before decorating.

Energy 203kcal/850kJ; Protein 3.9g; Carbohydrate 24.9g, of which sugars 6.6g; Fat 10.5g, of which saturates 6.4g; Cholesterol 39mg; Calcium 63mg; Fibre 1g; Sodium 90mg.

Raspberry crunch friands

In this recipe egg whites are combined with ground nuts, melted butter and very little flour. The raw mixture has quite a loose consistency, but don't worry – as the cakes bake they will become just as firm and well risen as other cakes with a higher proportion of flour.

MAKES 12

175g/6oz/¾ cup butter
115g/4oz/1 cup ground almonds
225g/8oz/2 cups icing
   (confectioners') sugar, sifted
65g/2½oz/9 tbsp plain (all-
   purpose) flour, sifted
6 egg whites
115g/4oz/1 cup fresh raspberries

For the crunchy sugar frosting
juice of 1 small lemon
150g/5oz/¾ cup caster
   (superfine) sugar
very finely cut strips of candied
   lemon rind (optional)

1 Preheat the oven to 200°C/400°F/ Gas 6. Grease the cups of a friand or bun tin (pan) with melted butter and dust lightly with flour. Turn the tin upside down and tap it sharply on the work surface to get rid of any excess flour.

2 Melt the butter, remove from the heat and set aside to cool slightly.

3 Put the ground almonds, sugar and flour in a mixing bowl and stir together.

4 In a separate bowl, beat the egg whites lightly for 15 seconds, or just enough to break them up.

5 Add the egg whites to the dry ingredients and mix. Add the melted butter to the bowl and mix lightly until just combined.

6 Pour the mixture into the cups and press one raspberry into the centre of each. Bake for 20–25 minutes until the friands are pale golden and springy to the touch. Leave to cool slightly then turn them out on to a wire rack.

7 To make the sugar frosting, mix the lemon juice with the sugar and set aside for 10 minutes for the sugar to partly dissolve. Drizzle over the tops of the cooled cakes and leave to set for several hours. Top with a few curls of candied lemon rind, if you like.

Energy 317kcal/1330kJ; Protein 4.4g; Carbohydrate 38.3g, of which sugars 33.6g; Fat 17.4g, of which saturates 8.4g; Cholesterol 34mg; Calcium 53mg; Fibre 1.1g; Sodium 143mg.

Little Madeira cakes with cream and jam

These cakes look as good as they taste. The Madeira cake mixture, enriched with ground almonds and Calvados, rises beautifully into a perfect dome. When the cakes have cooled the domes are sliced away to make room for a mouthwatering filling of buttercream and jam.

MAKES 14

225g/8oz/1 cup butter, softened
225g/8oz/generous 1 cup caster
  (superfine) sugar
4 eggs
225g/8oz/2 cups self-raising
  (self-rising) flour
115g/4oz/1 cup plain
  (all-purpose) flour
60ml/4 tbsp ground almonds
5ml/1 tsp finely grated lemon rind
30ml/2 tbsp Calvados, brandy
  or milk

For the filling
175g/6oz/¾ cup butter, softened
350g/12oz/3 cups icing
  (confectioners') sugar, double
  sifted, plus extra for dusting
20ml/4 tsp lemon juice
20ml/4 tsp warm water
60ml/4 tbsp raspberry jam

1 Preheat the oven to 180°C/350°F/
Gas 4. Line 14 cups of two muffin
tins (pans) with paper cases.

2 Cream the butter and caster sugar
together until light and fluffy.

3 Add two of the eggs, a little at a
time, mixing well after each addition.
Sprinkle 15ml/1 tbsp of the flour
into the mixture and beat it in. Add
the remaining eggs gradually, beating
well after each addition, then beat in
another 15ml/1 tbsp flour until just
combined. Sift the remaining flours
into the mixture and fold in lightly
with the ground almonds, lemon
rind and Calvados, brandy or milk.

4 Fill the prepared cups almost to
the top. Bake for 20–22 minutes
until the tops spring back when
touched and the cakes are light
golden. Transfer to a wire rack.

5 To make the buttercream, beat
the softened butter with the icing
sugar until it is smooth and fluffy.
Stir in the lemon juice and warm
water and continue to beat
until smooth.

6 When the cakes have cooled
completely, slice a round from the
top of each.

7 Using a large piping (pastry) bag
fitted with a plain nozzle, pipe a
circle of buttercream.

8 Add a spoonful of jam to fill each
cake before replacing the dome on
top. Just before serving, dust lightly
with sifted icing sugar.

Energy 574kcal/2406kJ; Protein 5.2g; Carbohydrate 75.5g, of which sugars 54g; Fat 29.5g, of which saturates 18.6g; Cholesterol 140mg; Calcium 81mg; Fibre 0.9g; Sodium 278mg.

Classic cakes

No afternoon tea table is complete without a stunning cake for a centrepiece. This delightful chapter includes all the classic recipes that make the perfect addition to a feast. There are light and airy recipes that are perfect for summer, such as Cherry Cake or Easy-all-in-one Sponge that is delicious served with a flavourful berry compote. For cold winter days choose Parkin or Sticky Gingerbread: the dense textures and complex flavours are perfect for this time of year. Included, too, are recipes that suit any occasion such as rich Boston Cream Pie, or the intriguing Battenberg, with its chequerboard marking.

Left: Cherry Cake and Lemon Roulade with Lemon-curd Cream are just two of the fantastic cakes this chapter offers: both are perfect for serving for afternoon tea.

Sticky gingerbread

This dark rich gingerbread cries out to be smothered in cool butter or swirls of cream cheese as a contrast to the cake's taste and texture. It tastes better when kept for a few days, so prepare ahead before serving with afternoon tea on a chilly winter's day.

MAKES 8 SLICES

225g/8oz/2 cups plain (all-purpose)
  flour
10ml/2 tsp ground ginger
5ml/1 tsp mixed (apple pie) spice
pinch of salt
2 pieces preserved stem ginger,
  drained and chopped
115g/4oz/½ cup butter, softened
115g/4oz/½ cup dark muscovado
  (molasses) sugar, sifted
275g/10oz/scant 1 cup black treacle
  (molasses)
2 eggs, beaten
2.5ml/½ tsp bicarbonate of soda
  (baking soda)
30ml/2 tbsp milk, warmed
butter or cream cheese, to serve

1 Preheat the oven to 160°C/325°F/ Gas 3. Grease and line an 18cm/7in square cake tin (pan), that measures about 7.5cm/3in deep.

2 Sift the flour, ground ginger, mixed spice and salt together into a bowl. Add the stem ginger and toss it in the flour to coat thoroughly.

3 In a separate bowl, cream the butter and sugar together until fluffy, then gradually beat in the treacle. Add the eggs and the flour mixture.

4 Dissolve the bicarbonate of soda in the milk and gradually beat into the batter. Pour into the prepared tin and bake for 45 minutes. Reduce the oven temperature to 150°C/300°F/ Gas 2 and bake for a further 30 minutes. To test whether the cake is cooked, insert a metal skewer into the middle: it should come out clean.

5 Cool for 5 minutes in the tin and then turn out on to a wire rack to cool completely. Keep for two to three days in an airtight container so that the gingerbread becomes sticky and moist. Cut into pieces and serve with butter or cream cheese.

Energy 373kcal/1572kJ; Protein 5.2g; Carbohydrate 60.9g, of which sugars 38.7g; Fat 13.9g, of which saturates 8.1g; Cholesterol 78.5mg; Calcium 253.6mg; Fibre 0.9g; Sodium 170.5mg.

Parkin

From the north of England, parkin contains oatmeal and lots of syrup and treacle. This exceptionally moist ginger cake improves in flavour and texture when stored in a tin for several days. It is perfect for autumnal tea parties. Keep for up to a week in an airtight container.

MAKES 16–20 SQUARES

300ml/½ pint/1¼ cups milk
225g/8oz/⅔ cup golden
  (light corn) syrup
225g/8oz/scant ¾ cup
  treacle (molasses)
115g/4oz/½ cup butter
50g/2oz/¼ cup soft dark
  brown sugar
450g/1lb/4 cups plain
  (all-purpose) flour
2.5ml/½ tsp bicarbonate of soda
  (baking soda)
7.5ml/1½ tsp ground ginger
350g/12oz/3 cups
  medium oatmeal
1 egg, beaten
icing (confectioners') sugar,
  for dusting

1 Preheat the oven to 180°C/350°F/ Gas 4. Grease and line a 20cm/8in square deep cake tin (pan).

2 Gently heat together the milk, syrup, treacle, butter and sugar, stirring until smooth; do not boil.

3 Sift the flour into a bowl, add the bicarbonate of soda, ginger and oatmeal. Make a well in the centre.

4 Allow the treacle mixture to cool in the pan slightly so that it is just warm. Add the mixture to the bowl with the egg, stirring to make a smooth batter.

5 Pour the batter into the tin and bake for 45 minutes, or until firm to the touch.

6 Cool slightly in the tin, then turn out on to a wire rack to go cold. Remove the lining paper. Dust with icing sugar and cut into squares.

COOK'S TIP
Parkin freezes well, wrapped in foil for up to 3 months. After this the spices lose their power.

Energy 273kcal/1152kJ; Protein 5.3g; Carbohydrate 50g, of which sugars 20.1g; Fat 7.1g, of which saturates 3.3g; Cholesterol 23mg; Calcium 127mg; Fibre 1.9g; Sodium 102mg.

Battenberg

Immediately identifiable, Battenberg cake has a characteristic light sponge that is set in a chequerboard arrangement of pink and yellow cake. It is encased in a smooth cover of marzipan and served in dainty slices – a perfect addition to the tea table.

SERVES 14

175g/6oz/¾ cup butter, softened
175g/6oz/scant 1 cup caster (superfine) sugar
3 large (US extra large) eggs, lightly beaten
175g/6oz/1½ cups self-raising (self-rising) flour, sifted
pinch of salt
2.5ml/½ tsp red food colouring
2.5ml/½ tsp rosewater
2.5ml/½ tsp orange flower water, or almond extract
450g/1lb marzipan
90ml/6 tbsp apricot jam
30ml/2 tbsp sugar

1 Preheat the oven to 190°C/375°F/ Gas 5. Lightly grease a Swiss roll tin (jelly roll pan), 30 x 20 x 2.5cm (12 x 8 x 1in). Lightly grease the base and line it with baking parchment.

2 Cut a strip of cardboard to fit the inside of the tin. Cover with foil, lightly grease and wedge in place. In a large bowl, beat the butter with the caster sugar until creamy. Add the eggs and beat well. Lightly fold in the flour and salt.

3 Put half the mixture in a clean bowl and mix in the red food colouring and rosewater until evenly tinted. Turn into one side of the tin.

4 Mix the orange flower water or almond extract into the remaining batter and turn into the empty side of the tin. Smooth into the corners.

5 Bake for 20 minutes until risen and firm to the touch. Leave to stand for 5 minutes. Slide the blade of a knife between cake, tin and foil strip, and turn out on to a wire rack lined with silicone paper. Remove the lining paper. Leave to go cold.

6 Trim the cake so that each half measures 28 x 9cm (11 x 3½in). Cut each slab in half lengthways so there are four equal pieces.

7 In a pan, bring the jam and sugar slowly to the boil, stirring constantly. Boil for 30–60 seconds. Remove from the heat.

8 To assemble the cake, brush the top of each plain cake strip with the syrup and press a pink strip on top. Brush one side of each cake stack with syrup and press them together to make a chequerboard pattern.

9 Roll out the marzipan to 28cm/ 11in square. Brush the cake top with syrup, and place the cake syrup-side down 1cm/½in from one edge of the marzipan. Brush the rest of the cake with syrup. Wrap the marzipan over and around the cake, smoothing it firmly with your hand. Press firmly at the join to seal. Trim away any excess marzipan.

Energy 355kcal/1492kJ; Protein 4.4g; Carbohydrate 51.2g, of which sugars 41.7g; Fat 15.7g, of which saturates 7.5g; Cholesterol 70mg; Calcium 55mg; Fibre 1g; Sodium 117mg.

Cherry cake

Both dried and glacé cherries are used in this elegant cake, partnered with the delicate flavour of almonds and decorated with a drizzle of icing. It is a combination that is perfect for a summer tea party. Store in an airtight container for up to five days. Freeze undecorated for two months.

SERVES 10

175g/6oz/¾ cup unsalted
   butter, softened
175g/6oz/scant 1 cup caster
   (superfine) sugar
3 eggs, beaten
150g/5oz/1¼ cups self-raising
   (self-rising) flour
50g/2oz/½ cup plain
   (all-purpose) flour
75g/3oz/¾ cup ground almonds
75g/3oz/scant ½ cup glacé
   (candied) cherries, washed, dried
   and halved
25g/1oz dried cherries
a few drops of almond extract

For the decoration
115g/4oz/1 cup icing
   (confectioners') sugar, sifted
5ml/1 tsp lemon juice
50g/2oz/½ cup flaked (sliced)
   almonds, toasted
10 natural glacé (candied) cherries

1 Preheat the oven to 160°C/325°F/ Gas 3. Grease and line a 20cm/8in round deep cake tin (pan).

2 In a bowl, beat the butter with the sugar until light and fluffy, using an electric whisk, if possible. Add the eggs a little at a time, including 5ml/1 tsp of flour with each addition.

3 Sift in the flours, the ground almonds and cherries. Stir well.

4 Add the flour and cherry mixture to the butter and sugar and fold together with the almond extract until smooth. Spoon into the cake tin and smooth level.

5 Bake for 45–50 minutes, or until a skewer inserted into the centre comes out clean. Cool slightly, then turn on to a wire rack to go cold. Remove the lining paper.

6 In a bowl, mix the icing sugar with the lemon juice, and 10–15ml/ 2–3 tsp water, to make a soft icing. Drizzle half over the cake top. Sprinkle the almonds into the centre. Place the cherries around the edge. Drizzle over the remaining icing.

Energy 367kcal/1535kJ; Protein 5g; Carbohydrate 43.7g, of which sugars 26.6g; Fat 20.4g, of which saturates 12g; Cholesterol 118mg; Calcium 75mg; Fibre 0.9g; Sodium 309mg.

Easy all-in-one sponge

This strawberry and 'cream' cake is so quick and easy to make. You'll find this simple topping handy for other cakes too, as you can make it from store-cupboard ingredients. Store for up to three days in an airtight container. Freeze the basic cakes undecorated for up to two months.

SERVES 12

175g/6oz/1½ cups self-raising
   (self-rising) flour
5ml/1 tsp baking powder
175g/6oz/¾ cup soft tub
   margarine
175g/6oz/scant 1 cup caster
   (superfine) sugar
3 eggs
15ml/1 tbsp milk
5ml/1 tsp vanilla extract

For the filling and topping
150g/5oz white chocolate chips
200g/7oz/scant 1 cup cream cheese
25g/1oz/¼ cup icing
   (confectioners') sugar
30ml/2 tbsp strawberry jam
12 strawberries

1 Preheat the oven to 180°C/350°F/ Gas 4. Grease and line two 20cm/8in round shallow cake tins (pans) with baking parchment.

2 Sift the flour and baking powder into a large bowl, then add all the remaining cake ingredients.

3 Beat until smooth, then divide between the tins and smooth level.

4 Bake for 20 minutes, or until the cakes spring back when pressed. Allow to stand for 5 minutes, then turn out on to a wire rack to go cold. Remove the lining papers.

5 To make the icing, melt the chocolate chips in a heatproof bowl over a pan of gently simmering water. Remove from the heat and cool slightly, then beat in the cream cheese and icing sugar.

6 Spread the top of one sponge with jam. Carefully spread one-third of the icing on top.

7 Slice 4 strawberries, then sprinkle over the jam. Put the cakes together.

8 Spread the remaining icing over the cake top. Decorate with the whole strawberries.

Energy 395kcal/1648kJ; Protein 4.7g; Carbohydrate 39.6g, of which sugars 28.5g; Fat 25.3g, of which saturates 15.2g; Cholesterol 94mg; Calcium 90mg; Fibre 0.5g; Sodium 173mg.

Apple cake

This recipe comes from the West of England and uses cooking apples to give the cake a moist texture and a refreshing sweet-and-sour flavour. You can use eating apples, if you prefer, for a sweeter result. Eat fresh with clotted cream or vanilla ice cream for a tea-time treat.

SERVES 8

225g/8oz cooking apples, peeled,
   cored and chopped
juice of ½ lemon
225g/8oz/2 cups plain
   (all-purpose) flour
7.5ml/1½ tsp baking powder
115g/4oz/½ cup butter, diced
165g/5½oz/scant ¾ cup soft light
   brown sugar
1 egg, beaten
30–45ml/2–3 tbsp milk
2.5ml/½ tsp ground cinnamon

1 Preheat the oven to 180°C/
350°F/Gas 4. Grease and line an
18cm/7in round cake tin (pan) with
baking parchment.

2 In a small bowl, toss the apples
with the lemon juice to stop them
from going brown.

3 Sift the flour and baking powder
into a large bowl.

4 With cold hands, rub the butter
into the flour mixture until it
resembles fine crumbs. Stir in
115g/4oz/½ cup of the sugar, and
the apples.

5 Add the egg and enough milk to
give a soft, dropping consistency.

6 Spoon into the prepared tin and
smooth the top level.

7 Mix together the remaining sugar
with the cinnamon, then sprinkle
over the cake batter.

8 Bake for 45–50 minutes, or until
firm to the touch. Leave to cool,
then turn out on to a wire rack to go
cold. Peel off the lining paper.

COOK'S TIP
Steps 3 and 4 can be made
ahead of time and the dry
crumbs stored in the refrigerator.

Energy 476kcal/2003kJ; Protein 4.5g; Carbohydrate 74.6g, of which sugars 56.5g; Fat 19.8g, of which saturates 8.5g; Cholesterol 32.5mg; Calcium 77.1mg; Fibre 2g; Sodium 104.8mg.

Mincemeat cake

If you have any fruit mincemeat and small oranges left over after the Christmas holiday, they make a great basis for a tangy, quick-and-easy cake. Enrich the batter with some plain chocolate to make the cake even more special. Keep for one week in an airtight container.

SERVES 8–10

115g/4oz/½ cup soft tub
  margarine
3 small mandarin or
  tangerine oranges
75g/3oz/⅓ cup soft dark
  brown sugar
2 eggs, beaten
175g/6oz/1½ cups self-raising
  (self-rising) flour
2.5ml/½ tsp baking powder
15ml/1 tbsp milk
225g/8oz/⅔ cup luxury
  fruit mincemeat
50g/2oz plain (semisweet)
  chocolate, grated

For the decoration
175g/6oz/1½ cups icing
  (confectioners') sugar

1 Preheat the oven to 160°C/325°F/
Gas 3. Grease and line a 20cm/8in
round deep cake tin (pan) with
baking parchment.

2 Finely grate the rind from two
oranges and put in a large bowl.

3 Pare long shreds of peel from the
third orange, then set aside.

4 Squeeze the juice from two
oranges and keep 30ml/2 tbsp aside
for the icing.

5 Put the remaining juice and all
the other cake ingredients into a
large bowl. Beat with a wooden
spoon for about 2 minutes, or until
the mixture is soft and smooth.
Spoon into the tin and smooth the
top level.

6 Bake for 40–45 minutes, or until
firm and a warmed skewer inserted
into the centre comes out clean.
Cool in the tin for 10 minutes, then
turn out to cool on a wire rack and
peel away the papers.

7 To make the decoration, mix the
icing sugar with the reserved orange
juice until smooth. Spread over the
top of the cold cake and allow
the icing to run in drizzles down the
sides. Sprinkle the orange shreds on
top of the cake and leave to set for
30 minutes.

Energy 292kcal/1227kJ; Protein 2g; Carbohydrate 44.6g, of which sugars 44.4g; Fat 13g, of which saturates 7.9g; Cholesterol 66mg; Calcium 37mg; Fibre 0.5g; Sodium 135mg.

Chocolate cake

A rich luxurious chocolate cake is a staple of every self-respecting tea table. Perennially popular, this chocolate cake has an intense taste and aroma that make it a feast for the senses. Sandwiched between two layers of cake is a sweet buttercream filling.

SERVES 8

225g/8oz/2 cups plain
  (all-purpose) flour
5ml/1 tsp bicarbonate of soda
  (baking soda)
50g/2oz/½ cup unsweetened
  cocoa powder
130g/4½oz/9 tbsp butter, softened
250g/9oz/1¼ cups caster
  (superfine) sugar
3 eggs, beaten
250ml/8fl oz/1 cup buttermilk

For the buttercream
175g/6oz/1½ cups icing
  (confectioners') sugar
115g/4oz/½ cup butter, softened
few drops of vanilla extract
50g/2oz dark (bittersweet)
  chocolate

1 Preheat the oven to 180°C/350°F/Gas 4. Grease two 20cm/8in cake tins (pans) and line the bases with baking parchment. Sift the flour with the bicarbonate of soda and cocoa.

2 In another bowl, beat the butter and sugar until light and fluffy. Gradually beat in the eggs, then beat in the flour and buttermilk.

3 Spoon into the prepared tins and bake for 30–35 minutes until firm to the touch. Turn out of the tins, peel off the paper and leave on a wire rack to cool completely.

4 To make the buttercream, sift the icing sugar into a bowl. In a separate bowl, beat the butter until very soft and creamy. Beat in half the sifted icing sugar until smooth and light. Gradually beat in the remaining sugar and the vanilla extract.

5 Break the chocolate into squares and put in a heatproof bowl set over a pan of gently simmering water until melted. Mix the chocolate into the buttercream. Use half to sandwich the cakes together, and spread the rest over the top.

Energy 430kcal/1790kJ; Protein 7.8g; Carbohydrate 29.5g, of which sugars 28.8g; Fat 32.1g, of which saturates 13.6g; Cholesterol 96mg; Calcium 92mg; Fibre 1.9g; Sodium 125mg.

Chocolate-orange marble cake

Relive your memories of childhood and make this magical cake with its clever marbled pattern. Two cake batters are swirled together to give the marbled effect, and, because one is flavoured with orange and the other chocolate, the overall taste is wonderful too.

SERVES 10

225g/8oz/1 cup butter, softened
225g/8oz/generous 1 cup caster
  (superfine) sugar
4 eggs, beaten
225g/8oz/2 cups self-raising
  (self-rising) flour
30ml/2 tbsp unsweetened
  cocoa powder
15ml/1 tbsp milk
grated rind from 1 large orange
15ml/1 tbsp orange juice

For the icing
115g/4oz plain (semisweet)
  or milk chocolate, melted
  and cooled
115g/4oz/½ cup unsalted butter
225g/8oz/2 cups icing
  (confectioners') sugar, sifted

1 Preheat the oven to 180°C/350°F/ Gas 4. Grease and line a 20cm/8in round deep cake tin (pan) with baking parchment.

2 In a large bowl, beat the butter and sugar together until pale and fluffy.

3 Beat in the eggs a little at a time. Fold the flour into the mixture. Put half of the batter into another bowl.

4 Sift the cocoa into one bowl of batter and mix well with the milk.

> **COOK'S TIP**
> The cake keeps up to 5 days in an airtight container.

5 Put the rind and orange juice into the other bowl and mix well.

6 Spoon alternate tablespoonfuls of each mixture into the cake tin. Swirl a knife through the mixture once, then smooth the top level.

7 Bake for 45 minutes, or until the centre springs back when pressed. Leave to cool. Remove the papers.

8 In another bowl, whisk the butter. Beat in the icing sugar. Stir in the chocolate. Spread over the cake.

Energy 505kcal/2109kJ; Protein 6.5g; Carbohydrate 48.1g, of which sugars 36.6g; Fat 32.9g, of which saturates 18.8g; Cholesterol 119mg; Calcium 98mg; Fibre 1.5g; Sodium 322mg.

Boston cream pie

Created by chef M. Sanzian at the Parker House Hotel in Boston in the 1850s, this famous 'pie' is unusual, because sandwiched between the two cake layers is a rich custard. With its chocolate glaze it is a very appealing addition to the tea table. Keep refrigerated for up to three days.

SERVES 8

225g/8oz/2 cups plain
  (all-purpose) flour
15ml/1 tbsp baking powder
pinch of salt
115g/4oz/½ cup butter, softened
200g/7oz/1 cup caster
  (superfine) sugar
2 eggs
5ml/1 tsp vanilla extract
175m/6fl oz/l/¾ cup milk

For the filling
250ml/8fl oz/1 cup milk
3 egg yolks
90g/3½oz/½ cup caster
  (superfine) sugar
25g/1oz/¼ cup plain
  (all-purpose) flour
15ml/1 tbsp butter
5ml/1 tsp vanilla extract

For the chocolate glaze
25g/1oz dark (bittersweet)
  chocolate
15g/½oz/1 tbsp butter
50g/2oz/½ cup icing
  (confectioners') sugar, plus extra
  for dusting
2.5ml/½ tsp vanilla extract
15ml/1 tbsp hot water

1 Preheat the oven to 190°C/375°F/Gas 5. Thoroughly grease and line two 20cm/8in round shallow cake tins (pans) with baking parchment.

2 Sift the flour with the baking powder and salt into a large mixing bowl.

3 In a large bowl, beat the butter and sugar together until light and fluffy. Beat in the eggs one at a time, beating well after each addition. Stir in the vanilla extract.

4 Add the milk and the dry ingredients, alternating the batches and mixing only enough to blend.

5 Divide the cake batter between the prepared tins and spread it out evenly.

6 Bake for 25 minutes, or until a skewer inserted into the centre comes out clean. Allow to stand in the tins for 5 minutes before turning out on to a wire rack to cool completely. Remove the lining.

7 To make the filling, in a small pan, heat the milk to boiling point and remove from the heat.

8 In a heatproof bowl, beat the egg yolks until smooth. Gradually add the sugar and continue beating until pale yellow, then beat in the flour.

9 Pour the hot milk into the egg yolk mixture while beating.

10 When all the milk has been added, put the bowl over a pan of boiling water. Heat, stirring constantly, until thickened. Cook for 2 minutes more, then remove from the heat.

11 Stir in the butter and vanilla extract. Leave to cool.

12 Slice off the domed top of each cake to create a flat surface. Put one cake on a serving plate and spread on the filling in a thick layer. Set the other cake on top, cut side down. Smooth the edge of the filling layer so that it is flush with the sides of the cake layers.

13 To make the chocolate glaze, melt the chocolate and butter in a heatproof bowl set over a pan of gently simmering water. Stir well.

14 When smooth, remove from the heat and beat in the icing sugar using a wooden spoon. Add the vanilla extract, then beat in a little hot water to give a spreadable consistency. Spread evenly over the top of the cake. When it is set dust the top with icing sugar.

Energy 499kcal/2100kJ; Protein 6g; Carbohydrate 77.1g, of which sugars 53.1g; Fat 20.3g, of which saturates 12.1g; Cholesterol 146mg; Calcium 112mg; Fibre 1g; Sodium 297mg.

Frosted walnut layer cake

Walnuts go very well in rich cakes, especially when combined with a sweet filling. This moist and nutty cake is layered with vanilla buttercream and then topped with swirls of a super-light and fluffy frosting. It is ideal for a special tea party. Keep for five days in an airtight container.

SERVES 12

225g/8oz/2 cups self-raising
   (self-rising) flour
5ml/1 tsp baking powder
225g/8oz/1 cup butter, softened
225g/8oz/1 cup soft light
   brown sugar
75g/3oz/¾ cup walnuts,
   finely chopped
4 eggs
15ml/1 tbsp treacle (molasses)

For the buttercream
75g/3oz/6 tbsp unsalted butter
5ml/1 tsp vanilla extract
175g/6oz/1½ cups icing
   (confectioners') sugar

For the meringue frosting
2 large (US extra large)
   egg whites
350g/12oz/1¾ cups golden caster
   (superfine) sugar
pinch of salt
pinch of cream of tartar
15ml/1 tbsp warm water
whole walnut halves, to decorate

1 Preheat the oven to 160°C/325°F/ Gas 3. Grease and line two 20cm/8in round shallow cake tins (pans) with baking parchment.

2 Sift the flour and baking powder into a large bowl, then add all the remaining ingredients.

3 Beat together for 2 minutes, or until smooth, then divide between the tins and spread level.

4 Bake for 25 minutes, or until golden and springy to the touch in the centre.

5 Allow to stand for 5 minutes, then turn out on to a wire rack to go cold. Remove the lining papers. Cut each cake in half horizontally using a long-bladed sharp knife.

6 To make the buttercream, in a large bowl, beat the butter, vanilla extract and icing sugar together until light and fluffy.

7 Spread a third thinly over one sponge half and place a sponge layer on top, then continue layering the sponges with the buttercream. Put the cake on to a serving plate.

8 To make the frosting, put the egg whites in a large heatproof bowl and add the caster sugar, salt, cream of tartar and water. Put the bowl over a pan of hot water and whisk with an electric mixer for 7 minutes, or until the mixture is thick and stands in peaks.

9 Immediately, use a metal spatula to swirl the frosting over the top and sides of the cake.

10 Arrange the walnut halves on top and leave to set for 10 minutes before serving.

Energy 563kcal/2349kJ; Protein 8.5g; Carbohydrate 50.6g, of which sugars 39.2g; Fat 35.3g, of which saturates 10.1g; Cholesterol 108mg; Calcium 114mg; Fibre 1.5g; Sodium 177mg.

Lemon roulade with lemon-curd cream

This feather-light roulade is flavoured with almonds and filled with a rich lemon-curd cream.
It makes a marvellous dessert or a tea-time treat. Use best-quality or homemade lemon curd for
that perfect touch. Eat this cake fresh for best taste. It will store chilled for 1–2 days.

SERVES 8

4 eggs, separated
115g/4oz/generous ½ cup caster
  (superfine) sugar
finely grated rind of 2 lemons,
  plus extra to decorate
5ml/1 tsp vanilla extract
40g/1½oz/⅓ cup plain
  (all-purpose) flour
25g/1oz/¼ cup ground almonds

For the lemon cream
300ml/½ pint/1¼ cups double
  (heavy) cream
60ml/4 tbsp lemon curd
45ml/3 tbsp icing (confectioners')
  sugar, for dusting

1 Preheat the oven to 190°C/375°F/
Gas 5. Grease and line a 33 × 23cm/
13 × 9in Swiss roll tin (jelly roll
pan) with baking parchment.

2 In a large bowl, beat the egg
yolks with half the sugar until
foamy. Beat in the lemon rind and
vanilla extract.

3 Sift the flour over the egg mixture
and lightly fold in with the ground
almonds, using a metal spoon.

4 Put the egg whites into a clean,
grease-free bowl and whisk until
they form stiff, glossy peaks.

5 Gradually whisk in the remaining
sugar to form a stiff meringue.

6 Stir half the meringue mixture into
the egg yolk mixture to slacken it.
When combined, fold in the
remainder of the mixture.

7 Pour the batter into the prepared
tin and smooth level.

8 Bake for 10 minutes, or until
risen and spongy to the touch.

9 Put the tin on a wire rack and
cover loosely with a sheet of baking
parchment and a damp dish towel.
Leave to cool.

10 To make the lemon cream, whip
the cream until it holds its shape,
then fold in the lemon curd.

11 Sift the icing sugar over a piece of
baking parchment. Turn the sponge
out on to it. Peel off the lining paper
and spread over the lemon cream.

12 Using the paper, roll up the
sponge from one long side. Sprinkle
with lemon rind.

Energy 337kcal/1401kJ; Protein 5g; Carbohydrate 24.5g, of which sugars 18.9g; Fat 25.1g, of which saturates 13.6g; Cholesterol 148mg; Calcium 55mg; Fibre 0.4g; Sodium 50mg.

Lemon drizzle cake

Wonderfully moist and lemony, this cake is a favourite at coffee mornings and afternoon tea.
A lemon and sugar syrup is poured over the cooked cake and allowed to soak through, so that
the whole cake is sweet and tangy. Store in an airtight container for up to five days.

3 In a large bowl, beat the butter with the lemon and sugar mixture until light and fluffy, then beat in the eggs one at a time.

4 Sift the flour and baking powder into the mixture in three batches and beat well.

5 Turn the batter into the prepared tin and smooth the top level. Bake for 1½ hours, or until golden brown and springy to the touch.

SERVES 6

finely grated rind of 2 lemons
175g/6oz/scant 1 cup caster (superfine) sugar, plus 5ml/1 tsp
225g/8oz/1 cup unsalted butter, softened
4 eggs
225g/8oz/2 cups self-raising (self-rising) flour
5ml/1 tsp baking powder
shredded rind of 1 lemon, to decorate

For the syrup
juice of 1 lemon
150g/5oz/¾ cup caster (superfine) sugar

1 Preheat the oven to 160°C/ 325°F/Gas 3. Grease and line the base and sides of an 18–20cm/ 7–8in round deep cake tin (pan) with baking parchment.

2 Mix the lemon rind and sugar together in a bowl.

6 To make the syrup, slowly heat the juice with the sugar until dissolved.

7 Prick the cake top with a skewer and pour over the syrup. Sprinkle over the shredded lemon rind and 5ml/1 tsp sugar, then leave to cool. Remove the lining paper.

Energy 659kcal/2765kJ; Protein 8g; Carbohydrate 84.1g, of which sugars 56.2g; Fat 34.8g, of which saturates 21.4g; Cholesterol 213mg; Calcium 184mg; Fibre 1.2g; Sodium 466mg.

Almond and raspberry-filled roll

This light and airy whisked sponge cake is rolled up with a gorgeous filling of fresh raspberries and cream, making it a perfect treat for tea in the garden in summer. It is also excellent filled with other soft fruits, such as small or sliced strawberries, or blackcurrants. Eat fresh.

SERVES 8

4 eggs
115g/4oz/generous ½ cup caster
    (superfine) sugar, plus extra
    for dusting
150g/5oz/1¼ cups plain
    (all-purpose) flour, sifted
25g/1oz/¼ cup ground almonds
toasted flaked (sliced) almonds,
    to decorate

For the filling
250ml/8fl oz/1 cup double
    (heavy) cream
275g/10oz/2½ cups fresh
    raspberries

1 Preheat the oven to 200°C/
400°F/Gas 6. Grease and line a
33 × 23cm/13 × 9in Swiss roll
tin (jelly roll pan) with baking
parchment.

2 Put the eggs and sugar in a large
bowl and beat with an electric whisk
for about 10 minutes, or until the
mixture is thick and pale.

3 Sift the flour over the mixture and
gently fold in with the ground
almonds, using a metal spoon.

4 Spoon the batter into the tin and
smooth level. Bake for 10–12
minutes, or until the sponge is well
risen and springy to the touch.

5 Dust a sheet of baking parchment
liberally with caster sugar. Turn out
the cake on to the paper, and leave
to cool with the tin still in place.

6 Lift the tin off the cooled cake and
carefully peel away the lining paper.

7 To make the filling, whip the
cream until it holds its shape. Fold
in 250g/8oz/1¼ cups of the
raspberries, and spread over the
cooled cake, leaving a border.

8 Carefully roll up the cake from a
narrow end, using the paper to lift
the sponge.

9 Dust with caster sugar. Serve
decorated with the remaining
raspberries and the toasted
flaked almonds.

Energy 271kcal/1127kJ; Protein 4.7g; Carbohydrate 16.7g, of which sugars 11.9g; Fat 21.1g, of which saturates 11.2g; Cholesterol 114mg; Calcium 56mg; Fibre 1.2g; Sodium 35mg.

Carrot cake with cream cheese icing

As well as keeping this well-known cake moist, grated carrot also adds its own sweetness. Here, this classic tea-time treat is topped with a zesty orange and cream cheese icing, which goes perfectly with the nutty flavour of the cake. Keep refrigerated for up to three days.

SERVES 10

90g/3½oz/¾ cup wholemeal
  (whole-wheat) flour
150g/5oz/1¼ cups plain
  (all-purpose) flour
10ml/2 tsp baking powder
5ml/1 tsp bicarbonate of soda
  (baking soda)
5ml/1 tsp ground cinnamon
2.5ml/½ tsp ground allspice
250g/9oz/1¼ cups soft light
  brown sugar
3 carrots, peeled and
  coarsely grated
115g/4oz/1 cup chopped walnuts
3 large (US extra large) eggs
juice of 1 orange
120ml/4fl oz/½ cup sunflower oil
shreds of pared orange rind,
  to decorate

For the icing
50g/2oz/¼ cup butter, softened
200g/7oz/scant 1 cup cream
  cheese, softened
grated rind of 1 orange
200g/7oz/1¾ cups icing
  (confectioners') sugar
5ml/1 tsp vanilla extract

1 Preheat the oven to 180°C/350°F/
Gas 4. Grease and line a 23cm/9in
round deep cake tin (pan) with
baking parchment.

2 Sift the flours, baking powder,
bicarbonate of soda, cinnamon and
allspice into a bowl, then add in the
bran from the sieve (strainer).

3 Add the brown sugar, carrots and
walnuts. Make a well in the centre.

4 In another bowl, beat together the
eggs and orange juice. Add the egg
mixture with the oil to the dry
ingredients. Mix well.

5 Spoon the batter into the prepared
tin and level the top. Bake for about
1 hour, or until risen and springy to
the touch.

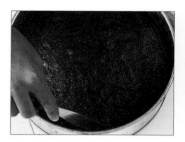

6 Leave the cake to set in the tin on
a wire rack for 10 minutes, then
slide a knife between the cake and
the tin to loosen it. Turn the cake
out on to a rack and remove the
lining paper. Leave to go cold, then
place on a serving plate.

7 To make the icing, beat the butter,
cream cheese and grated orange rind
in a large bowl.

8 Sift the icing sugar, then gradually
add to the bowl with the vanilla
extract, beating well after each
addition, until the mixture
is creamy.

9 Spread the icing on top of the
cake. Sprinkle the shreds of orange
rind over the top of the iced cake
to decorate.

Energy 397kcal/1664kJ; Protein 7.6g; Carbohydrate 49.2g, of which sugars 29.5g; Fat 20.3g, of which saturates 8.5g; Cholesterol 88mg; Calcium 75mg; Fibre 1.8g; Sodium 99mg.

Mini celebrations

Prettily decorated cupcakes always look lovely on a party table. A tiered cakestand holding small cakes is a charming and popular substitute for a traditional wedding cake, but there is a design here for every occasion, from iced cakes encrusted with brightly coloured candies for a children's birthday tea to sophisticated liqueur-laced creations for grown-up feasts. Everyone enjoys helping themselves to their own beautifully iced little cake.

Left: The decorations on these Mini Party Cakes can easily be tailored to suit the theme of the afternoon tea party celebration.

Christening cupcakes

Everyone will love these delicate little cakes, which are perfect for a christening tea party. Adorn the tops with cute decorations – rabbits, rocking horses and tiny spring flowers. For a small party halve the ingredients to make 24 bitesize cupcakes.

3 Add the sifted flour and fold it into the mixture using a metal spoon, until just combined.

4 Half-fill the paper cases with the cake mixture. Bake for 12–15 minutes until golden. Test by lightly pressing the centre of the cakes with your finger: the sponge should lightly spring back. Leave on a wire rack to cool.

MAKES 48 TINY CAKES

175g/6oz/¾ cup butter, softened
175g/6oz/scant 1 cup caster
  (superfine) sugar
4 eggs, lightly beaten
5ml/1 tsp vanilla extract
175g/6oz/1½ cups self-raising
  (self-rising) flour, sifted

For the clementine icing
150g/5oz/1¼ cups icing
  (confectioners') sugar, sifted
freshly squeezed juice of 1
  clementine or mandarin

For the decorations
115g/4oz sugarpaste divided and
  half tinted pink and half blue

1 Preheat the oven to 180°C/350°F/ Gas 4. Line the cups of four 12-cup mini cupcake trays with paper cases.

2 Place the softened butter and sugar in the bowl of an electric mixer and beat until light and creamy. Gradually add the beaten eggs in small amounts and beat well after each addition. Stir in the vanilla extract.

5 To make the icing, sift the sugar into a mixing bowl and stir in the clementine juice until the consistency is smooth and shiny. Spread a little icing over the top of each cake, coaxing it lightly with a knife to coat the surface evenly.

6 Cut out sugarpaste decorations and arrange before the icing sets.

Energy 78kcal/329kJ; Protein 0.9g; Carbohydrate 11.6g, of which sugars 8.9g; Fat 3.5g, of which saturates 2.1g; Cholesterol 24mg; Calcium 20mg; Fibre 0.1g; Sodium 47mg.

Mini party cakes

These little cakes look extremely pretty on the tea table decorated with icing and sugarpaste ornaments in different pastel colours. Once the cakes are iced a sherbet 'flying saucer' sweet is stuck on top of each one, before being decorated with butterflies and flowers.

MAKES 48 TINY CAKES

175g/6oz/¾ cup butter, softened
175g/6oz/scant 1 cup caster
  (superfine) sugar
4 eggs, lightly beaten
5ml/1 tsp vanilla extract
175g/6oz/1½ cups self-raising
  (self-rising) flour, sifted

For the icing
150g/5oz/1¼ cups icing
  (confectioners') sugar, sifted
food colouring in 4 colours: pink,
  pale blue, peach, green

For the decorations
115g/4oz white sugarpaste
food colouring in 4 colours: pink,
  pale blue, peach, green
sherbet-filled flying saucer sweets

1 Preheat the oven to 180°C/350°F/ Gas 4. Line the cups of four 12-cup mini cupcake trays with paper cases.

2 Place the softened butter and sugar in the bowl of an electric mixer and beat until light and creamy. Gradually add the eggs in small amounts and beat well after each addition.

3 Add the vanilla and sifted flour and fold it into the butter mixture until just combined.

4 Half-fill the paper cases with the mixture and bake for 12–15 minutes until golden. Test by pressing the centre of the cakes with your finger: the sponge should lightly spring back. Leave on a wire rack to cool completely.

5 Make the icing with just enough hot water (about 20ml/4 tsp) to make a soft glacé icing. Divide the icing between four bowls, then tint each with a different food colour, keeping the colours pale.

6 Ice each cake and coax it to the edges with the back of the spoon.

7 Decorate flying saucer sweets with tinted sprinkles and sugarpaste flowers, leaves and butterflies. Attach with glacé icing. Stick each to the top of a cupcake with glacé icing.

Energy 78kcal/329kJ; Protein 0.9g; Carbohydrate 11.6g, of which sugars 8.9g; Fat 3.5g, of which saturates 2.1g; Cholesterol 24mg; Calcium 20mg; Fibre 0.1g; Sodium 47mg.

Halloween treats with spooky frosting

No wonder kids love Halloween when there are treats like these to be enjoyed. These dark spicy muffins are very moist and make good use of the pumpkin flesh from the Jack-o-lanterns. Make them in advance if you can (without the topping), as the flavour will improve after a few days.

MAKES 10 STANDARD MUFFINS

100ml/3½fl oz/scant ½ cup olive oil
175g/6oz/¾ cup light muscovado
  (brown) sugar
50g/2oz/¼ cup soft dark
  brown sugar
1 egg, lightly beaten
7.5ml/1½ tsp vanilla extract
275g/10oz pumpkin flesh, grated
175g/6oz sultanas (golden raisins)
275g/10oz/2½ cups self-raising
  (self-rising) flour, sifted
10ml/2 tsp mixed (apple pie) spice
5ml/1 tsp ground ginger

For the ginger frosting
and decorations

250g/9oz/2¼ cups icing
  (confectioners') sugar, sifted
5ml/1 tsp ground ginger
15ml/1 tbsp lemon juice
30ml/2 tbsp ginger syrup from a jar
  of preserved stem ginger
175g/6oz white sugarpaste
mini marshmallows

1 Preheat the oven to 180°C/
350°F/Gas 4. Line the cups of a
muffin tin (pan) with 10 standard
paper cases.

2 In a large bowl, beat the oil with
the sugars. Add the egg and beat
well. Stir in the vanilla extract,
grated pumpkin and sultanas.

3 Sift the flour and spices into the
batter and stir until just mixed.

4 Divide the batter between the
paper cases. Bake for 28 minutes, or
until risen and golden. Leave to set.
Turn out on to a wire rack to go cold.

5 To make the ginger frosting, mix
the first four ingredients together in
a large bowl, then spoon over the
tops of the cakes and leave to set.

6 Roll out the sugarpaste and cut
out Halloween decorations. Stick
them to the tops of the muffins.
Serve sprinkled with marshmallows.

Energy 405kcal/1718kJ; Protein 4g; Carbohydrate 85.6g, of which sugars 65g; Fat 7.6g, of which saturates 1.2g; Cholesterol 19mg; Calcium 144mg; Fibre 1.5g; Sodium 120mg.

Kids' chocolate party cakes

A generous covering of bright and colourful sweets, sprinkles and marshmallows over a thick chocolate frosting is bound to go down well with children at a tea party. The kids will love to help decorate these luscious chocolate muffins. Keep for up to three days in the refrigerator.

MAKES 9–10 STANDARD MUFFINS

165g/5½oz/scant ¾ cup butter, softened
150g/5oz/¾ cup caster (superfine) sugar
5ml/1 tsp vanilla extract
150g/5oz/1¼ cups self-raising (self-rising) flour
20g/¾oz/scant ¼ cup unsweetened cocoa powder
7.5ml/1½ tsp baking powder
3 eggs, beaten
50–60 small sweets (candies)
coloured sprinkles

For the frosting
250ml/8fl oz/1 cup crème fraîche
225g/8oz plain (semisweet) chocolate, broken into pieces
75g/3oz/⅔ cup icing (confectioners') sugar

1 Preheat the oven to 180°C/350°F/Gas 4. Lightly grease the cups of a muffin tin (pan) or line them with paper cases.

2 In a large bowl, beat together the butter, sugar and vanilla until light and creamy.

3 Sift the flour, cocoa and baking powder into the butter and sugar mixture and beat to combine. Add the eggs and beat well.

4 Divide the batter between the paper cases and bake for 22–25 minutes or until risen and springy to the touch. Leave to stand for a few minutes then turn out on to a wire rack to go cold.

5 To make the frosting, heat the crème fraîche over low heat until hot, but not boiling. Remove from the heat.

6 Add the chocolate and stir until melted. Sift in the icing sugar and mix until smooth. Set aside to thicken slightly. Spread in swirls over the muffins.

7 Decorate with confectionery.

Energy 392kcal/1641kJ; Protein 5g; Carbohydrate 42.2g, of which sugars 30.5g; Fat 23.8g, of which saturates 14.8g; Cholesterol 111mg; Calcium 110mg; Fibre 0.7g; Sodium 235mg.

Lovebirds

Unashamedly romantic decorations make these cakes perfect for any occasion when love is in the air, from an intimate tryst to an engagement or anniversary tea party. They would also make a sweet gift for a loving couple, nestled in a pretty box.

MAKES 10

175g/6oz/¾ cup butter, softened
175g/6oz/scant 1 cup caster
    (superfine) sugar
4 eggs, lightly beaten
5ml/1 tsp vanilla extract
175g/6oz/1½ cups self-raising
    (self-rising) flour, sifted

For the icing and decorations
350g/12oz/3 cups icing
    (confectioners') sugar, sifted
115g/4oz white sugarpaste
food colour in different tints

1 Preheat the oven to 180°C/350°F/
Gas 4. Line a bun tin (pan) with
paper cases.

2 Beat the butter with the sugar
until creamy.

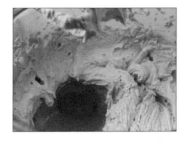

3 Beat in the eggs one at a time,
then stir in the vanilla and flour.

4 Half-fill the paper cases with the
batter. Bake for 20 minutes, until
golden. Cool on a wire rack.

5 Tint the sugarpaste and cut out
scalloped circles to fit the cake tops.

6 Make the glacé icing, then tint it
and spread a little on each cake.
Stick one scallop to each cake top.

7 Cut out lovebirds, hearts, flowers,
and leaves. Leave to dry flat.

8 Stick the decorations in place as
desired with sugarpaste and icing.

Energy 385kcal/1614kJ; Protein 4.9g; Carbohydrate 52.8g, of which sugars 38g; Fat 18.6g, of which saturates 11.2g; Cholesterol 129mg; Calcium 62mg; Fibre 0.6g; Sodium 180mg.

Valentine cupcakes

Pink and white sugared hearts make a classic cake decoration that's very easy to achieve, using a few cutters in different sizes. Just mix and match the colours and designs on a batch of cakes to give a contemporary twist to this traditional theme for a Valentine's Day tea gathering.

MAKES 10

175g/6oz/¾ cup butter, softened
175g/6oz/scant 1 cup caster
  (superfine) sugar
4 eggs, lightly beaten
5ml/1 tsp vanilla extract
175g/6oz/1½ cups self-raising
  (self-rising) flour, sifted

For the topping
350g/12oz/3 cups icing
  (confectioners') sugar, sifted
pink food colouring
115g/4oz white sugarpaste
pink candy sugar or sprinkles

1 Preheat the oven to 180°C/350°F/
Gas 4. Line the cups of a bun tin
(pan) with paper cases.

2 Beat the butter and sugar until
light and creamy. Gradually add the
beaten eggs in small amounts and
beat well after each addition. Stir in
the vanilla extract. Add the sifted
flour and fold it into the mixture
until just combined.

3 Spoon the mixture into the paper
cases. Bake in the centre of the oven
for 20 minutes until golden. Test by
lightly pressing the centre of the
cakes with your finger: the sponge
should lightly spring back. Leave on
a wire rack to cool completely.

4 To make the topping, mix the
sugar with enough hot water to
make a fairly thick icing. Divide
between two bowls and tint one
pink. Spread on to the cakes.

5 Tint the sugarpaste different
shades of pink. Roll out, then cut
out heart shapes using different size
cutters. Place on a flat surface to dry.

6 Stick the decorations on the iced
cakes. Paint some of the hearts with
water and cover with pink candy
sugar or sprinkles before attaching.

Energy 501kcal/2109kJ; Protein 5g; Carbohydrate 83.6g, of which sugars 68.8g; Fat 18.6g, of which saturates 11.2g; Cholesterol 129mg; Calcium 78mg; Fibre 0.6g; Sodium 181mg.

Marzipan-topped Easter cakes

These Easter cupcakes are irresistibly flavoured with fresh spices and orange rind and decorated with an embossed marzipan topping and cute little Easter motifs. If you are making the cakes for a tea party with children, you could soak the dried fruit in orange juice instead of sherry.

2 Preheat the oven to 180°C/350°F/ Gas 4. Line the cups of a bun tin (pan) with paper cases.

3 Beat the butter and sugar until creamy. Beat in an egg. Add 15ml/ 1 tbsp of flour and mix well before repeating with the second egg and another 15ml/1 tbsp flour. Fold in the remaining flour and mixed spice. Drain the dried fruit and stir it in with the orange rind and juice.

4 Fill the paper cases three-quarters full. Bake for 22–25 minutes until springy to the touch. Allow to cool completely. Slice off the tops level with the top of the cases.

5 Put the apricot glaze ingredients in a pan and melt over low heat.

6 Roll out the marzipan to 3mm/⅛in thick. Emboss with circular patterns. Cut out using a round cutter and attach to the cakes using the glaze.

MAKES 10–11

115g/4oz dried mango or pineapple or a mixture, finely chopped
115g/4oz sultanas (golden raisins)
50g/2oz mixed (candied) peel, chopped
100ml/3½ fl oz/scant ½ cup sherry
115g/4oz/½ cup butter, softened
115g/4oz/½ cup light muscovado (brown) sugar
2 eggs
225g/8oz/2 cups self-raising (self-rising) flour
7.5ml/1½ tsp mixed (apple pie) spice
finely grated rind of ½ large orange and juice of ¼ orange

For the apricot glaze
30ml/2 tbsp apricot jam
15ml/1 tbsp water
15ml/1 tbsp caster (superfine) sugar

For the topping
450g/1lb marzipan
small amounts of sugarpaste in white, primrose yellow, pale blue and pale pink
a little royal icing
sugared eggs

1 Place the dried fruits in a bowl with the mixed (candied) peel. Add the sherry and stir well. Leave for 24 hours.

7 Cut out and decorate a selection of motifs from sugarpaste and leave on a flat surface to dry before sticking in place with a little royal icing, along with a few sugared eggs.

Energy 452kcal/1903kJ; Protein 5.8g; Carbohydrate 73.7g, of which sugars 58.1g; Fat 15.1g, of which saturates 6.5g; Cholesterol 59mg; Calcium 85mg; Fibre 2g; Sodium 127mg.

You're a star

Mascarpone and Marsala add a delicious nuance to these mocha-flavoured cakes, which are topped with a velvety cream and chocolate stars for a dazzling display at the tea table. You can make the chocolate decorations in advance and keep in an airtight box in the refrigerator.

MAKES 8–10

150g/5oz/10 tbsp butter, softened
200g/7oz/1 cup golden caster
 (superfine) sugar
3 eggs
175g/6oz/¾ cup mascarpone
5ml/1 tsp grated lemon rind
30ml/2 tbsp buttermilk
15ml/1 tbsp unsweetened cocoa
 powder, plus extra for dusting
25ml/1½ tbsp espresso coffee
15ml/1 tbsp Marsala
250g/9oz/2¼ cups self-raising
 (self-rising) flour

For the topping
250ml/8fl oz/1 cup double
 (heavy) cream
225g/8oz/1 cup mascarpone
15ml/1 tbsp golden caster
 (superfine) sugar
15ml/1 tbsp Marsala
seeds from ½ vanilla pod (bean)
25g/1oz milk chocolate, melted

For the chocolate stars and leaves
100g/3¾oz plain (semisweet)
 chocolate
100g/3¾oz milk chocolate

1 Preheat the oven to 180°C/350°F/ Gas 4. Line a muffin tin (pan) with paper cases.

2 Beat the butter and sugar together until light and creamy. Gradually beat in the eggs, one at a time, beating well after each addition. Stir in the mascarpone, lemon rind, buttermilk, cocoa, coffee and Marsala, then fold in the flour.

3 Fill the prepared cups. Bake for 25 minutes, or until firm. Turn out on to a wire rack to cool.

4 Meanwhile make the topping, beat the cream with the mascarpone, sugar, Marsala and vanilla seeds. Lightly fold in the melted chocolate.

5 To make the decorations, melt the chocolates separately, then spread on baking parchment and chill until just set. Cut out the shapes.

6 Spoon the topping on to the cakes, and press on the decorations. Dust with cocoa powder.

Energy 718kcal/2990kJ; Protein 8g; Carbohydrate 56.8g, of which sugars 36.7g; Fat 53.7g, of which saturates 32.1g; Cholesterol 167mg; Calcium 146mg; Fibre 1g; Sodium 297mg.

Mother's Day fairy cakes with sugar roses

These deliciously featherlight sponge cakes are topped with delicately coloured icing scented with rose water and trimmed with a feminine melange of sugarpaste flower decorations. Silver foil cases add a touch of glamour to these very special cakes.

MAKES 10

3 eggs, separated
115g/4oz/generous ½ cup caster (superfine) sugar
juice of ½ lemon
grated rind of 1 mandarin
65g/2½oz/scant ½ cup fine semolina
15g/½oz/1 tbsp ground almonds

For the rose water icing
350g/12oz/3 cups icing (confectioners') sugar
5ml/1 tsp rose water
15ml/1 tbsp hot water

For the decorations
350g/12oz white sugarpaste
food colouring

1 Preheat the oven to 180°C/350°F/ Gas 4. Line the cups of a bun tin (pan) with foil or paper cases.

2 Beat the egg yolks with the sugar until light. Beat in the lemon juice and fold in the mandarin rind, semolina and almonds. In a separate bowl, whisk the egg whites until stiff. Fold into the mixture.

3 Pour into the cake cases until half full. Bake for 15 minutes, until the cakes are golden. Leave to cool, then turn out on to a wire rack.

4 To make the icing, mix the sugar with the rose water and enough hot water to make a flowing consistency. Spread it on top of the cooled cakes and leave to dry.

5 To make the sugarpaste roses, tint some paste pink and roll out three or four small circles very thinly; roll up the first to form the centre then add the other petals working around the central petal. Keep the petals open at the top so that they start to resemble a bud. Set all the flowers on a board covered with baking parchment to dry. Stick in place with a small blob of icing.

Energy 306kcal/1302kJ; Protein 3.2g; Carbohydrate 72g, of which sugars 66.9g; Fat 2.6g, of which saturates 0.5g; Cholesterol 57mg; Calcium 47mg; Fibre 0.3g; Sodium 26mg.

Summer cupcakes with fresh fruit icing

Add a touch of indulgence to a summer tea party with these gloriously pretty cupcakes. The recipe is simple and the cakes are topped with a trio of icings flavoured with fresh fruit juice, then decorated with sugarpaste flowers easily created using plunger cutters.

MAKES 12

225g/8oz/1 cup butter, softened
225g/8oz/generous 1 cup caster
   (superfine) sugar
4 eggs, lightly beaten
50g/2oz/½ cup plain
   (all-purpose) flour
150g/5oz/1¼ cups ground almonds
5ml/1 tsp vanilla extract
15ml/1 tbsp single (light) cream

For the decorations
350g/12oz white sugarpaste
food colouring
royal icing
artificial flower stamens
candy sugar, for sprinkling

For the icing
350g/12oz/3 cups icing
   (confectioners') sugar, sifted
15ml/1 tbsp fresh raspberry juice
15ml/1 tbsp fresh orange juice
15ml/1 tbsp fresh lime juice

1 Preheat the oven to 180°C/350°F/ Gas 4. Line the cups of a bun tin (pan) with paper cases.

2 Beat the butter and sugar until light and creamy. Add the eggs in small amounts, beating well after each addition. Sift in the flour and beat well. Add the ground almonds, vanilla extract and cream and combine.

3 Part fill the paper cases and bake for 20–25 minutes until the cakes are light golden brown and the centres feel firm to the touch.

4 Leave the cakes to cool in the tin for 5 minutes, then turn out on to a wire rack to cool completely.

5 To make the flowers, tint pieces of paste as desired. Roll out and stamp out individual petals. Stick together arranging them in a flower shape.

6 Mount some stamens in royal icing. Leave to dry. Cut out small flowers using plunger cutters.

7 When the decorations are dry, make the icing for the cake tops. Divide the sugar among three bowls and mix each batch with one of the fruit juices and about 5ml/1 tsp hot water to make a smooth fluid icing.

8 Spread each icing on top of the cakes, coaxing it out to the edges. Arrange the sugarpaste decorations on the cakes before the icing sets.

9 Once it is dry, sprinkle some of the cakes with a little candy sugar.

Energy 536kcal/2253kJ; Protein 5.6g; Carbohydrate 78.4g, of which sugars 74.9g; Fat 24.4g, of which saturates 11.4g; Cholesterol 107mg; Calcium 87mg; Fibre 1.1g; Sodium 171mg.

Iced cherry cakes

Glacé cherries are used in this almond cake mixture, but if you find them too sweet you could use sharp-tasting dried sour cherries, or even fresh cherries. You'll need a special textured rolling pin to achieve the lovely embossed basketweave design on the icing.

3 In another bowl beat the butter and sugar until creamy. Add one egg at a time and beat until the mixture is light and fluffy. Mix in the fruit rind, brandy and orange juice, then the dry ingredients and the cherries.

4 Fill the paper cases three-quarters full. Bake for 25 minutes or until golden and springy to the touch. Leave to cool a little before turning them out on to a wire rack.

MAKES 10

175g/6oz/1½ cups self-raising (self-rising) flour
10ml/2 tsp baking powder
75g/3oz/¾ cup ground almonds
175g/6oz/¾ cup butter, softened
175g/6oz/scant 1 cup golden caster (superfine) sugar
3 eggs, lightly beaten
finely grated rind of ½ lemon
finely grated rind of ½ orange
15ml/1 tbsp brandy or Calvados
60ml/4 tbsp orange juice
150g/5oz glacé (candied) cherries, halved

For the topping
350g/12oz sugarpaste
green food colouring

For the decorations
150g/5oz sugarpaste
red and brown food colouring
115g/4oz royal icing

1 Preheat the oven to 180°C/350°F/ Gas 4. Line the cups of a bun tin (pan) with paper cases.

2 Sift the flour and baking powder into a mixing bowl and stir in the ground almonds.

5 For the topping, colour the sugarpaste pale green and roll it out to a 6mm/¼in thickness. Emboss with a decorative rolling pin then cut out ten circles and stick them on the cooled cakes using royal icing. Roll 20 red sugarpaste cherries, 20 brown stems and some green leaves and stick in place.

Energy 548kcal/2308kJ; Protein 5.6g; Carbohydrate 90.4g, of which sugars 76.9g; Fat 20.4g, of which saturates 10.3g; Cholesterol 97mg; Calcium 96mg; Fibre 1.2g; Sodium 162mg.

Wedding cupcakes

The pink or peach sugarpaste circular toppings will stand slightly proud of the cakes, so make them a little in advance so that they firm up before they are applied, with royal icing, to the tops of the cakes. Use ready-made sugar flowers or make your own using a plunger cutter.

MAKES 12

225g/8oz marzipan
75g/3oz/6 tbsp butter, softened
100g/3½oz/½ cup caster
  (superfine) sugar
3 eggs, lightly beaten
15ml/1 tbsp brandy
100g/3¾oz/scant ½ cup ground
  almonds
150g/5oz/1¼ cups plain
  (all-purpose) flour
10ml/2 tsp baking powder

For the topping
450g/1lb white sugarpaste
paste food colouring in pink or
  peach and apple green
115g/4oz royal icing
sugarpaste flowers

1 To make the sugarpaste circles colour 175g/6oz of the sugarpaste shell pink or peach. Roll it out fairly thinly on a surface dusted with icing (confectioners') sugar. Using a round crinkle-edged cutter stamp out 12 circles and leave them to dry.

2 To make the scalloped circles roll out 140–175g/5–6oz of white sugarpaste fairly thinly. Stamp out 12 circles a little smaller than the pink circles. Leave to dry.

3 To make the leaves, colour the remaining 115g/4oz of sugarpaste apple green (or leave it white if you like). Roll it out thinly and using a leaf cutter stamp out 12 leaves. Lightly bend them into realistic shapes and leave to dry.

4 Preheat the oven to 180°C/350°F/ Gas 4. Line the cups of a muffin tin (pan) with paper cases.

5 Place the marzipan, butter and sugar together in the bowl of an electric mixer and mix well to a smooth even paste. Leaving the motor running, add the eggs in a very thin stream, beating well until the mixture is smooth.

6 Add the brandy and ground almonds, sift in the flour and baking powder and fold in.

7 Fill the cups three-quarters full with the cake mixture, and bake for 20–25 minutes until the cakes are golden and the centres are springy to the touch.

8 Leave to cool in the tin for 5 minutes, then turn the cakes out on to a wire rack and leave to cool completely.

9 Use a blob of royal icing to attach the scalloped circles to the cake toppings. Brush the cakes with a little more icing and press the circles on top, then decorate with sugarpaste leaves and flowers.

Energy 302kcal/1269kJ; Protein 5.6g; Carbohydrate 40.4g, of which sugars 30.6g; Fat 13.7g, of which saturates 4.4g; Cholesterol 62mg; Calcium 67mg; Fibre 1.4g; Sodium 71mg.

Welcome to your new home cupcakes

The hand-piped decorations on these cakes may look ambitious but with care you can achieve the pattern quite easily. You will need several small piping bags with fine plain nozzles filled with different coloured royal icing to infill the details of the houses and flower borders.

MAKES 12

2 eggs
115g/4oz/generous ½ cup caster
   (superfine) sugar
50ml/2fl oz/¼ cup double
   (heavy) cream
finely grated rind of 1 small lemon
finely grated rind of 1 small orange
115g/4oz/1 cup self-raising
   (self-rising) flour
2.5ml/½ tsp baking powder
50g/2oz/¼ cup butter, melted

For the icing
350g/12oz/3 cups icing
   (confectioners') sugar, sifted
15ml/1 tbsp clementine or orange
   juice, strained

For the decoration
sugarpaste coloured as desired
225g/8oz royal icing
food colouring in several shades

1 Preheat the oven to 180°C/350°F/ Gas 4. Line the cups of a 12-hole bun tin (pan) with paper cases.

2 Beat the eggs with the sugar until pale in colour. Beat in the cream, then add the grated lemon and orange rinds. Fold in the flour sifted with the baking powder, then fold in the warm melted butter.

3 Three-quarters fill the cases and bake for about 15 minutes, until golden. Leave to cool completely.

4 Roll out the sugarpaste on a light dusting of icing sugar and cut scallop edge circles to fit each cake.

5 Mix the icing sugar with enough fruit juice to make a thick, fluid consistency. Spread over the cakes and immediately stick a sugarpaste scallop to each.

6 To make the houses, tint the royal icing as desired to a soft consistency and fill several piping (icing) bags fitted with fine plain nozzles.

7 On to the sugarpaste scallop, pipe a square for the house shape. Fill with icing and smooth out any air bubbles. Add a roof and then a chimney in the same way.

8 Pipe all the decorative details.

Energy 305kcal/1290kJ; Protein 2.3g; Carbohydrate 63.3g, of which sugars 56g; Fat 6.7g, of which saturates 3.8g; Cholesterol 47mg; Calcium 49mg; Fibre 0.3g; Sodium 48mg.

Party number cakes

These delicious, moist Madeira cakes have a hidden centre of tangy lemon curd. The pretty pastel-coloured alphabet candies that decorate them can be arranged to spell out the names of your guests, if you wish. Look out for delicately coloured sweets and sprinkles to complete the effect.

MAKES 12

225g/8oz/1 cup butter, softened
225g/8oz/generous 1 cup caster
  (superfine) sugar
4 eggs
225g/8oz/2 cups self-raising
  (self-rising) flour
115g/4oz/1 cup plain
  (all-purpose) flour
60ml/4 tbsp ground almonds
25ml/1½ tbsp lemon juice
15ml/1 tbsp milk
60ml/4 tbsp lemon curd

For the sherbet icing
250g/9oz/2¼ cups icing
  (confectioners') sugar,
  double sifted
40g/1½oz/⅓ cup sherbet
30ml/2 tbsp lemon juice
20ml/4 tsp hot water
15ml/1 tbsp lemon curd

For the decorations
60 alphabet sweets (candies)
36 torpedo sweets (candies)
candy sugar or sprinkles

1 Preheat the oven to 180°C/350°F/ Gas 4. Line the cups of a 12-cup muffin tin (pan) with paper cases.

2 Cream the butter and sugar until light and fluffy. Beat in two eggs a little at a time, then 15ml/1 tbsp of the flour. Add the remaining eggs, and another 15ml/1 tbsp of flour.

3 Sift the remaining flours in, then fold them in lightly with the ground almonds, lemon juice and milk.

4 Fill the paper cups almost to the top. Bake for 20–25 minutes until the cakes are golden. Allow to cool.

5 To make the sherbet icing, sift the sugar and sherbet and combine with the remaining ingredients to make a soft icing that is just firm enough to hold its shape.

6 When the cakes are cold, slice a round from the top of each one. Insert 5ml/1 tsp lemon curd into each cake before replacing the top.

7 Spread each cake with a thick layer of sherbet icing. Press your choice of decorations into the icing while it is soft.

Energy 464kcal/1950kJ; Protein 6.2g; Carbohydrate 67.7g, of which sugars 44.6g; Fat 20.7g, of which saturates 11g; Cholesterol 108mg; Calcium 87mg; Fibre 1.3g; Sodium 173mg.

Wedding anniversary cakes

Delicious featherlight cakes and simple white and mauve sugarpaste hearts make an elegant presentation for an anniversary tea party. The decorations are easy to make with a heart-shaped cutter and a tiny flower-shaped plunger cutter.

MAKES 10

3 eggs, separated
115g/4oz/½ cup caster
   (superfine) sugar
juice of ½ lemon
grated rind of 1 mandarin
65g/2½oz/scant ½ cup fine
   semolina
15g/½oz/1 tbsp ground almonds

For the icing
350g/12oz/3 cups icing
   (confectioners') sugar
5ml/1 tsp grappa
15ml/1 tbsp hot water

For the decorations
350g/12oz white sugarpaste
mauve food colouring
a little royal icing

1 To make the decorations, divide the sugarpaste in half. Knead a little mauve food colouring into one piece until evenly coloured, then roll out both pieces separately. Cut out ten mauve hearts and ten white hearts.

2 Cut out 20 small flowers and pipe a little royal icing into each centre. Leave the decorations to dry.

3 Preheat the oven to 180°C/350°F/ Gas 4. Line the cups of a bun tin (pan) with paper cases.

4 Using an electric mixer, beat the egg yolks with the sugar until light and creamy. Add the lemon juice and beat until well mixed. Fold in the grated mandarin rind, semolina and ground almonds using a large spoon or spatula.

5 In a separate bowl, whisk the egg whites until stiff peaks form.

6 Lightly stir one heaped tablespoonful of the beaten egg white into the cake mixture to slacken the consistency, then gently fold in the remaining beaten egg white until the mixture is just combined. Do not overmix.

7 Spoon into the prepared cups until half full and bake for 15 minutes, until golden. Leave to cool, slightly then turn out on to a rack.

8 To make the icing, mix the ingredients together, adding enough of the water to form a soft liquid icing, and spread it on the cakes until it almost reaches the edges. While the icing is fresh quickly add the decorations, then leave to set.

COOK'S TIP
Remember to match the paper cake cases to the occasion for a special anniversary: silver for a silver wedding, red for a ruby wedding and so on.

Energy 346kcal/1471kJ; Protein 3.3g; Carbohydrate 82.5g, of which sugars 77.4g; Fat 2.6g, of which saturates 0.5g; Cholesterol 57mg; Calcium 53mg; Fibre 0.3g; Sodium 26mg.

Teapot decoration

This pretty teapot cupcake is sure to be a showstopper at any afternoon tea party, whether it's for a child's birthday or for a young-at-heart adult. The decoration is quite time-consuming to make but well worth the effort. Use any standard cupcake recipe you like.

10 cupcakes of your choice
scraps of sugarpaste
food pastes in pastel colours
small quantity glacé icing
icing (confectioners') sugar,
    for dusting

1 Tint small quantities of sugarpaste lilac, lemon, pink and brown for each component of the teapot and teacup design. Wrap each ball separately and tightly in clear film (plastic wrap) so that it does not dry out. Keep in a cool place.

2 Coat the top of each cake with white glacé icing to fill the case.

3 On sifted icing sugar, roll out a thin circle of white sugarpaste to fit just inside the paper case. Stamp out a circle using a scallop-edge cutter and stick in place while the glacé icing is wet.

4 Roll out a thin layer of lilac sugarpaste for the mat below the teapot. Cut a small circle using a scallop edge cutter.

5 Impress a design in it using a modelling tool and stick in place.

6 To make the body of the teapot, roll a ball of pale yellow paste so that it is smooth all over. Make another smaller ball for the lid. Flatten the bottom edge slightly and stick in place with water. Make a small sausage for the handle and another for the spout. Fix in place with water. Carefully smooth any joins with your fingers.

7 Cut out a flat disc for the saucer. Model a bowl for the cup and fill with glacé icing to represent a drink. Make a sausage handle. The teaspoon is a small sausage rolled thinly at one end and shaped with a ball tool. The cake on the saucer is made of layered sugarpaste balls.

Strawberry cakes

This pretty decorative design has to be assembled just before serving so that the fresh fruit doesn't discolour the sugarpaste topping. All the components can be made ahead of time though for speedy serving at a summer's day tea party. Use any standard cupcake recipe you like.

10 cupcakes of your choice
strawberry jam
small quantity sugarpaste
pink and green food colouring
2 sizes of strawberry flowers
icing (confectioners') sugar,
    for dusting
fresh strawberries

1 Coat the top of each cupcake with a generous layer of strawberry jam.

2 Tint some sugarpaste pink and roll it out thinly on a surface dusted lightly with icing sugar. Stamp out a circle to fit the top of the cupcake using a round scallop-edge cutter. Stick in place on top of the jam.

3 Tint another small amount of sugarpaste pale leaf green. Roll out and cut out leaves and calyx shapes.

4 Using glacé icing, stick the components in place. Stick a leaf in place on one side of the cupcake top. Decide where the strawberry will go and position the two strawberry flowers close by.

5 Wrap the sugarpaste calyx around the top of the strawberry. Use a blob of jam to hold it in place and stick in position on top of the cupcake just before serving.

Almond cupcakes with grapes

Bunches of marzipan grapes decorate these spectacular tea party cakes, but if you would prefer a simpler decoration you could finish the cakes elegantly with just a single green vine leaf laid on top. Brandy can be substituted for grappa in the recipe.

MAKES 10

225g/8oz marzipan
75g/3oz/6 tbsp butter, softened
100g/3¾oz/generous ½ cup caster (superfine) sugar
3 eggs, lightly beaten
15ml/1 tbsp grappa
100g/3½oz/scant ½ cup ground almonds
150g/5oz/1¼ cups plain (all-purpose) flour
10ml/2 tsp baking powder
10ml/2 tsp Seville orange marmalade, sieved

For the decoration
500g/1¼lb white marzipan
green and purple food colouring
50g/2oz royal icing
a little sieved apricot jam
10 dried or fresh apple stalks

1 Preheat the oven to 180°C/350°F/ Gas 4. Line the cups of a bun tin (pan) with paper cases.

2 Beat the marzipan, butter and sugar together to a smooth, even paste, using an electric mixer. With the whisk running, add the eggs in a very thin stream, beating well until the mixture is very smooth.

3 Fold in the grappa, almonds and flour sifted with the baking powder. Finally, stir in the marmalade.

4 Fill the paper cases a little over half full with the mixture and bake for 20–25 minutes until golden and springy to the touch in the centre. Leave to cool completely on a wire rack, then slice off the cake tops level with the tops of the cases.

5 For the marzipan topping, roll out 175g/6oz of marzipan fairly thinly on a board dusted with icing (confectioners') sugar. Using a crinkle-edged cutter, cut ten circles.

6 Colour 115g/4oz marzipan apple green. Roll it out thinly and cut out ten vine leaves.

7 Colour the remaining marzipan purple and roll it into nine smooth balls for each cake.

8 Heat the apricot jam and brush on the centre of each cake. Press the circles of marzipan on top. Brush the centre of each circle with hot apricot jam and stick on the grapes, stacked to resemble a small bunch, then attach a vine leaf with royal icing and push in an apple stalk.

Energy 572kcal/2404kJ; Protein 10.5g; Carbohydrate 76.9g, of which sugars 65g; Fat 25.7g, of which saturates 6.1g; Cholesterol 81mg; Calcium 122mg; Fibre 2.9g; Sodium 94mg.

Fairy cupcakes

These magical cupcakes will look stunning at a themed tea party. The delicate pearlized effect is achieved using edible lustre powder, available from sugarcraft suppliers. Add a tiny silver fairy decoration to complete the sparkly effect.

MAKES 8–9

175g/6oz/¾ cup butter, softened
175g/6oz/scant ¾ cup caster
  (superfine) sugar
5ml/1 tsp vanilla extract
4 eggs, lightly beaten
175g/6oz/1½ cups self-raising
  (self-rising) flour
silver dragées, fairy, and edible
  lustre powder, to decorate

For the buttercream
75g/3oz/6 tbsp butter, softened
175g/6oz/1½ cups icing
  (confectioners') sugar, double
  sifted, plus extra for dusting
½ vanilla pod (bean), split

1 Preheat the oven to 180°C/350°F/ Gas 4. Line the cups of a bun tin (pan) with paper cases.

2 Place the butter and sugar in a large bowl, and beat until light and creamy using an electric mixer. Add the vanilla extract and beat in the eggs in small amounts, beating well after each addition.

3 Sift the flour over and fold it gently into the mixture.

4 Spoon the mixture into the cases and bake for 20 minutes until the cakes are golden brown and the centres feel firm when pressed.

5 Leave the cakes in the tin for 5 minutes to cool, then transfer to a wire rack to cool completely.

6 To make the buttercream, beat the butter with the sugar and vanilla seeds until smooth and fluffy.

7 Spoon a thick blob of buttercream on to the top of each cake and smooth it over the surface, but not right up to the edges. Brush the tops of the cakes with edible lustre powder and top with silver dragées.

Energy 457kcal/1914kJ; Protein 4.9g; Carbohydrate 55.7g, of which sugars 40.9g; Fat 25.4g, of which saturates 15.7g; Cholesterol 148mg; Calcium 65mg; Fibre 0.6g; Sodium 242mg.

Christmas spice cupcakes

Mincemeat, brandy and freshly ground spices are the main ingredients in these delicious celebration cupcakes, which are ideal for those who love the rich spicy flavours of Christmas. The iced cupcake toppings will require a small snowflake or other Christmas themed cutter.

MAKES 14

2 eggs
115g/4oz/generous ½ cup golden caster (superfine) sugar
50ml/2fl oz/¼ cup double (heavy) cream
grated rind of 1 clementine
115g/4oz/⅓ cup mincemeat
115g/4oz/1 cup self-raising (self-rising) flour
2.5ml/½ tsp baking powder
5ml/1 tsp mixed (apple pie) spice
10ml/2 tsp brandy
50g/2oz/¼ cup butter, melted

For the icing
350g/12oz/3 cups icing (confectioners') sugar, sifted
15ml/1 tbsp hot water
red food colouring

To decorate
175g/6oz sugarpaste
red paste food colouring (or use 115g/4oz pre-coloured red sugarpaste)

1 Preheat the oven to 180°C/350°F/ Gas 4. Line the cups of a bun tin (pan) with paper cases.

2 Lightly beat the eggs with the sugar. Beat the cream into the egg mixture for about 1 minute, then add the grated clementine rind. Fold in the mincemeat. Sift in the flour, baking powder and mixed spice and fold in.

3 Finally add the brandy and the melted butter and stir to combine.

4 Half fill the paper cases with the batter. Place in the centre of the oven and bake for 12–15 minutes until risen and golden. Test by lightly pressing the centre of the cakes with your fingertips; the sponge should spring back. Leave on a wire rack to cool.

5 To make the icing, mix the sugar with just enough hot water to make a soft icing. Tint one-third of it with the red food colour and spoon over four of the cakes. Ice the remaining cakes with the white icing.

6 Set aside one-third of the sugarpaste and colour the rest red. Roll both out and stamp out ten red and four white snowflakes. Stick one on each cake before the icing sets.

Energy 272kcal/1153kJ; Protein 2g; Carbohydrate 56g, of which sugars 49.7g; Fat 6.1g, of which saturates 3.4g; Cholesterol 40mg; Calcium 43mg; Fibre 0.4g; Sodium 52mg.

Chocolate cupcakes with crème fraîche icing

These simple chocolate cakes have a sweet and sharp crème fraîche icing, which can be made using either dark or white chocolate. Cut the Christmas tree decorations out of contrasting chocolate, and bake the cakes in gold cases to sparkle on the festive tea table.

MAKES 20

150g/5oz dark (bittersweet)
  chocolate
175ml/6fl oz/¾ cup single
  (light) cream
5ml/1 tsp vanilla extract
225g/8oz/generous 1 cup golden
  caster (superfine) sugar
200g/7oz/scant 1 cup butter
3 eggs
225g/8oz/2 cups plain
  (all-purpose) flour
20g/¾oz/2 tbsp unsweetened
  cocoa powder
10ml/2 tsp baking powder

For the icing and decoration
200g/7oz dark (bittersweet) or
  white chocolate
50g/2oz/4 tbsp butter
250ml/8fl oz/1 cup crème fraîche
75g/3oz/⅔ cup icing
  (confectioners') sugar, sifted
225/8oz white or dark (bittersweet)
  chocolate, to decorate

1 Preheat the oven to 190°C/375°F/ Gas 5. Line the cups of two bun tins (pans) with paper cases.

2 Melt the chocolate with the cream over low heat, stirring constantly. Stir in the vanilla and set aside.

3 Beat the sugar and butter together until light and fluffy, then beat in the eggs one at a time. Sift the flour, cocoa powder and baking powder over the butter mixture and fold in, alternating with the chocolate cream, until the batter is combined.

4 Half fill the prepared cups and lightly smooth the tops level. Bake for 20–25 minutes, until the centres are firm. Cool on a wire rack.

5 To make the icing, melt the chocolate and butter over a pan of simmering water, stirring, until smooth. Leave to cool a little, then stir in the crème fraîche followed by the sugar. Spread the icing over the cupcakes with a metal spatula.

6 Melt the chocolate for the trees over a pan of simmering water and pour on to a tray lined with baking parchment. Chill until just set, then cut out the shapes and chill again until firm. Stick on to the cakes.

Energy 419kcal/1751kJ; Protein 4.2g; Carbohydrate 43.8g, of which sugars 33.6g; Fat 26.5g, of which saturates 16.4g; Cholesterol 79mg; Calcium 57mg; Fibre 0.5g; Sodium 125mg.

Sumptuous gateaux

Many of us have been tempted to buy beautiful gateaux from a pâtisserie and serve these as a dessert for a special occasion, but you can create these elegant specialities in your own kitchen. Gateaux do take a little more time and effort to make than many other cakes, but most can be prepared ahead or in stages. Allow plenty of time to enjoy the finishing stages. Although the cakes are a little more complicated, you will be surprised how simple skills can achieve a spectacular, mouthwatering centrepiece to the afternoon tea table.

Left: Coconut Lime Gateau and Raspberry and Hazelnut Meringue Cake.

Raspberry and hazelnut meringue cake

Toasted and ground hazelnuts add a nutty flavour to this simple cake of meringue rounds sandwiched together with fresh cream and raspberries. This combination will appeal to all dessert lovers. Store baked meringue bases, unfilled, for one week. Once filled, eat fresh.

SERVES 8

140g/5oz/1¼ cups hazelnuts
4 egg whites
200g/7oz/1 cup caster
  (superfine) sugar
2.5ml/½ tsp vanilla extract

For the filling
300ml/½ pint/1¼ cups
  whipping cream
700g/1lb 8oz/4 cups raspberries

1 Preheat the oven to 180°C/ 350°F/Gas 4. Thoroughly grease and line the bases of two 20cm/8in round cake tins (pans) with baking parchment.

2 Spread the hazelnuts on a baking sheet and bake for 8 minutes, or until lightly toasted. Leave to cool slightly. Rub the hazelnuts vigorously in a clean dish towel to remove the skins. Reduce the oven temperature to 150°C/ 300°F/Gas 2.

3 Grind the nuts in a food processor, until they are the consistency of coarse sand.

4 Put the egg whites into a clean, grease-free bowl and whisk until they form stiff peaks. Beat in 30ml/ 2 tbsp of the sugar, then, using a plastic spatula, fold in the remaining sugar, a few spoonfuls at a time.

5 Fold in the vanilla and hazelnuts.

6 Divide the mixture between the cake tins and smooth the top level. Bake for 1¼ hours until firm.

7 Leave to cool in the tin for 5 minutes, then run a knife around the inside edge of the tins to loosen the meringues. Turn out to cool on a wire rack.

8 For the filling, whip the cream. Spread half on one cake round and top with half the raspberries.

9 Top with the other cake round. Spread the remaining cream on top and arrange the rest of the raspberries over the top. Chill for 1 hour before serving.

Energy 298kcal/1252kJ; Protein 3.2g; Carbohydrate 39.5g, of which sugars 39.5g; Fat 15.3g, of which saturates 9.5g; Cholesterol 39mg; Calcium 55mg; Fibre 1.4g; Sodium 44mg.

Raspberry mousse cake

A lavish amount of raspberries gives this freezer gateau its vibrant colour and flavour. Make it at the height of summer when these deliciously scented fruits are plentiful and their flavour is at its best. Keep frozen for three months. To use, thaw in the refrigerator, slowly.

SERVES 8–10

2 eggs
50g/2oz/¼ cup sugar
50g/2oz/½ cup plain
   (all-purpose) flour
30ml/2 tbsp unsweetened
   cocoa powder
600g/1lb 6oz/4½ cups raspberries
115g/4oz/1 cup icing
   (confectioners') sugar
300ml/½ pint/1¼ cups
   whipping cream
2 egg whites

1 Preheat the oven to 180°C/350°F/ Gas 4. Grease and line a 23cm/9in round cake tin (pan).

2 Whisk the eggs and sugar in a bowl set over a pan of simmering water until the beaters leave a trail when lifted. Remove from the heat.

3 Sift over the flour and cocoa and fold it in with a metal spoon. Spoon into the tin. Bake for 12–15 minutes, or until just firm. Turn out to cool on a wire rack.

4 Reline the tin with baking paper and replace the cake. Freeze.

5 Set aside 175g/6oz/1 cup of raspberries.

6 Put the rest of the raspberries in a food processor bowl, stir in the icing sugar and process to a purée.

7 Whip the cream to form soft peaks.

8 Put the egg whites into a clean, grease-free bowl and whisk until they form stiff peaks.

9 Using a large metal spoon, fold the cream, then the egg whites into the raspberry purée.

10 Spread half the raspberry mixture on to the cake. Sprinkle with the reserved raspberries. Spread the remaining raspberry mixture on top. Freeze overnight, then thaw for at least 2 hours before serving.

Energy 238kcal/996kJ; Protein 4.4g; Carbohydrate 25g, of which sugars 20.9g; Fat 14.1g, of which saturates 8.3g; Cholesterol 70mg; Calcium 58mg; Fibre 2g; Sodium 65mg.

Iced raspberry pavlova roulade

This melt-in-the-mouth meringue, rolled around vanilla cream and luscious raspberries, is a star tea-party attraction, and is surprisingly quick and simple to make. Eat fresh or store in the freezer in a rigid plastic container. Keep frozen for up to three months. Defrost for four hours.

5 Spoon the mixture into the prepared tin and smooth it level.

6 Put the meringue in a cold oven and turn the temperature to 150°C/300°F/Gas 2. Bake for 1 hour, or until the top is crisp and the meringue feels springy.

7 Turn out on to baking parchment sprinkled with sifted icing sugar and leave to go cold.

8 Meanwhile, whip the cream and vanilla. Stir in the raspberries.

SERVES 6–8

10ml/2 tsp cornflour (cornstarch)
225g/8oz/generous 1 cup caster (superfine) sugar
4 egg whites, at room temperature
icing (confectioners') sugar, sifted, for dusting
300ml/½ pint/1¼ cups double (heavy) cream or whipping cream
a few drops of vanilla extract
175g/6oz/1½ cups raspberries, partly frozen, plus extra to serve

1 Line a 33 x 23cm/13 x 9in Swiss roll tin (jelly roll pan) with baking parchment.

2 Sift the cornflour into a bowl and blend evenly with the sugar.

3 Put the egg whites into a clean, grease-free bowl and whisk until stiff peaks form.

4 Whisk in the caster sugar, a few spoonfuls at a time, until the mixture becomes stiff and glossy.

VARIATIONS
• Flavour the cream with liqueur or lemon curd.
• Fill with soft ice cream.

9 Spread the raspberry cream over the meringue, then roll up, using the paper as a support. Freeze for 1 hour before serving. Dust with icing sugar and top with more raspberries, to serve.

Energy 243kcal/1015kJ; Protein 2g; Carbohydrate 26g, of which sugars 26g; Fat 15.3g, of which saturates 9.5g; Cholesterol 39mg; Calcium 34mg; Fibre 0.5g; Sodium 33mg.

Summer celebration shortcake

A departure from the usual summer shortcake, this tea-time treat contains crunchy almonds, which go particularly well with the juicy strawberries and cream filling. The top layer is already divided into portions, giving it an attractive appearance as well as making it easier to serve.

SERVES 8

175g/6oz/³⁄₄ cup butter
150g/5oz/1¹⁄₄ cups plain
  (all-purpose) flour
115g/4oz/1 cup ground almonds
50g/2oz/¹⁄₄ cup caster
  (superfine) sugar
25g/1oz/¹⁄₄ cup flaked
  (sliced) almonds

For the filling and decoration
450g/1lb/4 cups
  fresh strawberries
300ml/¹⁄₂ pint/1¹⁄₄ cups double
  (heavy) cream
15ml/1 tbsp amaretto (optional)
icing (confectioners') sugar,
  for dusting

1 Preheat the oven to 180°C/350°F/
Gas 4. Grease two baking sheets.

2 Rub the butter into the flour until it forms fine crumbs, then stir in the ground almonds and sugar. Mix to a soft dough and knead until smooth.

3 Roll half of the dough into a 20cm/8in round and cut out neatly. Put on a baking sheet and sprinkle over half the almonds.

4 Knead the trimmings and the rest of the dough to make a second shortcake round. Sprinkle over the almonds. Prick each with a fork.

5 Bake for 20 minutes, or until pale golden. While still warm, mark the flattest one into eight even triangles and leave to cool. Cut the triangles when cold.

6 For the filling, reserve nine strawberries. Hull and chop the rest.

7 Whip the cream until it forms soft peaks. Place a quarter in a piping (pastry) bag fitted with a star nozzle.

8 Fold the berries into the remaining cream with the liqueur, if using.

9 Put the whole shortbread on a serving plate. Pile the fruit filling on top and arrange the eight triangles on top with points facing inwards.

10 Pipe a cream rosette on each one and top with a strawberry, then put the last strawberry in the centre. Dust lightly with icing sugar. Serve immediately.

Energy 364kcal/1515kJ; Protein 4.3g; Carbohydrate 29.9g, of which sugars 8.5g; Fat 25.6g, of which saturates 15.6g; Cholesterol 87mg; Calcium 70mg; Fibre 1.2g; Sodium 76mg.

Chocolate brandy-snap gateau

Savour every mouthful of this sensational dark chocolate gateau. The cake is rich with chocolate and hazelnuts, and filled and topped with ganache – a cream and chocolate icing. Crisp brandy-snap frills look wonderful at the tea table and contrast beautifully with the soft cake. Eat fresh.

SERVES 8

225g/8oz plain (semisweet)
   chocolate, broken into pieces
225g/8oz/1 cup unsalted butter,
   softened
200g/7oz/scant 1 cup muscovado
   (molasses) sugar
6 eggs, separated
5ml/1 tsp vanilla extract
150g/5oz/1¼ cups ground
   hazelnuts
60ml/4 tbsp fresh white
   breadcrumbs
finely grated rind of 1 large orange
icing (confectioners') sugar,
   for dusting

For the brandy snaps
50g/2oz/¼ cup unsalted butter
50g/2oz/¼ cup caster
   (superfine) sugar
75g/3oz/¼ cup golden (light
   corn) syrup
50g/2oz/½ cup plain
   (all-purpose) flour
5ml/1 tsp brandy

For the chocolate ganache
250ml/8fl oz/1 cup double
   (heavy) cream
225g/8oz plain (semisweet)
   chocolate, broken into pieces

1 Preheat the oven to 180°C/
250°F/Gas 4.

2 Grease and line two 20cm/8in round shallow cake tins (pans) and two baking sheets with baking parchment.

3 To make the cake, melt the chocolate in a heatproof bowl set over a pan of gently simmering water. Stir occasionally. Remove from the heat to cool slightly.

4 Beat the butter and sugar in a large bowl until pale and fluffy. Beat in the egg yolks and vanilla extract. Add the melted chocolate and mix thoroughly.

5 Put the egg whites into a clean, grease-free bowl and whisk until they form soft peaks.

6 Fold a tablespoon of the whites into the chocolate mixture to slacken it, then fold in the rest in batches with the ground hazelnuts, breadcrumbs and orange rind.

7 Divide the cake batter between the prepared tins and smooth the tops level.

8 Bake for 25–30 minutes, or until well risen and firm, then turn out to cool on wire racks. Remove the lining paper.

9 To make the brandy snaps, melt the butter, sugar and syrup in a pan over low heat, stirring occasionally.

10 Remove from the heat and stir in the flour and brandy until smooth.

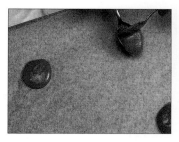

11 Place small spoonfuls well apart on the baking sheets with enough space to allow each biscuit to spread out, and bake for 10–15 minutes, or until golden.

Energy 870kcal/3622kJ; Protein 10.7g; Carbohydrate 70g, of which sugars 59g; Fat 62.7g, of which saturates 31.2g; Cholesterol 244mg; Calcium 102mg; Fibre 2.3g; Sodium 424mg.

12 Cool for a few seconds until firm enough to lift.

13 Immediately pinch the edges of each brandy snap to make a frilled effect. If the biscuits become too firm, pop them back into the oven for a few minutes. Leave to set on a wire rack.

14 Meanwhile, to make the chocolate ganache, heat the cream and chocolate together in a pan over low heat, stirring frequently until the chocolate has melted.

15 Pour into a bowl. Leave to cool, then stir until the mixture begins to hold its shape.

16 Sandwich the cake layers together with half the chocolate ganache, transfer to a plate and spread the remaining ganache on top.

17 Arrange the brandy snap frills over the gateau and dust with icing sugar. Serve immediately.

Layer cake

Three light cakes enclose a crushed raspberry layer and another of custard, all covered with vanilla-flavoured cream. It is an ideal tea-time cake for when raspberries are at their sweetest. Bake the cake layers the day before for the best flavour, then assemble the cake and eat fresh.

SERVES 10–12

115g/4oz/½ cup unsalted butter
200g/7oz/1 cup caster
  (superfine) sugar
4 eggs, separated
45ml/3 tbsp milk
175g/6oz/1½ cups plain
  (all-purpose) flour
25ml/1½ tbsp cornflour
  (cornstarch)
7.5ml/1½ tsp baking powder
5ml/1 tsp vanilla sugar
fresh raspberries, to decorate

For the custard filling
2 eggs
90g/3½oz/½ cup caster
  (superfine) sugar
15ml/1 tbsp cornflour
  (cornstarch)
350ml/12fl oz/1½ cups milk

For the cream topping
475ml/16fl oz/2 cups double
  (heavy) cream or whipping cream
25g/1oz/½ cup icing
  (confectioners') sugar
5ml/1 tsp vanilla sugar

For the raspberry filling
375g/13oz/generous 2 cups
  raspberries
sugar, to taste

COOK'S TIP
To make vanilla sugar, put a vanilla pod (bean) in a jar with a well-fitting lid, and fill with caster (superfine) sugar.

1 Preheat the oven to 230°C/450°F/ Gas 8. Lightly grease and flour three 23cm/9in shallow cake tins (pans).

2 Cream the butter with the sugar in a large bowl until light and fluffy. Beat in the egg yolks, one at a time. Stir in the milk until blended.

3 In a separate bowl, sift together the flour, cornflour, baking powder and vanilla sugar. Beat the flour mixture into the egg mixture.

4 Put the egg whites into a clean, grease-free bowl and whisk until they form stiff peaks. Gently fold the egg whites into the cake mixture.

5 Divide the batter evenly among the tins and smooth to the edges. Bake for 12 minutes. Leave the cakes to cool for 10 minutes, then turn out to cool on a wire rack.

6 To make the custard filling, whisk together the eggs and sugar in a pan. Whisk in the cornflour and the milk. Cook over low heat, stirring, for about 6 minutes or until thickened. Remove from the heat and leave to cool.

7 To make the topping, beat the cream in a bowl until soft peaks form. Stir in the icing sugar and vanilla sugar and beat until stiff.

8 To make the raspberry filling, crush the raspberries in a bowl and add a little sugar to taste.

9 To assemble the cake, place one layer on a serving plate and spread with the raspberry filling.

10 Place a second cake layer over the first and spread with the cooled custard. Top with the final layer.

11 Spread whipped cream over the sides and top of the cake.

12 Chill the cake until ready to serve, and decorate with raspberries.

Energy 433kcal/1811kJ; Protein 6.1g; Carbohydrate 44.6g, of which sugars 30.4g; Fat 27g, of which saturates 15.9g; Cholesterol 157mg; Calcium 86mg; Fibre 1.2g; Sodium 109mg.

Cinnamon apple gateau

Make this unusual cake for an autumn tea party. A light sponge is split and filled with a honey and cream cheese layer as well as softly cooked cinnamon apples and sultanas, then topped with glazed apples. Keep the sponge, unfilled, for two days in an airtight container. Fill and eat fresh.

SERVES 8–10

3 eggs
115g/4oz/generous ½ cup caster
  (superfine) sugar
75g/3oz/⅔ cup plain
  (all-purpose) flour
5ml/1 tsp ground cinnamon

For the filling and topping
4 large eating apples
60ml/4 tbsp clear honey
75g/3oz/generous ½ cup sultanas
  (golden raisins)
2.5ml/½ tsp ground cinnamon
350g/12oz/1½ cups
  soft cheese
60ml/4 tbsp fromage frais or
  crème fraîche
10ml/2 tsp lemon juice
45ml/3 tbsp sieved apricot glaze
mint sprigs, to decorate

1 Preheat the oven to 190°C/
375°F/Gas 5. Grease and line a
23cm/9in round cake tin (pan) with
baking parchment.

2 Put the eggs and sugar in a bowl
and beat with an electric whisk until
thick and mousse-like and the
beaters leave a trail on the surface.

3 Sift the flour and cinnamon over
the egg mixture and carefully fold in
with a large spoon.

4 Pour into the prepared tin and
bake for 25–30 minutes, or until
the cake springs back when lightly
pressed in the centre.

5 Slide a knife between the cake and
the tin to loosen the edge, then turn
the cake on to a wire rack to cool.

6 To make the filling, peel, core and
slice three apples and put them in a
pan. Add 30ml/ 2 tbsp of the honey
and 15ml/1 tbsp water. Cover and
cook over low heat for 10 minutes,
or until the apples have softened.

7 Add the sultanas and cinnamon,
stir, replace the lid and leave to cool.

8 Put the soft cheese in a bowl with
the remaining honey, the fromage
frais or crème fraîche and half the
lemon juice. Beat until smooth.

9 Cut the cake into two equal
rounds. Put half on a plate and
drizzle over any liquid from
the apples.

10 Spread with two-thirds of the
cheese mixture, then top with
the apple filling. Fit the top of the
cake in place.

11 Swirl the remaining cheese
mixture over the top of the sponge.
Core and slice the remaining apple,
sprinkle with lemon juice and use to
decorate the edge of the cake. Brush
the apple with apricot glaze and
place mint sprigs on top to decorate.

Energy 239kcal/1010kJ; Protein 10.8g; Carbohydrate 39.9g, of which sugars 32.8g; Fat 5.8g, of which saturates 2.9g; Cholesterol 82mg; Calcium 97mg; Fibre 1.1g; Sodium 225mg.

Sponge cake with strawberries and cream

This classic treat is delicious in the summer, filled with ripe, fragrant strawberries. The sponge is exceptionally light because it is made without fat. To ensure you have a perfect sponge, have all the ingredients at room temperature. Eat fresh after filling with fruit and cream.

SERVES 8–10

115g/4oz/generous ½ cup caster
   (superfine) sugar, plus extra
   for dusting
90g/3½oz/¾ cup plain
   (all-purpose) flour, sifted, plus
   extra for dusting
4 eggs
icing (confectioners') sugar,
   for dusting

For the filling
300ml/½ pint/1¼ cups double
   (heavy) cream
about 5ml/1 tsp icing
   (confectioners') sugar, sifted
450g/1lb/4 cups strawberries,
   washed and hulled
a little Cointreau (optional)

1 Preheat the oven to 190°C/375°F/ Gas 5. Grease a round 20cm/8in cake tin (pan). Dust the tin with 10ml/2 tsp caster sugar and flour combined. Tap out the excess.

COOK'S TIP
Freeze unfilled for 2 months.

2 Put the eggs and sugar into a bowl and use an electric whisk at high speed until it is light and thick, and the mixture leaves a trail as it drops from the whisk. (To whisk by hand; set the bowl over a pan a quarter filled with hot water and whisk until thick and creamy, then remove from the heat.)

3 Sift the flour over the whisked eggs and carefully fold it in with a metal spoon, mixing thoroughly but losing as little volume as possible.

4 Pour the batter into the cake tin and smooth the top level. Bake for 25–30 minutes, or until the sponge feels springy to the touch.

5 Leave in the tin for 5 minutes to set slightly, then loosen the sides with a knife and invert on to a wire rack to go cold.

6 To make the filling, whip the cream with a little icing sugar until it is stiff enough to hold its shape.

7 Slice the sponge across the middle with a long sharp knife to make two even layers.

8 Divide half the cream between the two inner cut sides of the sandwich.

9 Reserve some strawberries for the cake top, and then slice the rest.

10 Put the first sponge half on a serving plate and arrange the sliced strawberries on the cream. Sprinkle with liqueur, if using.

11 Cover with the second cake half and press down gently.

12 Spread the remaining cream on top of the cake, and arrange the reserved strawberries, whole or halved according to size, on top.

13 Set aside for an hour or so for the flavours to develop, then dust lightly with icing sugar and serve.

Energy 333kcal/1387kJ; Protein 5.3g; Carbohydrate 27.8g, of which sugars 19.2g; Fat 23.1g, of which saturates 13.3g; Cholesterol 147mg; Calcium 65mg; Fibre 1g; Sodium 48mg.

Coconut lime gateau

American frosting is what makes this zesty lime and coconut gateau so attractive. Made by whisking egg white and a sugar mixture over heat, the frosting is like a soft meringue icing. It tastes divine scattered with toasted coconut. Eat fresh or refrigerate for two days.

SERVES 10–12

225g/8oz/2 cups plain
   (all-purpose) flour
12.5ml/2½ tsp baking powder
225g/8oz/1 cup butter, at
   room temperature
225g/8oz/generous 1 cup caster
   (superfine) sugar
grated rind of 2 limes
4 eggs
60ml/4 tbsp fresh lime juice (from
   about 2 limes)
75g/3oz/1 cup desiccated (dry
   unsweetened) coconut

For the frosting
275g/10oz/scant 1½ cups caster
   (superfine) sugar
2.5ml/½ tsp/½ tsp cream of tartar
2 egg whites
60ml/4 tbsp cold water
15ml/1 tbsp liquid glucose
10ml/2 tsp vanilla extract

1 Preheat the oven to 180°C/350°F/ Gas 4. Grease and line two 23cm/9in round shallow cake tins (pans) with baking parchment.

2 Sift together the flour and baking powder into a bowl.

3 In another large bowl, beat the butter until soft. Add the sugar and lime rind, then beat until pale and fluffy. Beat in the eggs, one at a time, adding 5ml/1 tsp of the flour mixture with each addition to stop the batter from curdling. Beat the mixture well between each addition.

4 Using a wooden spoon, fold in the flour mixture in small batches, alternating with the lime juice. When the batter is smooth, stir in two-thirds of the coconut.

5 Divide the batter between the tins and spread it evenly to the sides.

6 Bake for 30–35 minutes, or until a skewer inserted into the centre comes out clean. Leave to cool in the tins for 10 minutes, then turn out to cool on a wire rack. Remove the lining paper. Leave to go cold.

7 Spread the remaining coconut in another cake tin. Bake until golden brown, stirring occasionally. Watch carefully so that the coconut does not get too dark. Allow to cool in the tin.

8 To make the frosting, put the sugar in a large heatproof bowl and add the cream of tartar, egg whites, water and glucose. Stir to mix.

9 Set the bowl over a pan of boiling water. Beat with an electric whisk at high speed for 7 minutes or until thick and stiff peaks form. Remove from the heat.

10 Add the vanilla extract and continue beating for 3 minutes or until the frosting has cooled slightly.

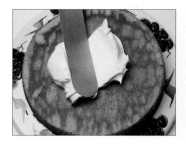

11 Put a cake on a serving plate. Spread a layer of frosting on top.

12 Set the second cake on top. Swirl the rest of the frosting all over the cake. Sprinkle with the toasted coconut and leave to set.

Energy 732kcal/3079kJ; Protein 7.3g; Carbohydrate 111g, of which sugars 59g; Fat 32g, of which saturates 20.5g; Cholesterol 155mg; Calcium 105.7mg; Fibre 2.1g; Sodium 221mg.

Iced Victoria sponge

Crystallized roses grace this splendid Victoria sandwich. Filled with rose-scented buttercream, it makes a breath-taking centrepiece. You could use jam and buttercream to sandwich the layers.

SERVES 10–12

225g/8oz/1 cup butter, softened
225g/8oz/generous 1 cup caster
   (superfine) sugar
4 eggs
225g/8oz/2 cups self-raising
   (self-rising) flour
5ml/1 tsp baking powder

For the filling
115g/4oz/½ cup butter, softened
115g/4oz/1 cup icing
   (confectioners') sugar
60ml/4 tbsp sweetly scented
   rose petals

For the topping
225g/8oz/2 cups icing
   (confectioners') sugar
30–45ml/2–3 tbsp rose water
crystallized roses and rose petals

1 Preheat the oven to 180°C/350°F/ Gas 4. Lightly grease and line two 20cm/8in round sandwich tins (layer pans).

2 Beat the butter with the caster sugar until light and fluffy. Add the eggs one at a time, beating well after each. Sift over the flour and baking powder together, and beat well.

3 Divide the mixture between the two sandwich tins and bake for 25 minutes until firm to the touch. Transfer to a wire rack to cool.

4 To make the filling, beat the softened butter until light and creamy. Add the icing sugar until all has been incorporated.

5 Chop the rose petals finely and add to the butter mixture. Spread between the two halves of the cooled cake.

6 To make the topping, beat the icing sugar in a bowl with 30ml/ 2 tbsp of the rose water to give a consistency that thickly coats the back of a spoon. Add more rose water, drop by drop, if necessary.

7 Spoon the icing over the cake, allowing it to run down the sides. Decorate with a circle of crystallized roses and petals.

CAUTION
Raw eggs should not be consumed by pregnant women, the young and elderly.

CRYSTALLIZED ROSES

1 egg white, or reconstituted
   powdered egg white
50g/2oz/¼ cup caster
   (superfine) sugar
6–8 pink roses, and several
   rose petals

1 Gather your flowers and petals when dry. Remove the white heel at the base of any individual petals as it tastes bitter.

2 Lightly beat the egg white and place in a saucer. Put the caster sugar in a separate saucer.

3 Using an artist's brush, paint the flowerhead, or petals front and back, with egg white.

4 Dredge with caster sugar until all are well coated.

5 Lay individual petals and flowers on sheets of baking parchment and keep them in a warm, dry place overnight, or until crisp. Store in a sealed container for up to 2 days.

Energy 557kcal/2339kJ; Protein 4.3g; Carbohydrate 83.4g, of which sugars 69.1g; Fat 25.2g, of which saturates 15.9g; Cholesterol 129mg; Calcium 75mg; Fibre 0.6g; Sodium 240mg.

Index

This edition is published by Hermes House
an imprint of Anness Publishing Ltd
info@anness.com
www.hermeshouse.com; www.annesspublishing.com

If you like the images in this book and would like to investigate using them for publishing, promotions or advertising,
please visit our website www.practicalpictures.com for more information.

© Anness Publishing Ltd 2023

Publisher: Joanna Lorenz
Editorial Director: Helen Sudell
Editor: Simona Hill
Production: Ben Worley
Photographers: William Lingwood, Charlie Richards, Craig Robertson
Home Economists: Belinda Alternoxel, Lucy McKelvie
Styling: Liz Hippisley, Helen Trent

COOK'S NOTES

Bracketed terms are intended for American readers.
For all recipes, quantities are given in both metric and imperial measures and, where appropriate, in standard cups and spoons.
Follow one set of measures, but not a mixture, because they are not interchangeable.
Standard spoon and cup measures are level. 1 tsp = 5ml, 1 tbsp = 15ml, 1 cup = 250ml/8fl oz.
Australian standard tablespoons are 20ml. Australian readers should use 3 tsp in place of 1 tbsp for measuring small quantities.
American pints are 16fl oz/2 cups. American readers should use 20fl oz/2.5 cups in place of 1 pint when measuring liquids.
Electric oven temperatures in this book are for conventional ovens. When using a fan oven, the temperature will probably need to be reduced by about
10–20°C/20–40°F. Since ovens vary, you should check with your manufacturer's instruction book for guidance.
The nutritional analysis given for each recipe is calculated per portion (i.e. serving or item), unless otherwise stated. If the recipe gives a range,
such as Serves 4–6, then the nutritional analysis will be for the smaller portion size, i.e. 6 servings.
The analysis does not include optional ingredients, such as salt added to taste.
Medium (US large) eggs are used unless otherwise stated.

PUBLISHER'S NOTE